Metaphor

A Computational Perspective

Synthesis Lectures on Human Language Technologies

Editor
Graeme Hirst, *University of Toronto*

Synthesis Lectures on Human Language Technologies is edited by Graeme Hirst of the University of Toronto. The series consists of 50- to 150-page monographs on topics relating to natural language processing, computational linguistics, information retrieval, and spoken language understanding. Emphasis is on important new techniques, on new applications, and on topics that combine two or more HLT subfields.

Metaphor: A Computational Perspective
Tony Veale, Ekaterina Shutova, and Beata Beigman Klebanov
2016

Grammatical Inference for Computational Linguistics
Jeffrey Heinz, Colin de la Higuera, and Menno van Zaanen
2015

Automatic Detection of Verbal Deception
Eileen Fitzpatrick, Joan Bachenko, and Tommaso Fornaciari
2015

Natural Language Processing for Social Media
Atefeh Farzindar and Diana Inkpen
2015

Semantic Similarity from Natural Language and Ontology Analysis
Sébastien Harispe, Sylvie Ranwez, Stefan Janaqi, and Jacky Montmain
2015

Learning to Rank for Information Retrieval and Natural Language Processing, Second Edition
Hang Li
2014

Ontology-Based Interpretation of Natural Language
Philipp Cimiano, Christina Unger, and John McCrae
2014

Metaphor: A Computational Perspective

Tony Veale, Ekaterina Shutova, and Beata Beigman Klebanov

ISBN: 978-3-031-01032-3   paperback
ISBN: 978-3-031-02160-2   ebook

DOI 10.1007/978-3-031-02160-2

A Publication in the Springer series
SYNTHESIS LECTURES ON HUMAN LANGUAGE TECHNOLOGIES

Lecture #31
Series Editor: Graeme Hirst, *University of Toronto*
Series ISSN
Print 1947-4040   Electronic 1947-4059

Metaphor

A Computational Perspective

Tony Veale
University College Dublin

Ekaterina Shutova
University of Cambridge

Beata Beigman Klebanov
Educational Testing Service

SYNTHESIS LECTURES ON HUMAN LANGUAGE TECHNOLOGIES #31

ABSTRACT

The literary imagination may take flight on the wings of metaphor, but hard-headed scientists are just as likely as doe-eyed poets to reach for a metaphor when the descriptive need arises. Metaphor is a pervasive aspect of every genre of text and every register of speech, and is as useful for describing the inner workings of a "black hole" (itself a metaphor) as it is the affairs of the human heart. The ubiquity of metaphor in natural language thus poses a significant challenge for Natural Language Processing (NLP) systems and their builders, who cannot afford to wait until the problems of literal language have been solved before turning their attention to figurative phenomena. This book offers a comprehensive approach to the computational treatment of metaphor and its figurative brethren—including simile, analogy, and conceptual blending—that does not shy away from their important cognitive and philosophical dimensions. Veale, Shutova, and Beigman Klebanov approach metaphor from multiple computational perspectives, providing coverage of both symbolic and statistical approaches to interpretation and paraphrase generation, while also considering key contributions from philosophy on what constitutes the "meaning" of a metaphor. This book also surveys available metaphor corpora and discusses protocols for metaphor annotation. Any reader with an interest in metaphor, from beginning researchers to seasoned scholars, will find this book to be an invaluable guide to what is a fascinating linguistic phenomenon.

KEYWORDS

metaphor, simile, analogy, blending, figurative language processing

Contents

Preface

The aim of this book is to introduce metaphor research to the wider NLP community, and to survey the state-of-the-art in computational methods in a way that may also be helpful to those approaching metaphor from a perspective that is not principally informed by work in Artificial Intelligence (AI). We focus on the history, methods, and goals of past research into this fascinating phenomenon in the hope of making metaphor a more accessible topic of future research, thereby pushing it further up the NLP community's wait-list. Our treatment will provide a condensed history of metaphor research that introduces the main theories of metaphor that survive, in one form or another, in contemporary analysis. Our coverage will include the main AI contributions to the field, which are modern attempts to give algorithmic form to views on metaphor that range from the ancient to the contemporary. And, just as contemporary AI research has taken on a distinctly web-colored hue, we shall explore the role of the Web in metaphor research, both as a source of data and as a computational platform for our metaphor-capable NLP systems. Computational linguistics and AI alike have each embraced statistical models as a means of improving robustness, exploiting rich veins of user data, and reducing a system's dependence on hand-crafted knowledge and rules. Metaphor research offers no exception to this trend, and so our book will also explore the role of statistical approaches in the analysis of metaphorical language. Since such approaches are ultimately only as good as the data over which they operate, we shall also focus on the contributions of corpus linguistics to the construction of annotated metaphor corpora. Finally, we shall draw these strands together to offer an application-oriented view of metaphor, asking whether there is a killer application for metaphor research, and whether (and how) computational approaches to metaphor can help advance not only the field of NLP, but other fields as well, such as the social sciences and education.

The ultimate goal of this book is not to make you believe, as we do, that metaphor is the very soul of language, though the growing field of metaphor research is always eager to welcome new converts. We will consider this book a success if readers take away a desire to address metaphor head on, in some form or another in their research, and find in this book the necessary tools to make this engagement a practical reality.

Tony Veale, Ekaterina Shutova, and Beata Beigman Klebanov
January 2016

CHAPTER 1

Introducing Metaphor

Language would be a dull and brittle thing without metaphor. It is metaphor and its figurative kin—simile, analogy, blending, irony, understatement, hyperbole, and the like—that lend language its vitality and elasticity. It is metaphor and its kin that allow us to suggest much more than we actually say, and to invent new ways of saying it, when conventional language shows us its limits. It is metaphor and its kin that allow us to communicate not just information, but also real feelings and complex attitudes. Metaphor does not just report the result of personal insights, but also prompts and inspires listeners to have these insights for themselves. Each metaphor is a concise but highly productive *way of saying* that communicates a new and productive *way of seeing*.

But what exactly are metaphors and where do we look for them? Although metaphors are products of our faculty for creative thinking, metaphors in the wild can range from the scintillating to the banal. Just as repeated usage dulls the blade of a trusty knife, or repeated telling robs a once-funny joke of its ability to raise a laugh, repetition takes the bloom off a metaphor and turns it from an eye-catching flower into just another piece of the undergrowth. So metaphors are everywhere, in language, in film, in music, or in any system of signs that allows us to express ourselves creatively. These metaphors range from the novel to the conventional, and indeed some are so conventional as to escape our attention altogether. Nonetheless, even highly conventionalized metaphors retain a spark of the creativity that forged them, and in the right hands this spark can be fanned into a roaring fire. Consider the following example, which was used as the title of a popular science book by German rocket scientist Wernher von Braun: *"I Aim For The Stars!"* Since the heavens are filled with stars in any direction we care to look, von Braun could not have intended to use the word "aim" literally, which is to say *"I look and/or point in the specific direction of the stars"* or even (for he was a master pragmatist) *"I intend to move myself physically closer to the stars."* Rather, von Braun—who was attempting to popularize the concept of space travel with the American public, and thereby win state funding for his expensive scientific work—employed a basic metaphor that allows speakers to treat PURPOSES AS DESTINATIONS. Thus, von Braun saw the achievement of interstellar space travel as his goal, and expressed this goal using the language of physical destinations.

But von Braun, an ex-member of the Nazi party, was also the controversial creator of the German V-2 missiles that rained down on Britain during World War II. (He had been spirited away to the U.S. as part of *operation paperclip* at the end of the war, when the American and Russian militaries competed to round up the brains of the German rocket program.) The comedian

Mort Sahl took full advantage of this fact, and of von Braun's use of the PURPOSES ARE DESTI-NATIONS metaphor, to cheekily propose an alternative title for the scientist's book: *"I aim for the stars but I keep hitting London."* Clearly, the generic and highly reusable metaphor PURPOSES ARE DESTINATIONS is of a different character than the specific utterances that are constructed from it. Researchers refer to the former as a *conceptual metaphor*, for it resides at the level of thinking and ideas, and to the latter as a linguistic metaphor. Explicating the relationship between the former and the latter is one of the goals of contemporary cognitive and computational approaches to metaphor, and so we shall return to this relationship many times in this book. We'll also meet the conceptual metaphor PURPOSES ARE DESTINATIONS again in a later chapter.

We each use conventional metaphors every day, perhaps without even realizing it, yet we each have the ability to elaborate on these standard-issue constructions in our own way, to inject our own voice and personality into what we say. Consider the following quote from Twitter co-founder Biz Stone, who writes in his autobiography of how he came to be an early employee of Google:

> *I didn't know it at the time, but behind the scenes Evan [Williams] had to pull strings in order to hire me [at Google]* (Stone [2014]).

The idea of exerting influence on others by *pulling [their] strings* is deeply entrenched in the English language. We describe a bargain or an offer of special treatment as *"no strings attached"* when we believe the giver is not seeking to unduly influence us, which is to say *"to pull our strings."* An emotional appeal that hits its mark is said to *"tug at our heartstrings,"* while we might describe a master manipulator as being able to *"play someone like a violin."* A mother's continued influence on an adult child is often given metaphoric form with the phrase *"apron strings,"* and any effort (by mother or child) to curtail this influence is described as *"cutting the apron strings."* Stone's use of the *strings* metaphor in the context of the idiom *"behind the scenes"* might also bring to mind images of the pulleys and ropes with which stagehands lower and raise the curtain in a theatrical production (indeed, the word *"scene"* gets its meaning from the piece of cloth that was draped behind the stage in ancient theatres). Metaphors are much more than the stuff of fancy wordplay, and we use them to do much more than give our messages an attractive sheen: metaphors engage fully with the mechanisms of thought, allowing us to spark associations, insights, and other metaphors in the mind of a hearer even when we are using the most conventionalized of figures. We can think of these figures as being made of clay; convention has given them their shape, but we can add fine detail of our own, or bend them further to our own meanings. Let's look at the larger context of Stone's metaphor:

> *I didn't know it at the time, but behind the scenes Evan had to pull strings in order to hire me. Actually, they were more like ropes. Or cables—the kind that hold up suspension bridges* (Stone [2014]).

This elaboration should dispel any doubts about whether the *pulling [one's] strings* metaphor is nothing more than an arbitrary idiom that speakers learn to repeat in whatever context that suits.

Rather, a metaphor—even a highly conventional metaphor—establishes a frame of thought that encourages us to think in a particular way. Once it has our attention and draws us in, we are free to explore it, question it, and customize it as we see fit. For instance, we might ask how pulling on metaphorical strings might influence another person. If this other person is a weak-willed *puppet*, a *lightweight* player, or a minor *cog* in the machine (notice how effortlessly one metaphor leads to others), then not much effort is needed to exert influence, and so its strings will be light and easy to pull. But if this other person is a significant cog—a so-called *big wheel* or a *heavyweight* player—greater effort is needed to achieve any influence, requiring strings of greater thickness and tensile strength. Notice how the metaphor encourages us to think in the *source* domain (the domain of strings, cogs, pulleys, puppets, etc.) and to transfer our insights from here into the *target* domain (the domain of corporate decision-making). In Stone's example, his metaphor leads us to believe that his friend Evan needed to perform Herculean efforts on his behalf, to influence some very powerful people at Google by pulling on some very heavy-duty strings. As we'll see repeatedly throughout this book, even the most innocuous metaphors conceal a wealth of complexity, both in terms of their underlying representations and the cognitive/computational processes that are needed to understand them. This hidden complexity is a large part of what gives metaphors their allure for the computationalist.

However, although metaphor has a long and illustrious history of academic study, in both philosophy and linguistics, it remains a niche area in the computational study of language. For although most Natural Language Processing (NLP) researchers would readily acknowledge the ubiquity of metaphor in language, metaphor is a complex phenomenon and a hard engineering problem that continues, for the most part, to be wait-listed by the NLP community. To the application-minded, there are simply too many other problems of more practical and immediate interest—concerning syntax, semantics, inference, sentiment, co-reference, under-specification, and so on—that jump to the top of the community's collective to-do list. That metaphor touches on all of these problems and more is often seen as beside the point, although ultimately it is very much to the point: the problem of metaphor is just too big, too unwieldy, and too knowledge-hungry to be tackled first. Better to get a handle on all the other problems first, to obtain an algorithmic understanding of the workings of language that can later be enriched by a computational model of metaphor. This makes good engineering sense, if little philosophical or cognitive sense.

The purpose of this book is to demonstrate that this conventional wisdom is predicated upon a false dichotomy: researchers can build figurative-language processing systems that are practical and efficient *and* cognitively plausible, and which also reflect an understanding of the profound philosophical issues involved. Indeed, it is difficult for the computationally-minded researcher to explore aspects of metaphor that have *not* been previously visited by philosophers or psychologists or by earlier computationalists in its long and illustrious history of academic analysis. If there is little in the field of metaphor that one can truly call "virgin territory," it is nonetheless a field of many interesting landmarks that rewards careful viewing and repeat visits. We have written this book to be a comprehensive guide to the major landmarks in the computational treatment of metaphor and hope the reader will find it a useful map to this fascinating phenomenon's many attractions.

CHAPTER 2

Computational Approaches to Metaphor: Theoretical Foundations

2.1 THE *WHAT*, *WHY* AND *HOW* OF METAPHOR

Metaphor is both pervasive and evasive: ubiquitous in language, yet remarkably hard to pin down in formal terms. Yet the fact that there exists no single, definitive perspective on metaphor is very much in keeping with its chimerical nature. For metaphor is a highly productive mechanism that allows us to create a panoply of viewpoints on any concept we care to consider, including metaphor itself. Indeed, it scarcely seems possible to say anything meaningful at all about metaphor without first resorting to one kind of metaphor or another. So we talk of tenors and vehicles, sources and targets, spaces and domains, mappings and projections, metaphors that are living or dead, those that are fresh but soon stale, or of seeing one idea with the aid of another. Many of our metaphors for metaphor are metaphors of seeing, for seeing often leads to knowing, or at least to an impression of knowing. So a metaphor can be a viewfinder, a magnifying glass, a microscope, a lens, a window, a pair of conceptual spectacles, a distorting fun-house mirror, and even a set of conceptual blinders. Max Black, the philosopher who more than anyone else kickstarted the modern resurgence in metaphor research, described a metaphor as working much like a blackened piece of glass onto which a specific pattern of lines has been etched [Black, 1962]. Looking through this bespoke glass, we see only those parts of a target domain that the etched pattern allows us to see, and see these parts in clearer relation to each other precisely because we are not distracted by the many parts we cannot see. Metaphor prompts us to look, helps us to see, and then controls what we can see.

Metaphor has existed longer than our need to describe its function, and much longer than our need to name it as a distinct linguistic or cognitive phenomenon. Indeed, the word "metaphor" is itself founded on a metaphor, to carry (*-phor*) above and across (*meta-*) a signifier from one realm of experience to another. The Greek philosopher Aristotle, to whom we can trace the earliest use of the term, effectively describes metaphor as a form of semiotic displacement, in which our agreed signifier for one object, idea, or experience is deliberately displaced onto another. But metaphor is not the only kind of semiotic displacement in language. Punning, for instance, involves the temporary replacement of one signifier with another, based on the phonetic similarity of the two, as in "mail" and "male" (e.g., "Q: Is that the *mail* plane coming in to land? A: Of course it's a *male* plane, can't you see its undercarriage?"). Synecdoche licenses the displacement of a signifier of a part onto the whole to which it belongs (e.g., "brains" stands for clever (or *brainy*) people in "the American and Russian militaries competed to round up the *brains* of the German rocket program"), while metonymy licenses a more general displacement of a signifier onto an object or idea that is functionally or conceptually related to its conventional signification (e.g., when Raymond Chandler's private investigator Philip Marlowe says "Trouble is my business," he means "My business concerns other people's troubles, which invariably cause trouble for me;" so the metonymy tightens the relation between Marlowe and trouble). Aristotle is thus careful to enumerate the particular kinds of displacement that constitute a metaphor, as opposed to any other kind of semiotic play, and in his *Poetics* he offers the following schematic specification (as translated by Hutton [1982]):

Metaphor is the application to one thing of the name belonging to another. We may apply:

(a) *the name of a genus to one of its species, or*

(b) *the name of one species to its genus, or*

(c) *the name of one species to another of the same genus, or*

(d) *the transfer may be based on a proportion.*

The target of the name shift is typically called the *topic*, the *tenor*, or simply the *target* of the metaphor, while the source of the shift—the name belonging to another—is typically called the *vehicle* or simply the *source* of the metaphor. The designations *source* and *target* are generally preferred in the analogical literature (e.g., Gentner [1983]), although *vehicle* is more in keeping with Aristotle's view of metaphor as a carrier of meaning across domains. Throughout this book we shall use the terminology of *source domain* and *target domain* to denote the space of ideas associated with the source (or vehicle) and the target (or tenor) respectively. The word *domain* has no formal definition; we use it, as others do, to designate the cluster of related concepts, properties, and norms that attach to a particular source or target so that we may later speak of transferring, mapping, or projecting content from one domain onto another. With this in mind, Aristotle offers an illustrative use-case for each of his four displacement strategies.

(a) Genus to species: "*Here stands my ship*" employs the generic (genus) term "*to stand still*" as a replacement for its specialization (species) "*to be at anchor.*"

(b) Species to genus: "*Truly ten thousand noble deeds hath Odysseus done*" uses "*ten thousand deeds*" as a specialization of the vague genus term "*large number.*"

(c) Species to species: "*Drawing off the life with bronze*" and "*Cutting off the water with unwearied bronze*" each employ a specialization of the genus "*to take away.*"

(d) Proportional analogy: "*The wine cup is to Dionysus as the shield is to Ares*" is an obvious statement of the proportion *Dionysus:Cup::Ares:Shield*, yet it supports more subtle allusions, such as the poetic use of "*the cup of Ares*" to refer to a battle shield, or "*the shield of Dionysus*" to refer to a wine cup.

So, metaphor distinguishes itself from other forms of semiotic displacement by its reliance on the vertical operations of generalization and specialization. Metaphor allows us to move signifiers up and down a hierarchy of concepts, and supports the sideways movement of signifiers only insofar as they achieve such movement by climbing up from one domain so as to climb down into another. In effect, Aristotle provides a strong account of the "*what*" of metaphor, and a reasonable account of the "*how*," but offers very little on the "*why*" of metaphor, other than to suggest that it is done in a spirit of semiotic sport. The strategies in (a) to (d) above focus mainly on those uses of metaphor where the vehicle is explicitly given (e.g., the *cup of Ares* or *ten thousand deeds*) and a listener must work out the identity of the implied tenor (e.g., a *shield*, or a *large number*). But what of metaphors where tenor/target and vehicle/source are both explicitly given, as in the copula metaphor "*marriage is slavery?*"

Such metaphors appear to instantiate strategy (c) in Aristotle's scheme, in which one species of an unstated genus is mapped to another of the same genus. Presumably it is the identification of this unstated genus term—perhaps *cruel practice* or *social institution* in the case of *marriage as slavery*—that offers the key to the metaphor. Yet, if so, the metaphor degenerates into an example of strategy (b) and communicates only as much information as this genus can offer. In fact, if the listener does not possess the same conceptual hierarchy as the speaker—for instance, the listener may not view even slavery as a cruel practice, much less marriage—then the metaphor will fail. However, one need not agree with a metaphor to understand its purpose, and many metaphors are designed to change a listener's conceptual structures rather than to merely reflect them. So, in an important sense, the "*why*" of metaphor is precisely this: speakers often use metaphors to align the conceptual systems of others to that of their own.

For a metaphor is not a statement of fact, and most are more than the mere expression of a subjective viewpoint. Rather, a metaphor is an invitation to build a joint meaning space, as framed by the given viewpoint. The metaphor "*marriage is slavery*" is a communicative gambit that asks the listener to think about, and perhaps argue about, the idea that our concept of marriage can be meaningfully framed by our concept of slavery. In other words, the metaphor aims to establish what Brennan and Clark [1996] call a *conceptual pact*, and is a request that can be paraphrased as follows: "*let us agree to talk about marriage using the words and ideas we normally associate with slavery; to this end, let us go so far as to suspend disbelief and assume that marriage really is a kind of slavery, and thereby explore the extent to which our concept of marriage can be subsumed under our concept of slavery.*" The longwindedness of this paraphrase goes some way toward conveying the true utility of metaphor as much more than a flourish of language or a playful exercise in semiotic sport.

The metaphor "*marriage is slavery*" is an effective prompt to build a complex meaning space because "*slavery*" is itself an effective shorthand for a rich body of cultural knowledge and expectations. Wrapped up in our concept of slavery is a knowledge of the history of the practice, of the physical and emotional suffering of those who are caught in it, and of the motivations of those who practice it. In other words, slavery is a *dense descriptor*, an idea that is easily referenced and that brings with it a slew of properties, feelings, norms, and expectations. The use of a dense descriptor in a metaphor prompts a listener to unpack those aspects of the descriptor that seem relevant to the target/tenor. This conciseness comes at a price, as the listener may associate different feelings and properties with a concept like *slavery*, or may unpack the descriptor to focus on different aspects than those of interest to the speaker. For instance, a speaker may employ the concept of slavery to focus on the domestic abuse, emotional and physical, suffered by one who is trapped in a bad marriage, while the listener may instead unpack the reference to focus on the institutionalized nature of marriage and slavery. Yet the indeterminate nature of metaphor, a natural consequence of its concision, is often a desirable quality of a conceptual pact. One rarely uses metaphor to communicate a rigid set of facts or beliefs. Rather, metaphors introduce a set of *talking points* for a target, so that speaker and listener might converge toward a mutual understanding, if not of a target idea then of each other's views of the target. The indeterminacy of metaphor makes it a flexible form of communication. While literal language commits a speaker to a fixed interpretation, and offers little scope for the listener to contribute to the joint construction of meaning, metaphorical language suggests a looser but potentially richer meaning that is amenable to collaborative elaboration by each participant in a conversation.

The densest descriptors are the familiar stereotypes that get used time and again in our metaphors and our similes. Although every concept has the potential to be used figuratively, casual metaphors tend to draw their dense descriptors from the large pool of stereotypes shared by most speakers of a language (see Taylor [1954]). Because so many familiar stereotypes have polarizing qualities—think of the endearing and not-so-endearing qualities of babies, for instance—they serve as ideal vehicles for a metaphor that aims to convey a strong affective stance toward a topic. Even when stereotypes are not used figuratively, as in the assertion "*Steve Jobs was a great leader,*" they are often likely to elicit metaphors in response, such as "*yes, a pioneer,*" or "*a true artist!*" or even "*but what a tyrant!*" Familiar proper-named entities can also be used as dense descriptors, as when Steve Jobs is compared to the fictional inventor Tony Stark, or Apple is compared to Scientology, or Google to Microsoft. Metaphors are flexible conceits that draw on dense descriptors to concisely suggest a position on a target idea while seeking elaboration or refutation of this position from others. Our computational models for the interpretation of metaphors must thus allow speakers to exploit the same flexibility of expression when interacting with machines as they enjoy with other humans. Such a goal clearly requires a computational system to possess, or acquire, a great deal of knowledge, usefully clustered into dense pockets of properties, feelings, and expectations that can be evoked with a single word or idea.

2.2   THE "MEANING" OF METAPHOR

If metaphor is as much a process as a product, what then is the meaning of any given metaphor? We can point to the linguistic rendering of a metaphor and say that this string is a linguistic metaphor. We can point to the conceptual structure underpinning this linguistic rendering—and to other renderings of the same conceit—and say that this deep structure is a conceptual metaphor. But to what can we point and say: this is the *meaning* of this metaphor? The problem of metaphor meaning can be approached from a number of perspectives. We can talk of the truth value of a metaphor, much as we can talk of the truth value of any proposition. We can talk of a specific interpretation of a metaphor. Or, we can talk of the specific inferences that a metaphor licenses in the mind of the hearer, as well as the emotions for the target that it is likely to engender in a hearer.

Although most metaphors are literally false, truth value is a remarkably poor guide to the metaphorical nature of any statement. The assertion that *"Barack Obama is a Muslim"* is no more a metaphor because it is false than *"Al Gore is not a robot"* is not a metaphor because it is true. For logicians and philosophers, meaning resides not in truth values but in *truth conditions*, the set of criteria that, if true, would make a statement true as a whole. For instance, in semantic theory in which *"Barack Obama"* denotes the President of the United States in 2015, and in which *"Muslim"* denotes the set of all people who profess faith in the religion of Islam, the key truth condition for *"Barack Obama is a Muslim"* is whether the former individual is a member of the latter set. Different speakers may bring different definitions and denotations to bear on an utterance, and so it is sufficient for some political critics to define the truth condition of *"being a Muslim"* as membership in the set of people born of at least one Muslim parent, or as membership in the set of people born or raised in predominantly Muslim countries. However one finesses the denotations, *"Barack Obama is a Muslim"* has different truth conditions than *"Barack Obama is a socialist,"* as each hinges on membership in different (albeit possibly overlapping) sets, regardless of whether both statements ultimately have the same truth value.

As if defining the literal truth conditions of a predication such as *"being a Muslim"* or *"being a socialist"* weren't hard enough, metaphor poses a further, rather special challenge to the truth-conditional view of meaning. What, for instance, are the truth conditions of the statement *"Barack Obama is the Cicero of the 21st Century?"* One often needs as much creativity to assign truth conditions to a metaphor as to invent one in the first place. For truth conditions are neither as authoritative or as absolute as they seem, nor are they designed by experts to be shared by all. Rather, truth conditions are often speaker-relative and context-sensitive. One speaker may think that to truthfully call one a socialist, it is enough that this person openly espouse socialist values. Another may think it sufficient for one to act like a socialist, whether one actually thinks of oneself as a socialist or not. These speakers are likely to disagree over the truth conditions of the statement *"Barack Obama is a socialist,"* yet this is not a problem for metaphor or for language. The truth conditions of a metaphor often arise from a tacit negotiation between speaker and hearer of the meaning of the metaphor, rather than the other way around.

Philosophers who are otherwise bullish about truth conditional semantics are often bearish toward the idea in the context of metaphor. Donald Davidson, for instance, questions the usefulness of truth conditions for arriving at the meaning of a metaphor. For Davidson [1978], a metaphor does not so much communicate a meaning as inspire a meaning, leading him to argue that "*the attempt to give literal expression to the content of the metaphor is simply misguided.*" Thus, in the metaphor "*my car drinks gasoline,*" only some of the truth conditions associated with literal uses of the verb *to drink* will be applicable in the metaphorical context of a drinking car, but none of these carry the weight of the interpretation that the speaker hopes to inspire in the listener (for instance, that my car requires *too much* gasoline to operate). These truth conditions include, for instance, the expectation that the drinker is an animate creature, that the substance consumed is a potable liquid, and that the drinker both consumes the liquid and derives some chemical benefit from it. Just two of these truth conditions are sensible for the metaphor "*my car drinks gasoline,*" namely that my car consumes gasoline and derives some chemical value from it. In effect, this is the truth-conditional equivalent of Aristotle's strategy (b), whereby the species *to drink* is displaced onto its genus *to consume*. However, to suggest that this banal observation is the speaker's intended meaning is to fly in the face of Grice's *maxim of informativeness* (see Grice [1978]), since the claim of gasoline consumption holds for most cars and is hardly worth mentioning in the context of this car. Rather, as we can expect most listeners to know that cars consume gasoline, that people generally only drink what they want to drink (and thus drink what they like), then the speaker's most likely meaning is *my car likes to drink gasoline and thus consumes a lot of gasoline, rather more than I would prefer*. This meaning cannot be derived from the truth-conditional semantics of the words in the metaphor, but can only emerge from a pragmatic understanding of the world knowledge behind the words.

Black [1962] proposes an *interactionist* view of metaphor that explains how the meaning of a metaphor emerges from a heuristic, common-sense consideration of possible interactions between the ideas raised by the metaphor. For Black, the meaning of a metaphor is more than the sum of the meaning of its parts, and a surprising meaning may thus emerge from the juxtaposition of two rather familiar ideas (in this sense, Black foreshadows the notion of emergent meaning developed by Fauconnier and Turner [2002] in the context of their theory of *conceptual blending*). The use of common-sense knowledge—such as cultural associations, folk beliefs, conventional implicatures, and so on—offers a much richer and open-ended basis for exploring the associations and beliefs that emerge in the mind of the listener in response to a metaphor than a purely truth-conditional approach based on denotations and set membership. As in the more contemporary take on Black's interaction view of metaphor offered by Indurkhya [1992], metaphor is not so much a user of pre-existing similarity as a creator of new similarities, insofar as the meaning that emerges from a metaphorical juxtaposition reveals the source and target to be more similar than the listener may have previously realized. Davidson and Black (and later researchers such as Indurkhya) agree that what makes metaphor special is not the truth conditions imposed by its words on the semantics of the specific utterance, but the system of ideas and associations that are evoked—in response to the metaphor—in the mind of a "suitable" listener in a "suitable" context. A key question for Davidson is whether this system of ideas and associations can be considered the *secondary* or *special meaning* of the metaphor (where the literal interpretation serves as the primary meaning), or indeed whether it is well-founded to consider a metaphor as having such a secondary meaning. As Davidson [1978] points out, similes do their work without the need for a secondary meaning—they typically mean what they purport to mean on the surface—so why should metaphors be any different?

Specifically, Black and Davidson disagree on the extent to which it is sensible to speak of the special meaning of a metaphor (as opposed to the literal meaning that resides on the surface) as a parcel of cognitive content that is communicated from speaker to listener. Davidson [1978] explicitly denies the position (which he attributes to Black) that a metaphor "asserts or implies certain complex things by dint of a special meaning and *thus* accomplishes its job of yielding an insight" (his italics). For Davidson, to speak of the meaning of a metaphor as a distinct message or insight is simply wrong-headed, as misguided as speaking about the definitive meaning of a poem, a joke, or a theatrical play. For instance, what does it mean to speak of the meaning of a play? At one level, the only level at which Davidson argues that it is sensible to speak of the meaning of a metaphor, a play means just what its words and sentences purport to mean, although it may also nudge a viewer to think certain thoughts or consider certain possibilities about the world. The deeper meaning of a play, what one might call its message to the audience, is not contained in the text itself, but is inspired in the mind of a viewer. Davidson's view is reminiscent of the angry response by the Irish playwright Brendan Behan to an interviewer who had asked him to summarize the message of his most recent work: "*Message? What the hell do you think I am, a postman?*" However, the fact that two viewers may find themselves in agreement in their responses to a play, and find that their responses agree with those intended by the playwright, suggests that playwrights may nonetheless be successfully asserting some secondary meaning via their work. Likewise, the fact that listeners may agree as to the insights delivered by a metaphor, and agree with the speaker as to the nature of these insights, speaks to the reality that speakers often do aim to assert something with their metaphors that is not to be found in the literal meaning of their statements. Indeed, as Black [1979] notes, the fact that listeners may disagree with each other, or with a speaker, in their response to a metaphor suggests that speakers do wish to assert some measure of propositional content with their metaphors. The difficulty of precisely pinpointing and circumscribing this propositional content (or the impossibility of doing this *in principle* for all metaphors) should not lead us to infer that it never exists, or give up on the task of trying to pinpoint (formally or computationally) at least part of this meaning.

2.3   PARAPHRASING METAPHOR

Most discussions about the meaning of a given metaphor inevitably turn on our ability to produce a convincing paraphrase. Yet Davidson [1978] raises a cautionary note when he argues that "what we attempt in 'paraphrasing' a metaphor cannot be to give its meaning, as that lies on the surface; rather, we attempt to evoke what the metaphor brings to our attention." So just what is a paraphrase then? If we take what "lies on the surface" of a metaphor to be its literal content in the source domain, and what it "brings to our attention" to be its literal focal point in the target domain, then what we mean by a literal paraphrase is a *target-domain* paraphrase. This distinction, although perhaps obvious, is an important one. After all, many metaphors—such as negative metaphors—are literally true. In the case of negative metaphors such as "*I am not Superman,*" "*Money does not grow on trees,*" and "*Your father is not an ATM,*" the surface meaning from the source-domain of each is literally true and just as informative as the corresponding metaphor, but it cannot usefully be taken as a literal paraphrase of the metaphor. Likewise, a paraphrase that merely transforms a metaphor into a simile—such as "*it's like my car drinks gasoline*"—may yield a reformulation that is literally true, but it does nothing to shift the focus of our attention to the relevant area of the target-domain. (The relation of metaphor to simile, and the ability to expand/compress/paraphrase one as the other, is the subject of ongoing debate; see e.g., Glucksberg and Haught [2006]; Utsumi [2007]; and Barnden [2012] for a flavor of this debate.) In other words, it is not the literalness of a paraphrase that makes it a useful guide to a metaphor, but its literalness with respect to the target domain.

Because concise metaphors are often the most under-specified, they frequently offer the most open-ended interpretations and require the most complex target-domain paraphrases. Indeed, this richness of possible paraphrases may not be an accidental feature of metaphor but a driving force in its interpretation. Utsumi [2007, 2011] refers to this richness as the *interpretative diversity* of a metaphor. Utsumi argues that listeners often choose an interpretation strategy (such as, e.g., a comparison of source to target, or a categorization of the target under a category suggested by the source) that increases the diversity of the resulting interpretation. Consider the metaphor "*wishes are children*" from the musical *Into The Woods*. This metaphor, coupled with the narrative context in which it is used—a fairy-tale world in which wishes come true with unexpected consequences—can evoke a diversity of more-or-less mutually consistent thoughts about wishes and their fulfillment, which might be paraphrased thus: "*wishes are born of our deepest desires;*" "*wishes have lives of their own and grow to follow their own paths;*" "*wishes can bring us pain as well as joy;*" "*we give life to our wishes and so are responsible for their consequences;*" etc. Related figurative phenomena, such as metonymy, may also play a role in paraphrasing a metaphor. For instance, one might consider wishes to be the stuff of childish optimism, and thus consider wish-makers to be child-like in their approach to life. Childless couples often wish for children, and so their wishes—when they come true, as in the case of one sub-plot of *Into The Woods*—actually become children. However, for Davidson at least, the metaphor means just what it says on the surface: that is, in truth-conditional terms, for every wish w there exists a child c such that $w = c$. As such, none of those prior statements is a paraphrase of the metaphor, rather they are a prior justification for it or a posterior response to it.

Davidson's injunction against "*attempt[s] to give literal expression to the content of [a] metaphor*" further reminds us that metaphor is never reducible to a literal restatement, no matter how detailed that restatement may be. This fact is tautological in its obviousness, for, by definition, any literal restatement is *not* a metaphor, does not resonate with the same semantic tension as a metaphor, does not tease and thrill with the same ambiguity and under-specification as a metaphor, and does not pose a comparable challenge to our conceptual systems. Moreover, any literal restatement is not a paraphrase of the actual meaning of the metaphor, but a paraphrase of just one interpretation. The meaning of a metaphor resides not in a single authoritative interpretation, but in a whole space of possible interpretations. The indeterminacy and interpretative diversity of metaphor lends it an elasticity that cannot be captured in literal language. No matter how detailed our paraphrase, a metaphor always holds out the promise of more—more detail, more mappings, more associations—if we would only deepen our search. Finally, a paraphrase does not propose the same conceptual pact to an audience, and so is unable to serve the same communicative role as the metaphor it replaces.

One important communicative role that is not captured by an explicit paraphrase is *plausible deniability*, wherein a speaker uses metaphor to communicate a tendentious claim, and subsequently appeals to the ambiguity of metaphor to deflect criticism if this claim is ill-received by an audience. Consider the case of Republican presidential candidate Donald Trump, who was challenged on his alleged record of sexism by FOX-News reporter Megyn Kelly during the first televised GOP debate in 2015. Trump rebutted the charge and complained of mistreatment at the hands of the debate moderators, later claiming in an interview that "*you could see there was blood coming out of her* [Kelly's] *eyes, blood coming out of her wherever.*" Many commentators in the media took Trump's comments to be a potent mixture of metaphor, metonymy, hyperbole, and bombast. Although Trump painted a picture of a woman possessed by a demon, bleeding uncontrollably from every orifice, and thus lacking control over her own physical and mental state, his under-specified reference to a woman bleeding from "*her wherever*" was widely taken to be a metonymic reference to menstruation. Trump, it was claimed, was simply giving new form to the old charge that a woman who behaves aggressively to a man must be in the irrational grip of premenstrual tension. In a daring move, Trump was seemingly fighting charges of sexism with more sexism, yet when pressed on the matter, he defended himself with this tweet: "*Re Megyn Kelly quote: 'you could see there was blood coming out of her eyes, blood coming out of her wherever' (NOSE). Just got on w/thought.*" He elaborated further in a subsequent statement, claiming that "*Only a deviant would think anything else.*" Although we can debate Trump's actual intentions for his blood metaphor, it does seem that its non-literal under-specification was an essential part of its communicative function, allowing Trump to push a provocative idea into the public sphere while denying that this idea was ever part of his intended message. Another issue with literal paraphrases then is that they sometimes render in plain speech an opinion that was never intended to be plainly expressed or openly interrogated in the first place.

Yet, for all this, there is little to be gained from being a radical skeptic on the matter of literal restatement. Paraphrases may be necessarily imperfect, but they possess a practical utility for researchers and speakers alike. For, in establishing a conceptual pact, a metaphorical utterance may prompt a listener to produce a paraphrase in response, as the listener's own contribution to the construction of a joint meaning space. By doing so, the listener may propose a particular reading of a metaphor that enriches and elaborates upon the speaker's own viewpoint. In effect, this exchange of paraphrases serves to align the understanding of both speaker and listener, and allows each to arrive at a deeper appreciation of a metaphor. For similar reasons, and for others that are distinctly computational, the ability to produce a literal paraphrase of a figurative statement is also of some practical value in a computational setting. Not only does paraphrasing allow a computer to explain its interpretation of a metaphor, in a way that allows users to detect a failure of interpretation, it also allows a computer to directly assign a semantic representation to a metaphor that is consistent with the system's own axioms, so that then it can reason safely about the metaphor's contents. Indeed, in a wide range of NLP systems—such as for sentiment analysis, information retrieval and extraction, question answering, and summarization—literal paraphrasing can support a perfectly adequate approach to metaphor meaning that is just as deep as the system's treatment of literal texts and literal meanings.

As shown in our earlier discussion of the metaphor "*wishes are children*," we need not limit ourselves to purely literal statements when paraphrasing a metaphor, and so, perhaps, neither should our NLP systems. The value of any paraphrase lies in its ability to explain a challenging turn of phrase using more conventional and less taxing language. This is so whether the text to be paraphrased uses the non-literal language of poetry or the literal language of legalistic jargon (as found, say, in a legal contract or a patent application). Indeed, the latter demonstrates that the most natural and most useful paraphrase is not always the most literal, and less challenging forms of figurative expression, such as a familiar conventional metaphor, may better convey the intended meaning of a metaphor. For example, when paraphrasing a metaphorical description of a wine as "*muscular*," it is more helpful than not to exploit the conventional if metaphorical view of wines as possessing a "*body*." Or consider the metaphor "*to pick up a touch of the flu*," which in turn contains a pair of tactile metaphors, "*to pick up*" and "*touch*." The first of these is perhaps more naturally paraphrased using the conventional metaphor "*to catch*," which is very commonly used with infections, rather than the strictly literal and somewhat dramatic "*become infected by*" or "*to suffer from*." The second is perhaps best paraphrased using the modifier "*mild*" for "*flu*," even though the idea of mildness is likely a metaphor itself in this context. Indeed, it is hard to find a concise literal rendering for the tactile metaphor "*touch*:" a touch suggests a glancing contact, which implies a contact of short duration that lacks force. So a "*touch of flu*" implies a short-lived infection that does not manifest the worst symptoms of the ailment.

An acceptance of the occasional conventional metaphor in a supposedly literal paraphrase is especially useful in the context of statistical models of metaphor, for it is in the nature of conventional metaphor to be used habitually and to assume the status of normative, literal language over time, to the extent that the two are hard to separate on statistical grounds alone. Indeed, much of what we consider literal was once a newly minted figurative form that, as the philosopher Nietzsche put it, has become the base metal of literal coinage through oft-repeated usage. An NLP system that aims to remove all metaphor from language will find much—perhaps too much—to remove, and will be left with precious little with which to compose its paraphrases. In contrast to the divide between the figurative and the literal, the unconventional/conventional divide has an observable reality in large text corpora that is conducive to statistical analysis (e.g., Shutova et al. [2012], Bollegala and Shutova [2013]). It is a quantifiable reality that allows a paraphrasing system to learn to do as human paraphrasers do: to generate helpful conventional paraphrases from unconventional metaphors. If such paraphrases contain conventional metaphors, as they are very likely to do, this need not pose a serious challenge to the semantic representations of an NLP system. Conventional metaphors are part of the furniture of language, and can easily be accommodated—with some design forethought—in a system's core representations. For instance, both the *MIDAS* system of Martin [1990] and the *ATT-META* system of Barnden and Lee [2002], and Barnden [2006] put a semantic representation of conventional metaphors at the heart of their metaphor interpretation systems. *MIDAS* and *ATT-META* each show, through their different uses of schematic structures, how an NLP system can support a wider range of inferences, and, thus, a fuller interpretation of a metaphor, by reserving a place for the metaphor in its semantic and conceptual representation of an utterance.

2.4   METAPHOR AND SIMILE

Since the worldview communicated by a metaphor is often shaped by a speaker's perception of a situation or an interlocutor, simile—the figurative device most often called upon to simultaneously communicate and explain our perceptions—can be of particular use when paraphrasing a metaphorical worldview. Consider the metaphor "*marriage is slavery*:" while there is little insight to be gained by paraphrasing this metaphor with the simile "*marriage is like slavery*," there is much to be gained from the paraphrase "*this marriage is like the relationship between a slaver and his slave: you act like you own me, and treat me like your slave*." The use of similes imbues this paraphrase with three interesting qualities. First, the similes bring a desirable emotional distance to the description of an undesirable relationship, for the assertion "*you act like you own me*" conveys a very different affect than "*you own me*" or "*you are my owner*." Second, the paraphrasing similes are not freighted with the same semantic tension as the original metaphor, since similes merely assert the similarity of two ideas and openly admit—through their use of "*as*" or "*like*"—to the counterfactuality of a viewpoint. That is, every simile "A is like B" asserts not just that *A is similar to B*, but that *A is very much not B*. Finally, the similes not only explain the meaning of the metaphor, but offer a rationale for it too: the paraphrase suggests that the metaphor is the speaker's way of making sense of the bad behavior of others.

The implicit negation in every simile makes simile a particularly good choice for paraphrasing a negative metaphor. For, just as explicit similes contain tacit negations, explicit negations often suggest tacit similes, especially when the negation emphasizes the figurative qualities of a descriptor. Since most negative metaphors are trivially true in a literal sense, insofar as the underlying positive metaphor is literally absurd, then each negative metaphor is also its own literal paraphrase. Thus, it really is the case that no man is an island; that your wife is not your maid; that your overbearing boss does not own you; that your college fund is not an ATM; etc. Yet there is more to a negative metaphor than the negation of an obvious falsehood. A negative metaphor is not so much a disavowal of an explicit metaphor, or of the tacit conceptual pact that it implies, as it is an explicit repudiation of someone else's implicit simile. Why else would we need to say something that is so obviously true? So, the frustrated wife who cries at her boorish spouse "*I am not your maid!*" is in fact saying "*Do not treat me like your maid!*" The moody teenager who snaps at a concerned neighbor "*You are not my father*" is in fact saying "*Stop acting like my father.*" And the man who needs to be told that "*No man is an island*" is no doubt acting like someone who believes the opposite. Similes allow a speaker to be abundantly clear as to the perceptual foundations of a figurative viewpoint, and clear in ways that are hard to achieve in metaphor.

Giora et al. [2010] argue that negation, when used to convey such apparently obvious facts, is a *metaphor-inducing operation*. So, like metaphors and similes, negations of the false or the absurd are much more likely to activate the figurative aspects of a descriptor than any literal qualities. Metaphor involves highly selective inference (see Hobbs [1981]) and the assertion "*I'm no Superman*" selectively activates the qualities of the cultural icon (and very dense descriptor) *Superman* that are most often projected by a metaphor or a simile, such as *strength*, *resilience*, and *speed*, rather than any literal quality related to appearance (e.g., wearing a red cape, or red underwear on the outside) or behavior (e.g., fighting crime, working in disguise as a reporter, etc.). Precisely what these figurative qualities are for a given descriptor is something that one would have difficulty discerning from only metaphorical uses of the descriptor, as metaphors rarely make explicit the qualities that are projected onto the target. This brings us then to another aspect of similes that makes them so useful to the computational modeling of metaphor. Not only do similes explicitly mark their figurative status with "*like*" or "*as*," and frequently indicate the perceptual roots of their viewpoint with qualifiers such as "*act like*," "*smell like*," "*look like*," etc., they also often explicitly identify the qualities that are transferred from the source/vehicle to the target/tenor.

The scholar Quintilian saw the difference between metaphor and simile as the difference between an implicit and an explicit comparison. Not only does a simile mark the comparison between a *comparandum* and its *comparatum*, it may also provide a third element, a *tertium*, to state the reasons why both are seen as similar [Roberts, 2007]. In the English simile frame "*X is as Y as Z*" the tertium is given by the *[Y]* element, although a speaker may omit the tertium to say simply that "*X is like Z.*" But when the tertium is explicit, as it always is in "*as-as*" similes, a listener can acquire from the similes of others a sense of the properties of a *[Z]* that are most likely to be activated in a figurative comparison. In this way, similes become an important vector for the transmission of cultural knowledge via language; as Charles Dickens puts it in the opening page of *A Christmas Carol*, "*the wisdom of our ancestors is in the simile.*" Dickens was referring to the swirl of stock similes that were common currency in the language and culture of his day, but the modern scholar, or modern NLP system, now has access to a long-tail of diverse similes—

and diverse tertia—for a wide range of useful descriptors on the Web. Consider again the dense descriptor *Superman*: a Google search for the phrasal query "*as * as Superman*" (here * denotes a wildcard that can match any token in a text) returns web documents that fill the tertium * position with the following values: *strong, powerful, fast, mighty, invulnerable, resilient, cool*, and *American*. As these properties are frequently highlighted in figurative similes, it seems reasonable to assume that a metaphorical use of Superman will draw on the same properties.

The relationship between metaphor and simile is itself best described as a simile. Metaphor is like simile but it is not simile; nor is it wholly reducible to simile. Nonetheless, each concerns itself with the similarity of two ideas, and each focuses on qualities that readily extend across domains. So, just as similes can be used to make explicit the qualities that go unsaid in a metaphor, they can also be used to learn those very qualities, to provide—as we shall see later—the large set of dense descriptors that is required by any metaphor processing system.

2.5 METAPHOR AND ANALOGY

From Aristotle to Cicero to Quintilian, the earliest treatments of metaphor put similarity at the heart of the phenomenon, but agree on no single approach to formalizing similarity. Recall that Aristotle's four-fold scheme posits three ways in which inter-category similarity can be used to form a metaphor (strategies (a) to (c)) and a single way in which analogical similarity can be used (strategy (d)). Yet these strategies are not claimed to be mutually exclusive, and so, we can imagine a metaphor simultaneously exploiting both categorization and analogy together. It is thus useful to see the metaphor "*marriage is slavery*" as both a categorization statement (putting marriage in the same category of unpleasant situations as slavery) and as an analogy (so husbands are to wives, or wives are to husbands, as owners are to slaves). Yet the dichotomy between, on one hand, similarity arising from shared category membership, and on the other, similarity based on analogical proportion, is one that still separates modern theories of metaphor production and interpretation.

Aristotle's category membership approach survives, in a more finessed form, in Glucksberg's [1998, 2008] *category inclusion* view of metaphor. Whereas Aristotle's scheme (c)—in which the name of one species is applied to another of the same genus—presumes that source and target share a pre-existing membership in a common genus, Glucksberg argues this sharing is a *result* of the metaphor and not a cause. Moreover, since the Aristotelian scheme is easily trivialized when applied within a well-connected category hierarchy that ultimately places every concept under an all-embracing category root, Glucksberg's category inclusion view argues that the source and target categories cannot simply share, or be made to share, just any genus category. The point of metaphor, after all, is not just to assert that two ideas happen to share a common category; at the very least, a metaphor must also suggest a means of naming the specific category that the speaker has in mind. For Glucksberg, then, the source of a metaphor does not so much represent itself but the broader category of which it is a highly representative member. As such, "*slavery*" does not literally denote either the legal or historical sense of *slavery* in the metaphor "*marriage is slavery*," but any institutionalized system of exploitation and oppression. In contrast to the classical view of categorization, which models categories as simple mathematical sets, modern cognitive psychologists adopt a textured view of category structure in which some members are more central than others. The most central members may be so associated with a category—such as *shark* and *wolf* for the category of *ruthless predators*, *jail* for *oppressive and confining situations*, *slavery* for *cruel and exploitative relationships*—that they offer a more evocative, concise, and convenient way of naming that category than any literal alternative.

Yet Aristotle's strategy (d), analogical proportion, suggests how we might side-step this search for a mediating category altogether. For there is no need to find a common genus to unite the source and the target if the two can be reconciled by means of direct, unmediated relational similarities. By this reckoning, metaphors are made from the same stuff as scientific analogies: one observes a pattern of relationships in one domain, the tenor or target domain, and is reminded of a parallel set of relationships in another, the vehicle or source domain. But, as argued by the structure-mapping school of analogy [Gentner, 1983], a good analogy is more than a set of observed correspondences between domains. Rather, these correspondences—systematically linking two different conceptual structures—are just the starting point of an analogy. Having anchored elements of the source domain to the target domain, these correspondences then guide the transfer of additional material from the source into the target. For example, the Bohr/Rutherford analogy of atomic structure views the nucleus of the atom as occupying a relationally parallel position to the sun in a solar system, so that the electrons that orbit around the nucleus are the nanoscopic equivalent of the planets that orbit around the sun. Having established these correspondences, the analogy can now suggest a causal explanation for the orbit of electrons, by importing the causal explanation for the orbit of planets around a sun: for, just as the sun keeps speeding planets in orbit via a cosmic force, gravity, a comparable force must be attracting speeding electrons to stay in orbit around a nucleus. Gentner argues that many metaphors also work in this way: a source is chosen because of its analogical parallels to the target, and because it contains additional conceptual material that a speaker also wishes to assert of the target. A listener unpacks the metaphor by uncovering much the same parallels, and by then using these as a guide to the transfer of additional material from the source.

Consider again the metaphor "*marriage is slavery.*" A systematic analogy between *marriage* and *slavery* will identify abusive behaviors in both domains and create mappings between the protagonists and agonists of these behaviors. Thus, abusive husbands may be slave-owners and abused wives their slaves, while matchmakers can be mapped to slave dealers, family homes to plantations, wedding rings to shackles, marriage licenses to ownership papers, etc. A particular mapping is systematic if its elements are well-connected to each other, especially if they are connected via parallel causal relationships that explain how the various parts of a domain influence other parts of the same domain. Having established correspondences between ideas in the source and target domains, an analogy can now transplant onto the target any relationships that link these ideas in the source domain, to provide new insights as to the cause of these behaviors in the target domain. For instance, slave owners beat their slaves while abusive husbands beat their wives. But slave owners beat their slaves because they believe they own them, and see them as mere physical objects to mistreat as they see fit. By analogy, abusive husbands may beat their wives because they, too, believe they own them, and because they, too, view them as mere physical objects.

Any model of metaphor that hinges on the identification of a common genus, whether it has the simplicity of Aristotle's earliest scheme or the sophistication of Glucksberg's category inclusion model, operates by reducing the specific to the generic. Such approaches are best suited to the generation and interpretation of familiar metaphors, or to apparently novel metaphors that dress up old conceits in new ways. In contrast, the structure-mapping approach does not aim to see, or need to see, the generic in the specific, and so, *ceteris paribus*, is just as capable of seeing the analogical proportions between the source and target ideas of a truly original metaphor as it is for those of a wholly conventional pairing. However, this also means that the analogical approach will fail to capture the sense of familiarity that one experiences when faced with a timeworn combination of ideas, just as it must fail to capture the thrill that accompanies a truly original pairing. Of course, even the most hackneyed metaphor was once fresh and novel, and, although time does not change the substance of our metaphors, it does change the way we see them, and perhaps even the way we process them.

With two alternate approaches to choose from, each of which is better suited to a different kind, or historical *stage*, of metaphor, it makes sense to view these not as competing but as complementary approaches. As proposed by Bowdle and Gentner [2005] in their *career of metaphor* hypothesis, fresh metaphors that do not obviously instantiate a familiar conceit are more naturally understood as analogies. Structure-mapping analysis allows listeners to identify the parallel relationships in source and target domains that contribute to a new metaphor, thus allowing them to abstract from the source those parts of its meaning that are most likely to contribute to other metaphors. As speakers become habituated to a given metaphor, and to other metaphors that use the same source for similar ends, they come to think of the source as a vehicle for those parts of its conceptual structure that are transferable across domains. In effect, they form an abstracted representation of the source that ultimately allows the metaphor, and similar metaphors with the same source, to be understood in category inclusion terms.

The earliest account of metaphor, as offered by Aristotle, acknowledges that metaphor is a complex phenomenon that calls for a varied approach. Although any mixed model that recognizes the *career* of metaphor will inevitably lack the parsimony of a one-size-fits-all approach, it is surely preferable to tailor our models to the phenomenon than to cut the phenomenon to fit our models.

2.5.1   DOMAIN REPRESENTATIONS IN METAPHOR AND ANALOGY

As much as language unites us in our use of words to describe the world to each other, we are all free to think what we will about the world, or at least those aspects of the world that interest us the most. Different speakers may thus employ very different representations of the same domains, leading to strong disagreements about the most natural interpretation of a metaphor or an analogy involving those domains. Consider this exchange from the film *Jurassic Park*, between the owner and operator of the park (Hammond) and a mathematician (Malcolm) who has been tasked with evaluating the park:

> **John Hammond**: All major theme parks have delays. When they opened Disneyland in 1956, nothing worked!

> **Dr. Ian Malcolm**: Yeah, but, John, if The Pirates of the Caribbean breaks down, the pirates don't eat the tourists.

Here we see Hammond attempt to mitigate problems with his park by comparing them to the teething difficulties experienced in perhaps the most prototypical theme park of all, *Disneyland*. His representation of both domains (*Disneyland* and *Jurassic Park*) is thus high-level and generic, and so the resulting analogy lacks detail. If it is not so very different from an analogy comparing *Amazon.com* to *Barnes and Noble*, this blandness speaks to Hammond's larger goal in using this analogy. In response, Malcolm focuses on the specific problems at hand (namely, the hungry dinosaurs running amok all about them), and so brings to mind a very specific representation of *Disneyland* to suit the very specific representation of *Jurassic Park* that circumstances have forced upon him. Had Malcolm made an additional joke about both parks suffering very different kinds of *teething* problems, this pun would require an even more detailed representation of the source and target domains (e.g., technical glitches in the representation of *Disneyland* could map to the problems wrought by the dinosaurs' sharp teeth in the representation of *Jurassic Park*). Analogies and metaphors that are used to persuade are not simple one-shot efforts at communication. Rather, as argued in Cameron [2007], they form part of a larger framework of negotiation and alignment that allows speaker and listener to focus on the same aspects of a domain (or to at least see the other's point of view). As highlighted by this example, the representation of the domains in an analogy (and thus any metaphor based on an analogy) is open to negotiation by the speakers during the formation and interpretation of the analogy. It is not realistic to assume that these representations are pre-formed before the analogy is made and simply retrieved from memory to participate in a process of structure mapping. Rather, it seems more accurate to suppose that the search processes required by analogy involve more than a search through the space of possible alignments between two representations, but also a search through the space of possible representations to align.

2.6 CONCEPTUAL METAPHOR THEORY

Black and Davidson each tell us that the meaning of metaphor is not to be found in word meanings, but in the world itself, or at least in our models of the world. Lexical semantics can only take an NLP system so far, and the crucial ingredient in any metaphor-processing system is its array of conceptual representations. The field of cognitive linguistics, as exemplified by the work of Mark Johnson and George Lakoff [Johnson, 1987, Lakoff and Johnson, 1980], goes further still in emphasizing the role of world knowledge. A metaphor-processing system—whether human or machine—must possess an *embodied* understanding of the world: it must understand the mind's relation to the body and the body's relation to the world. These relationships are not literal, but are themselves governed by foundational metaphors that are grounded in our physical understanding of space, orientation, movement, and containment. These schematic structures—embodied concepts such as *Path* and *Container* and the metaphors built on top of them—are independent of language. Indeed, Lakoff and Johnson argue that metaphor is not primarily a linguistic phenomenon at all. Language is merely the stage on which metaphor does its most noticeable work.

The conceptual perspective sees metaphors as more than the finished products of creative language but as the very building blocks of thought itself. Complex world-views can be constructed from these conceptual metaphors, just as complex metaphors can themselves be constructed from simpler, lower-level metaphors. Grady [1997] argues that physical embodiment is the key to acquiring the latter kind of metaphor, which he dubs *"primary."* For instance, from a young age we come to associate—or as Johnson [1999] puts it, *conflate*—affection with physical closeness and shared bodily warmth, and continue throughout our lives to express affection through physical touch. It is unsurprising then that we develop the primary metaphor (Emotional) Affection is (Physical) Warmth, which allows us to talk of close relationships as *warm* relationships, of distant relationships as *cold* relationships, of giving someone *"the cold shoulder"* or *"a warm welcome."* Primary metaphors are not arbitrary: rather, just as they are born of past physical experience they also offer a useful prediction of future physical experience. Thus, we can expect a *warm welcome* to involve a physical embrace, while we can also expect those who give us the *cold shoulder* to keep their distance from us.

So the physical world serves as a sand-box in which a cognitive agent learns to associate cause and effect and to fit cognitive structures to concrete reality. For instance, we learn that objects are usefully grouped into piles; that adding to a pile makes it bigger and higher; that taking from a pile makes it smaller and lower; and thus, more generally, that more of anything implies upward accumulation, while less of anything implies downward reduction. In other words, we learn that More is Up and Less is Down. Likewise, our interactions with physical containers informs us of their affordances and limitations, and allows us to generalize a more abstract notion of containment that is conducive to cross-domain metaphorical reasoning. To appreciate the power of conceptual metaphors in a physical, non-linguistic setting, consider this tale of the Parsis and how they first came to settle in India. *Time Out Guide to Mumbai* offers a concise version of the legend:

> *They* [The Parsis] *arrived in Gujarat in the eighth or ninth century and sought asylum from the local king. He is said to have sent them away with a glass of milk full to the brim—his way of saying that his kingdom was full. The Parsi elders conferred, added some sugar to the milk and sent it back—to suggest that they would mix thoroughly and sweeten the life of the community.*

So, with the right objects to hand, one does not need words to communicate with metaphors. The glass proves to be a remarkably versatile vehicle of meaning, for both the king's message and that of the Parsi elders, because it instantiates a highly productive cognitive structure called the CONTAINER schema (see Johnson [1987]). The king uses the glass to represent a country: a country, like a glass, is a container, not just of liquids but of people and places and resources. Like a typical container, a country has physical boundaries that mark its extent; like a typical container, one can put things into a country or one can take them out again; and, like a typical container, a country can be full (of people) or it can be empty. Thus, the king uses a full glass of milk to convey the conceptual metaphor A COUNTRY IS A CONTAINER, but with the kicker "*this one is full.*" As the glass shuttles back and forth, it is used to carry subtly different meanings, each pivoting on the figurative affordances of the CONTAINER schema. The Parsis fashion their riposte from a different CONTAINER metaphor, LIFE IS A CONTAINER, one that can be figuratively filled with diverse events, relationships, and feelings. In contrast to the physical affordances of the COUNTRY IS A CONTAINER metaphor, which implies that countries are physical containers with physical limits on the amount of physical contents they can hold, LIFE IS A CONTAINER is a more abstract metaphor that places no such limits on its abstract contents. If LIFE IS A CONTAINER, it is a container with an unbounded capacity for emotional and cultural possibilities. The king and the Parsis are effectively playing a game of tropes, where the Parsis trump the king's use of the CONTAINER schema with a more creative metaphor of their own.

The CONTAINER schema is ubiquitous in language and thought. We talk of minds as containers of beliefs (perhaps "*bursting with ideas*"), of lives as containers of events (allowing some to live "*a full life*"), of texts as containers of words, and words as containers of meanings. Our relationships can be figuratively conceived as containers, too (as in "*there were three of us in that marriage*"), although we most often anchor our metaphors for personal relationships in the SOURCE-PATH-GOAL (or SPG) schema. Thus, we talk of relationships that "*are going nowhere,*" of relationships that have "*gone through a rough patch*" and are still "*on the rocks,*" or those that have "*hit the buffers*" or even "*come off the rails.*" Purposeful activities of all kinds are conceptually anchored in the SPG schema [Johnson, 1987], allowing us to talk of "*career paths,*" of being "*held back,*" and of "*getting ahead.*" Schemas such as SPG and CONTAINER allow us to talk of the big intangible ideas, such as LIFE and LOVE, in terms of physical objects that we can see and grasp and follow. When said out loud, SPG-based conceptual metaphors such as LIFE IS A JOURNEY sound like the most hackneyed of clichés, yet, as Lakoff and Johnson [1980] demonstrate, they exude a powerful influence on the way we see and talk about the world. They are evident in the way our thoughts and our texts often cohere around a single unifying metaphor. Although conceptual metaphors are most apparent in our clichés, they underpin even our most creative efforts. Whenever we riff on a creative metaphor, as the Parsis did with the king's figurative use of a physical container, we are instantiating and extending a conceptual metaphor.

Unsurprisingly, Conceptual Metaphor Theory (CMT) has significant implications for the computational modeling of metaphor in language [Lakoff, 1994, Lakoff and Johnson, 1980].

CMT-inspired computational models of metaphor range from symbolic approaches that focus on high-level data structures and knowledge-representations (e.g., Martin [1990]), to cognitive and neurological approaches that focus on lower-level arrangements of neuron-like activation elements and their interconnections (e.g., Feldman [2006]). But, regardless of which view of CMT is implemented, it is not enough that an NLP system goes beyond mere lexical semantics to embrace rich conceptual representations of target and source domains. It must embrace the *right kinds* of conceptual representations. Most theories of metaphor that lend themselves to a computational realization are ultimately agnostic about conceptual structure. Although they stipulate that such structures are necessary, and provide the general form of these structures—whether the set-theoretic genus/species representations of Aristotle, the graph-theoretic representations of Gentner's analogical structure-mapping approach, or the textured category representations of Glucksberg's category inclusion model—they do not make ontological commitments to the representations of particular concepts, such as CONTAINER, PATH, ORIENTATION, FORCE, etc. CMT argues that, for any agent to make and understand metaphors like a human, it must have the same conceptual biases as a human, and anchor its model of the world in the same foundational schemas. However, while these schematic concepts have an embodied basis in human cognition, this is not to suggest that an NLP system must also be embodied in the same way. Developmental roboticists may find some value in embodying a computational realization of CMT in an anthropomorphic robot, but this is neither necessary nor useful for a metaphor-capable NLP system. Such schemas are the conceptual products of physical embodiment, and it is enough that our systems also contain representations of these schemas that afford the same kinds of conceptual inferences.

For example, the *MIDAS* system of Martin [1990] employs the basic schematic structures of CMT to anchor and guide its interpretation of conventional metaphors and variations thereof. A single conventional metaphor may be instantiated in a wide range of domain-specific variations, as Martin demonstrates in the context of a dialogue system for offering Unix advice. This domain offers ample opportunity for the use of physically motivated conceptual schemas to describe otherwise intangible phenomena, since, e.g., computer users conventionally conceive of software processes as living things (prompting the metaphor "*How do I kill a runaway process?*") and software environments as containers (prompting the metaphor "*How do I get out of Emacs?*"). In another CMT-inspired approach, Veale and Keane [1992] employ the schemas of ORIENTATION and CONTAINER as semantic primitives in a lexico-conceptual representation they call a *Conceptual Scaffolding*. In contrast to other systems of semantic primitives, which conventionally employ such primitives as final, irreducible components of utterance meaning, these operators are intermediate placeholders that are designed to be replaced by domain-specific constructs during subsequent processes of interpretation and inference. Scaffolding operators are always replaced in this way, whether the speaker intends an utterance to be read literally or figuratively. Literal and metaphoric uses of image-schematic notions of containment (such as "*falling into a manhole*" vs. "*falling into debt*") and orientation (such as "*sliding down the hill*" vs. "*sliding down the polls*") will thus use precisely the same operators in precisely the same way in their respective scaffolding structures. The versatility of the CMT schemas allows the scaffolding construction process to be agnostic as to the literal or figurative status of an utterance, and pushes a decision on this distinction into the realm of inference and common-sense reasoning, where Black [1962] and Davidson [1978] each say it belongs. Alternatively, one can use CMT's schematic structures as a cognitively grounded vocabulary for tagging linguistic metaphors in large corpora with the appropriate conceptual annotations. A large corpus of metaphors annotated in this fashion may allow a computational system to learn to recognize and categorize unseen variations on these metaphors in free text, or to, perhaps, even generate novel variations of their own.

2.7   CONCEPTUAL INTEGRATION AND BLENDING

If figurative phenomena blur the boundaries between very different concepts and domains, we should not be surprised if they also blur the boundaries between themselves. It can be quite a challenge, even for a seasoned researcher, to determine precisely what figurative mechanism is at work in any given example of non-literal language. Metonymy and metaphor are often tightly bound up together, with metonymy providing the subtle glue to seamlessly tie metaphors to their targets. Thus, in the news headlines *"Chipotle shares hit by E. Coli scare"* and *"Nike jumps on share buyback,"* the metonymies *company* → *share* and *share* → *share_price* are necessary for the respective metaphors, HITTING IS DIMINISHING and JUMPING IS INCREASING, to take hold (note also the punning humor of the verb *"jump"* in the context of Nike, a maker of basketball shoes; Brône and Feyaerts [2005] describe this phenomenon as *double grounding*). Different kinds of figurative phenomena are not always marked at the linguistic level, and so an implicit comparison, in which the source and target are not explicitly identified with each other in the same utterance, may be taken as a metaphor by some, a simile by others, or an analogy by dissenters to both of these views. Moreover, what seems like a comparison to some may be taken as a categorization by others. Consider again our earlier example from the movie *Jurassic Park*. In particular, consider again the quote from the park owner, John Hammond:

> **Hammond**: All major theme parks have delays. When they opened Disneyland in 1956, nothing worked!

It makes sense here to understand Hammond's observation as an implicit comparison between Disneyland and Jurassic Park, although the latter is not explicitly mentioned. Nothing is seemingly working in Jurassic Park, but nothing worked in 1956 at Disneyland either, yet the latter turned out to be a monumental financial and cultural success. With this statement, Hammond thus implies comparable future success for his own troubled venture. However, note the generalization that precedes this comparison: *"All major theme parks have delays."* Hammond here seems to be establishing a categorization, in which Jurassic Park and Disneyland are to be placed in the same category, namely the category for which Disneyland is prototypical: a major theme park that started life inauspiciously but went on to win the hearts and wallets of America.

If Hammond's metaphor is simultaneously both a comparison and a categorization (and not one *or* the other) then Malcolm's rejoinder seems to be an entirely different species of figurative beast:

Malcolm: Yeah, but, John, if The Pirates of the Caribbean breaks down, the pirates don't eat the tourists.

In fact, Malcolm's conversational gambit is best described as a *conceptual blend* (see Fauconnier and Turner [2002]). Not only does it operate on the same domains as Hammond's gambit—Disneyland and Jurassic Park—it also thoroughly integrates a selection of elements from each of these domains to create an entirely new conceptual structure, one that contains emergent ideas and images that arise from neither input alone. Once again, Malcolm's remark is intended to be understood in the context of a juxtaposition of Disneyland and Jurassic Park, but it is much more than a comparison, categorization, or analogy. It involves analogy, of course, as a constituent process: thus, The Pirates of the Caribbean is implicitly aligned with the attractions of Jurassic Park, and so the animatronic pirates of the former are aligned with the genetically-engineered dinosaurs of the latter. But the salient behaviors of the latter—such as eating people willy-nilly—are also integrated with the protagonists of the former, to generate a delightful counterfactual image of mechanical pirates eating hapless tourists in mouse-earred caps. In the terminology of Fauconnier and Turner [2002], Malcolm is *running the blend*, which is to say he is conducting a mental simulation within the blend space that results from the integration of the inputs, to stimulate his imagination into recognizing the emergent possibilities that were hitherto just latent in the blend.

Metaphor has traditionally been modeled as a two-space phenomenon, in which conceptual content in one mental space—representing the vehicle or source domain—is projected onto, or mapped onto, the corresponding content in another space representing the tenor or target domain. Conceptual blending theory adds to the number of spaces that are implicated in figurative processing and further clarifies the notion of a mental space. Thus, a *generic space* provides low-level schematic structures (such as the SPG and CONTAINER schemas) that can serve to unite the disparate elements of the input spaces, while the *blend space* is a new space, distinct from any of the input spaces, in which content from the inputs is selectively projected and integrated. When Malcolm *runs* the blend to imagine pirates eating tourists, his mental simulation takes place here, in the newly constructed blend space. The set of all spaces that contribute to a blend, and the connections that link them, is called a *conceptual integration network*. Following Fauconnier [1994, 1997], a mental space is defined to be an ad-hoc bundle of domain-related information that a speaker or listener brings to the comprehension process. Notice, in the example above, Hammond and Malcolm both refer to the domain of Jurassic Park (qua theme park), but each builds a different mental space for this domain. For Hammond, the park is a business venture beset by temporary technical glitches; for Malcolm, the park is a place born of hubris and beset by rampaging carnivores. As shown by Malcolm's rejoinder, blending is especially suited to the construction and comprehension of counterfactual scenarios, since the blend space serves as a mental sand-box in which one can playfully experiment with the consequences of any given mapping between input spaces.

Blending theory also provides a relatively seamless framework for exploring and understanding the interactions between metaphor, analogy, metonymy, and concept invention. Indeed, one might argue that it is this seamlessness that often makes these phenomena so difficult to tease apart in the context of real examples (see Barnden [2010], who explores the "*slippery*" linkage between metaphor and metonymy). Consider the compound noun "*dinosaur hunter*," commonly used in the media to describe those paleontologists that seek out the skeletal remains of prehistoric creatures. Is the word "*hunter*" used metaphorically here, as in the compound "*bargain hunter*," or—since dinosaurs are animals every bit as fierce as elephants, rhinos, and lions—is it used literally (if a trifle unconventionally)? We can sidestep this question, while still arriving at an acceptable interpretation, by viewing the compound as a blend, in which the space of paleontology is integrated with the space of hunting to produce a new kind of hunter:prey relationship, one in which the hunter is temporally separated from his prey by 65 million years. That these hunters never actually see their prey in the flesh is beside the point, since metonymy allows us to conflate these long-dead dinosaurs with their skeletons. Indeed, Fauconnier and Turner [2002] argue that a common side-effect of conceptual blending is *metonymic tightening*, whereby the chains of associations that link the input spaces are compressed to create a tighter integration of conceptual content. So, when dinosaur skeletons are displayed in natural history museums, they are typically displayed as full-fledged dinosaurs, not as the mere parts of dinosaurs. If such displays are expertly framed so as to compress the holonymic relationship between a dinosaur and its bones into an identity relationship, blends such as "*dinosaur hunter*" do as much with language to achieve the same effect.

Fauconnier and Turner's [2002] blending theory (or the theory of *conceptual integration networks* to give it its formal title) sets out to explain—via a general architecture of constraints and optimality principles—how blended spaces are constructed via the selective projection of elements from multiple input spaces. But, how are those input spaces constructed in the first place? In the case of blends such as "*dinosaur hunter*," it is not unreasonable to assume that the mental spaces for *dinosaur* and *hunter* are derived, in part at least, from the corresponding entries in our mental lexicons. In other cases, these inputs may be the products of lower-level processes, such as the processes of conflation and differentiation that lead to the development of primary metaphors [Grady, 2005]. Lakoff and Johnson [1999] argue, for instance, that the neurally grounded processes that give rise to primary metaphors are complemented by conceptual processes that blend these primary inputs into more complex metaphors. For example, the conceptual metaphor LIFE IS A (PURPOSEFUL) JOURNEY can be considered a blend of the primary metaphors PURPOSES ARE DESTINATIONS (which we saw earlier in Wernher von Braun's metaphor of "*aiming for the stars*") and ACTIONS ARE MOTIONS (as when, e.g., a plan becomes reality when it is "*put in motion*"). In yet other cases, the inputs to a blend may themselves be the products of conceptual blending, which is to say, the blend space of one conceptual integration network may serve as an input space to another. Blends are conceptual products, after all, and successful blends may gain currency in a culture, so that they are given an evocative name or paired with a linguistic form to yield a reusable construction that achieves the status of a cultural trope.

Consider the following description of the film director Sam Mendes from a British newspaper in 2010: "*appearance: like the painting in George Clooney's attic.*" The newspaper was moved to sarcastic commentary after Mendes had been announced as the director of the next movie in the *James Bond* franchise, named *Skyfall*, and this sarcasm extended to its wry perspective on Clooney's carefully-constructed media image. The use of the definite article "*the*" before "*painting*" would suggest that this is a picture previously known to us, but, lacking any knowledge of Clooney's attic or of his taste in art, we must fall back on more general, cultural knowledge instead. Fortunately, the linguistic construction "*painting in [the] attic*" is strongly evocative of Oscar Wilde's morality tale *The Picture of Dorian Gray*, not because we remember the actual text of the story but because we are familiar with the phrase's repeated use in popular cultural as a shorthand for hidden excess and unnatural youthfulness. Recall that Wilde's novel centers around the gilded youth of the title and his bargain with fate: as Dorian remains forever young and beautiful on the outside, the ravages that time, sin, and excess should have wrought on his appearance are instead reflected in his portrait, which Gray wisely conceals in his attic. The story is so entrenched in the popular imagination that it takes just the merest mention of "*the*" painting in the attic to bring this particular picture to mind. Like the *Da...Dum...Da..Dum..DaDumDaDum* theme from the movie *Jaws*, or Monty Norman's signature theme from the *James Bond* movies, this simple construction evokes a wealth of unspoken narrative expectations. Of course, the fictitious painting lurking in Clooney's attic is not literally a painting of Dorian Gray; rather, it is a painting of Clooney as Gray, which is to say, the painting of a counterfactual Clooney who has committed to the same body-for-soul deal with fate as Wilde's anti-hero. In other words, "*the painting in George Clooney's attic*" is a cue to create a conceptual blend from the input spaces *George Clooney* and *Dorian Gray*. A visual representation of the resulting integration network is presented in Figure 2.1.

The blend space of this integration network now becomes available as input to the higher-level blend, where it is integrated with the target of the original simile, *Sam Mendes*. Because blends allow partial and highly selective projection of elements from their inputs onto their resulting blend spaces, what gets projected from this newly minted input space is the notion of a picture of George Clooney that differs significantly from the public perception of the actor. In the blend space of this new integration network, Mendes is identified with the figure in the painting—which, following the logic of Wilde's novel, we imagine as portraying Clooney as an older, wrinklier, flabbier, and generally more dissolute version of himself. So, in this blend space, Mendes is *not* identified with Clooney as we see him in the media and on the silver screen, but with this far less attractive counterfactual version of Clooney. Figure 2.2 shows the combination of both integration networks that a reader must construct to obtain the meaning of the original simile (which, at its most reductive, asserts that Mendes resembles an older, wrinklier, flabbier, and generally more dissolute version of Clooney). Note that we have elided from our analysis

Input space 1: George Clooney   Input space 2: Dorian Gray

Blend space: Clooney as Dorian

Figure 2.1: A conceptual integration of two mental spaces, one containing George Clooney and one containing Dorian Gray (reproduced from Veale [2012a]).

here the metonymy that is necessary to understand a comparison between a person and a painting: Mendes does not look like the painting itself (a flat painted surface in a decorative frame) but like the person that we imagine to be depicted in the painting. So, lurking beneath this simple-seeming simile is a blend within a blend, which in turn hinges on a metaphor (identifying Clooney and his imagined lifestyle choices with Gray and his soul-consuming narcissism), another simile (between Mendes and a less attractive version of Clooney), and a metonymy (allowing portraits to stand for their subjects).

Fauconnier and Turner [2002] effectively espouse a non-Davidsonian approach to figurative language, inasmuch as they propose that beneath the surface of every such utterance there is a cognitive content that one can call its *meaning*. So the integration network illustrated in Figure 2.2—with its component spaces and the many cross-connections between them—represents the cognitive content that listeners must construct for themselves in order to claim to have understood the meaning of "*appearance: like the painting in George Clooney's attic*" in the context of its target, *Sam Mendes*. Davidson argues that the meaning of a metaphor is essentially open-ended, but so too is the meaning of a blend. Listeners can, for instance, *run the blend* for themselves to

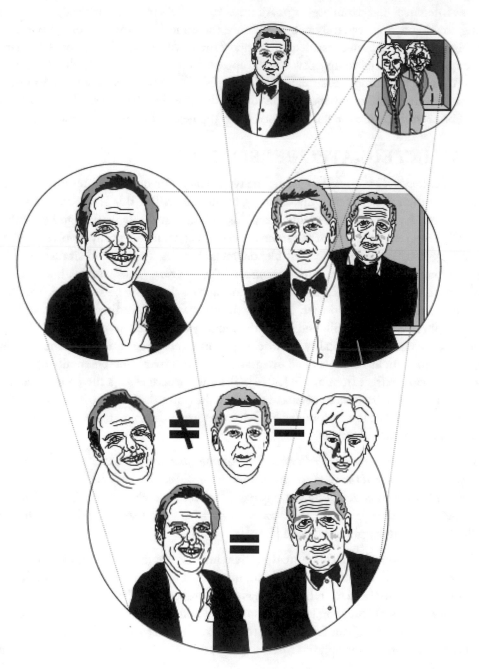

Figure 2.2: A conceptual integration of two mental spaces, one containing Sam Mendes and one containing the blend space from Figure 2.1 (reproduced from Veale [2012a]).

make new inferences and see emergent possibilities that others may have missed, but each of these meaning-making actions can only take place once the underlying integration network—such as that of Figure 2.2—has been constructed to support them. What is perhaps most surprising about this example is not just its complexity, but the apparent effortlessness with which readers understand it. After all, this composite simile/blend/metaphor/metonymy was used as a throwaway quip in a humorous "in brief" newspaper article[1] on the director Sam Mendes, where it was expected to raise a brief smile before the reader passed on to the next tidbit of gossip and snark.

2.8   AN INTEGRATED PERSPECTIVE

As the label *conceptual integration* suggests, the typical blend involves a tighter integration of conceptual spaces than the typical simile, analogy, or metaphor. But this is not to imply that those other figurative devices—which, as a text unfolds, might seamlessly work together with a blend to gradually reveal deeper layers of the same conceptual conceit—typically involve no integration at all. Rather, it seems truer to say that blends, metaphors, analogies, and similes each typically reside at different points on the same *continuum of integration*. Thus, similes hold their sources at arm's length from their targets by merely pointing to a similarity between the two. Analogies yoke both domains together so that, facing each other, we can see the reflection of one in the other. Metaphors are bolder still, and assert the identity of source and target, while blends make this identity a counterfactual reality by stitching source and target into the same linguistic and conceptual frame. For an example of an integration network that is incrementally tightened, consider the following extract from Stone [2014]. The author here evokes the conceptual metaphor PURPOSES ARE DESTINATIONS to persuasively make the point that one must choose one's path in life for oneself. As Stone is a co-founder of Twitter, he grounds his metaphor in the language and ideas of mobile phone technology:

> *Adopting a career because it's lucrative, or because your parents want you to …It's like someone else punched the GPS coordinates into your phone. You're locked onto your course, but you don't even know where you're going. When the route doesn't feel right, when your autopilot is leading you astray, then you must question your destination.* Hey! Who put "law degree" in my phone? (Stone [2014]).

Notice how Stone begins his entreaty with a simile. Although the PURPOSES ARE DESTINATIONS metaphor is widely used in English—for instance, it underpins the polysemy of the verb "to aim," it unites the spatial and the telic meanings of the prepositions "to" and "for,"[2] and it is evoked whenever one speaks of "standing between [someone] and their goal"—his GPS-enriched variation is perhaps novel enough on first reading to be better served by a gentle introduction via simile than a bold assertion via metaphor. Creative integration requires confidence from a writer and

---

[1]http://www.theguardian.com/film/2010/jan/06/sam-mendes-james-bond-notes
[2]A clear demonstration of how PURPOSES ARE DESTINATIONS attaches itself to the preposition "for" can be found on shampoo bottles. Those that are marked "for shiny hair" use "for" to indicate a PURPOSE, while those marked "for greasy hair" indicate a DESTINATION. It takes common-sense to know that greasy hair is not a desirable goal.

trust from a reader, and, lacking the back-and-forth negotiation described in Cameron [2007], a writer may seek to earn a reader's trust incrementally. So, having established the relevance of the GPS domain, Stone now elaborates his theme with a metaphor in which "course" and "route" are implicitly used to speak of LIFE and CAREER rather than spatial coordinates. All of the necessary conceptual elements are now in play for Stone to venture forth with a blend that binds them together into a unified whole. Note that the idea of typing "law degree" into someone's phone is not in the least semantically anomalous, and requires no re-imagining of how mobile phones work. However, getting the reader to imagine someone entering this setting *into a GPS application*, and getting meaningful results, requires a willing suspension of disbelief. So, having gradually ratcheted up the integration that can be achieved for the conceit PURPOSES ARE DESTINATIONS, first with a simile, then a metaphor, then a blend, Stone has guided us to a point where one's career path can be naturally re-imagined as a changeable (and indeed *hack*able) setting on a modern phone. Simile, metaphor, and blending are made to work together here to achieve a larger pragmatic goal: to communicate life advice to readers that have come to see the world through the affordances offered by their technological devices.

Clearly, figurative language presents a far greater challenge to the workings of open-domain NLP systems than our occasional refusal to use words in their dictionary senses. There can be no superficial approach to metaphor that can accommodate the kinds of examples we have just analyzed; neither does it seem sensible to look for a data source big enough for a *big data* solution to single-handedly provide the kind of carefully structured analyses and interpretations that are explored above and illustrated in Figures 2.1 and 2.2. Nonetheless, as we shall see next, as most AI/NLP developers are engineers first and theorists second, they have traditionally taken a pragmatic approach to the incorporation of figurative capabilities into their systems. While these capabilities are necessarily limited in scope and ambition, they are, collectively, richly informative as to what can be achieved with different trade-offs between theory and practice.

CHAPTER 3

Artificial Intelligence and Metaphor

Approaches to metaphor processing in artificial intelligence (AI) fall broadly into three categories: *corrective* approaches, in which metaphor is seen as a deviation from literal language that must be corrected if the meaning of a figurative text is to be captured in a semantic representation that is designed for literal language; *analogical* approaches, in which metaphor is seen as a systematic mapping of conceptual representations from a source domain (in which the vehicle resides) onto a target domain (in which the tenor resides); and *schematic* approaches, in which each instance of a metaphoric expression is understood as an instantiation of a more general metaphorical schema. In this section we briefly survey a variety of AI systems that are representative of these different kinds of approach.

3.1 CORRECTIVE APPROACHES: METAPHOR DIAGNOSIS AND REPAIR

The earliest AI approaches to NLP were characterized by their *engineering-first, cognition-second* philosophy, and in this respect the earliest AI approaches to metaphor processing were no exception. Such systems operated under the assumption that the core of language is literal; that the default mode of linguistic expression is literal; and that the semantic system underlying language—of frames, types, and roles—onto which the meaning of each utterance is mapped, is principally designed to accommodate literal meanings. Metaphor represents a ubiquitous challenge to the design intuitions of any system built on a literalist view of language, so it is hardly surprising that the earliest AI approaches treated metaphor as an aberration, a deviation that must be corrected if an NLP system is to robustly do its job. Inevitably, NLP systems built on a literalist foundation can only accommodate metaphors by first substituting them with literal paraphrases of their meaning. Yet, before this substitution can even be made, a literalist system must first recognize that a substitution is necessary, by diagnosing a metaphorical text as a deviation in need of a corrective remedy. The function of metaphor interpretation within a corrective approach is thus to perform the necessary course of correction whenever the standard interpretation processes, which have been optimized for literal expressions, map an utterance onto an anomalous, constraint-defying semantic representation.

One of the earliest and most representative AI instantiations of the corrective approach is offered by the *preference semantics* of Yorick Wilks. Wilks [1975] described how a semantic dictionary might be used to map an utterance onto a pseudo-logical formula that is part case-frame, part semantic template, and part literal paraphrase. Each formula contains slots that may be filled, with semantic tokens or with other formulae, so the semantic representation of the utterance as a whole is constructed from a patchwork of smaller formulae suggested by the words found in the utterance. The slots in a semantic formula impose *soft* constraints on the materials that can fill them, allowing the parsing process to construct the interpretation of an utterance that is most logically consistent with the syntactic and semantic intuitions of the system designer. These soft constraints are called *preferences*, and Wilks argues that the violation of preferences is the norm rather than the exception in even banal, non-figurative language. By searching for the interpretation that entails the least number of preference violations, Wilks [1975] shows that an NLP system using preference semantics can make a wide range of nuanced, semantics-influenced decisions, from prepositional attachment to word-sense disambiguation. In the case of lexicalized metaphors, in which the figurative meaning of a word is coded in the semantic dictionary as a separate sense, this minimization of preference violations allows an NLP system to choose the correct, figurative sense of a word.

But novel metaphors that extend our words to convey new senses cannot be handled in this way, as there is no pre-existing formula for a truly novel usage. Wilks [1978] thus broadened the remit of preference semantics to find a more appropriate semantic representation for the meaning of fresh figurative statements. He did this by allowing the semantic interpreter to search for an alternative representation that is not suggested by the dictionary definitions of the words in the utterance. To guide this search for a corrective remedy, Wilks [1978] introduced the notion of a *pseudo-text*, a bundle of complementary semantic formulae that demonstrates the correct semantic usage of a concept in a variety of contexts as viewed from a variety of salient perspectives. Pseudo-texts essentially circumscribe the spectrum of valid semantic usages, associations, and contexts in which a concept may be employed. For example, a pseudo-text for the concept CAR might encode the beliefs that cars consume gasoline, transport people and goods from place to place, travel at medium to high speeds, and often become embroiled in traffic jams. When a preference violation is unavoidably triggered, it becomes the task of the metaphor interpretation system to consider how an ill-fitting formula might be replaced with another from the relevant pseudo-text. For example, when given the now time-worn metaphor "*My car drinks gasoline*," a violation of the semantic preferences that DRINK expresses for an animate agent and a potable patient is triggered, prompting the metaphor interpretation process to kick in and select the alternative formula for the action *Consume gasoline* from the pseudo-text for CAR.

Fass [1988] builds upon the preference-breaking model in his *Collative Semantics* approach, to offer a unified account of coherence, metonymy, metaphor, and lexical ambiguity within a single semantic framework. Rather than project from a preference-breaking semantic formula onto a better-fitting formula in a related pseudo-text, however, Fass advocates—in shades of Aristotle's strategy (c)—that an abstraction hierarchy be used to map an ill-fitting case-frame onto one that represents a more semantically apropos action, situation, or relation. However, in the final analysis, the effect is much the same, and in the classic thirsty car metaphor the metaphoric use of DRINK is mapped onto the respectably literal case frame for the verb TO CONSUME. A related approach was later offered by Iverson and Helmreich [1992], who combined preference/collative semantics with marker-passing[1] to further extend the interpretative reach of their system for handling both metaphor and metonymy.

Since antiquity, scholars have found it useful to think of metaphor as a sideways move in a hierarchical meaning system. Aristotle saw metaphor as a lateral move of linguistic labels, from one species of idea to another of the same genus. Wilks and Fass and subsequent researchers have explained how this sideways move of labels, such as from DRINK to CONSUME, must also be accompanied by a sideways transfer of semantic structures (Nunberg [1995]), if the actual meaning of a metaphor is to be found. This movement of semantics is not arbitrary, but guided by a similarity in meaning, so key to metaphor interpretation is the partial invariance of meaning between the literal and figurative readings of an utterance. So, if part of the meaning of a word like "*drink*" is preserved invariant when it is used figuratively, why not capture this fact explicitly, in the semantic definition of the word? This is the approach adopted by Aarts and Calbert [1979], who use a semantic marker model of meaning (sometimes called, pejoratively, *markerese*) to capture not just the conventional meaning of a word, but its extended and invariant meanings too.

Marker models of meaning were first proposed by interpretative semanticists working within Chomsky's transformational framework (see Katz and Fodor [1964]), to explain the incongruity of otherwise well-formed sentences such as "*Colorless green ideas sleep furiously*," while simultaneously providing a means of lexical ambiguity resolution (to, e.g., select the correct reading of "*bachelor*" from among the possibilities "*unmarried man*," "*young male seal*," and "*primary college degree*"). Marker advocates argue that the meaning of a word can be captured by a componential definition comprising a list of atomic semantic features, such as +*Male*, +*Adult*, and −*Animate*. These markers are polarized to capture the basic semantic oppositions that underpin our intuitions about word meaning; thus, the definitions of *Man* and *Boy* share the features +*Male*, +*Animate*, +*Human*, and +*Physical*, and differ only in the polarization of the feature *Adult*. Semantic congruity is enforced in language by having words impose marker-based selectional constraints on each other as directed by the underlying syntactic structure. Thus, "*green ideas*" is considered aberrant because *Green* imposes the selectional constraint +*Physical* on a word for which this marker is not defined. Likewise, selectional constraints also filter out the incompatible readings of a polysemous word, thereby resolving lexical ambiguities. Although Katz and Fodor, as well as Aarts and Calbert, view marker-based constraints as hard constraints, there is no rea-

---

[1]Marker passing [Norvig, 1987] is a technique for identifying those aspects of a semantic/conceptual representation that are salient in the processing of a given concept in a graph representation of meaning (such as a semantic network). Simply, symbolic *markers* are passed from concept to concept, starting from the given concept and then spreading to all its associates, to the associates of those associates, and so on in parallel. Different markers may be spread from different starting points, with a view to finding the concepts at which different markers meet each other.

son in principle why they cannot also be used to express soft preferences in the manner of Wilks [1975, 1978].

The model of Aarts and Calbert [1979] further compartmentalizes the componential definition of each word into four different feature sets. The primary feature set holds the literal semantic markers called for under the original Katz and Fodor scheme. The secondary feature set holds the markers that capture the lexicalized metaphoric extensions of the word, that is, dead metaphors. For example, while the word "*red*" is primarily defined as a color (with selectional constraints for +*Physical* and +*Visible*), its secondary compartment also contains a marker representation for "*Communist*" (with the selectional constraint +*Human*). The generative feature set then contains markers that allow for the word to be used in a different, but related sense, as when the word is used in a synecdoche or metonymy. (In this respect, the approach bears some comparison to the *Generative Lexicon* of Pustejovsky [1991, 1995].) However, the most interesting compartment, from a metaphor perspective, is the transfer feature set, whose semantic markers may be projected into the representation of the target in metaphoric situations. These transfer features are intended to capture the abstract, invariant semantic notions that underpin everyday word use. For example, while the words "*big*" and "*heavy*" expect to be applied to concepts with the marker +*Physical*, they each also contain the feature +*Intense* in their transfer compartment. A marker-based system can thus arrive at the same interpretation for the abstract metaphors "*big problem*" and "*heavy problem*," by applying the marker +*Intense* to the concept *Problem* in the underlying semantic structure of the utterance.

Russell [1992] describes an approach to metaphor interpretation, called MAP, that is founded on the same principles of meaning transfer and invariance. As in the approach of Aarts and Calbert, Russell defines concepts in terms of specific, non-extensible domain-dependent features, and more abstract, extensible domain-independent features. In the terminology of Aarts and Calbert, these partitions correspond to the primary feature set and the transfer set respectively, inasmuch as the primary or non-extensible set defines our literal expectations of a concept, while the transfer or extensible set captures the invariant essence of the concept, a transferable distillation of abstract meaning that allows a concept or relation to be projected onto other domains. Once an initial semantic structure is built for a metaphoric utterance, using the semantic information associated with verbs and nouns in a semantic dictionary, Russell's MAP system then proceeds to project this structure out of the ill-suited source domain into the more apropos target domain. The basis for this mapping is an abstract structure created from the extensible features of the concepts involved. Thus, while non-extensible features are variable, insofar as they are expected to change when moving to a new domain, extensible features are to be considered invariant, as it is they that provide the common ground between the source and target domains.

MAP provides extensible features not just for adjectives and nouns, as in Aarts and Calbert [1979], but also for verbs and the semantic primitives that underpin them. For instance, the *Conceptual Dependency* (or CD; Schank and Abelson [1977]) primitives *atrans* (abstract transfer), *ptrans* (physical transfer), and *mtrans* (mental transfer) are all assigned the extensible feature

+*Transfer*, indicating that these primitives all involve some form of content movement, whether abstract, physical, or mental. A structure-mapping algorithm exploits these extensible features to shift semantic representations from one domain to another. For example, in interpreting the metaphor "*He gave her his opinion*," a representational shift occurs from the first, anomalous representation of the utterance, which posits a physical transference reading of "*give*" based on the *ptrans* primitive, to an alternative communication reading, which exploits a mental transference reading of "*give*" that uses *mtrans* instead. While the former reading is anomalous, the latter is semantically correct insofar as it violates none of the constraints imposed by the connectives of the system's representations.

Most corrective approaches are *top-down* approaches: they build representations that are in need of corrective remedy because they zealously bring top-down expectations to bear on the meaning of an utterance. When these expectations are violated by the figurative uses of words, the initial semantic representation must be repaired. Yet the most useful aspects of the corrective approach can also be employed in a *bottom-up* fashion, to yield an under-specified first-cut representation that can later be elaborated to complete a fleshed-out representation of utterance meaning. Cater [1985] provides one such bottom-up rethink of metaphor interpretation, arguing that the first-cut representation of meaning—what Martin [1990] calls a *primal representation*—can be constructed from abstract semantic connectives that are neither literal nor figurative. So, for example, an NLP system should not commit itself to a choice amongst *ptrans*, *mtrans*, or *atrans* when building an initial interpretation of a "*give*" event, but should simply use the vague abstraction *trans* instead. If the arguments of *trans* turn out to be physical objects, then *trans* can later be replaced with *ptrans*; if they are sentient and mental respectively, it can be replaced with *mtrans*; and so on, in a bottom-up construction of meaning. A similar approach is adopted by Veale and Keane [1992], whose under-specified meaning connectives are not abstracted from Schank's CD primitives, but inspired by the metaphor schemas of Lakoff and Johnson [1980], such as CON-TAINER and ORIENTATION. In each case, the bottom-up philosophy is the same: rather than rush toward an incorrect, top-down representation that subsequently needs to be fixed, a bottom-up system builds an under-specified scaffolding instead, one that guides the incremental construction of the appropriate meaning without any corrective *u-turns*.

Another corrective approach that avoids the need for interpretative u-turns was sketched in Cottrell [1987], who humorously described his unimplemented approach as *hopeware*. Cottrell saw metaphor as a natural functionality of artificial neural networks (ANNs) that are used to implement identity-mapping networks. Such networks are trained to map an input layer of features onto an output layer of the same features, as mediated by a lattice of weighted connections to and from a layer of hidden units (the *hidden layer*). These hidden units and their connections—*from* the input layer and *to* the output layer—allow the network to generalize over its many training examples, and to thus provide sensible outputs even when presented with novel inputs (provided, of course, that these novel inputs contain some familiar elements). Now suppose the input layer is given a feature representation of a statement paired to its literal meaning (how precisely this combined representation is chosen is a matter of implementation), and the network is trained to map many different instances of this input representation onto the very same features in the output layer. For instance, it may be trained to map a representation of the statement *cars run on gasoline* and its meaning (e.g., *consume(car, gasoline)*) onto itself. Later, when a partial representation is presented at the input layer, such as the representation of the statement *buses run on diesel*, the network will complete the representation on the output layer, to produce a representation of its meaning (i.e., *consume(bus, diesel)*). This completion functionality, which is a natural byproduct of identity-mapping in an ANN, can also be used to complete partial metaphoric inputs, such as the representation of the statement *cars drink gasoline*. In this approach, correction is achieved organically, without the need to first recognize a semantic anomaly. Rather, the network maps the partial input via the weighted connections it has been trained to develop, onto the nearest representation that it has been trained to produce (such as *consume(car, gasoline)*). At this point, however, we find ourselves faced with the same dilemma that afflicts the approach of Wilks [1978]: is *consume(car, gasoline)* really the most natural and sensible interpretation of *my car drinks gasoline*?

The essence of a corrective approach is that the figurative meaning of a metaphor bears some resemblance to its surface, literal meaning, so this resemblance can serve as a guide when nudging an inappropriate meaning toward one that is more apt for the metaphor. This similarity is either captured via a taxonomy (as in the case of Wilks [1978], and, to an extent, Cater [1985]) or via overlaps in a lower-level feature encoding (as in Aarts and Calbert [1979]; Cottrell [1987]; and Russell [1992]). Kintsch [2000, 2001] presents a statistical approach that forms part of a larger theory of predication more generally, in which a vector-space model[2] (VSM) of meaning based on Latent Semantic Analysis[3] (LSA; see Landauer and Dumais [1997]) is used "to adjust the meaning of a predicate as it is applied to different arguments." Because Kintsch [2001] presents a general algorithm for use in metaphorical and non-metaphorical predications alike—the general case being a proposition $P(A)$ in which a predicate P is applied to an argument A (e.g., where A is *selfies* and P is *go viral*)—one might say with some justification that this approach is not strictly *corrective*, in the sense that the approach does not first build a mistaken representation, or generate a semantic anomaly, that must subsequently be corrected. Nonetheless, the VSM/LSA approach of Kintsch [2001] uses similarity to nudge a metaphorical predication toward a more accommodating representation of utterance meaning, and so we will treat it here as a corrective approach.

Kintsch's [2001] predicative approach serves as the basis for Utsumi's [2011] categorization algorithm. In essence, a compressed vector space of reduced dimensionality (courtesy of LSA) is

---

[2]A vector-space model of text represents the meanings of words as vectors in an n-dimensional space, so that words with similar meanings and distributional patterns will have similar vector representations. The similarity of two vectors can be measured as the cosine of the angle between them. The dimensions of a vector space may themselves correspond to words, so that, e.g., the n dimensions correspond to the n different word types in a document set, and each of the n dimensions n_i of a vector for a given word w correspond to the number of documents in which w co-occurs with the corresponding dimension-word n_i.

[3]LSA is a vector-space model that dramatically reduces the number of its dimensions using a mathematical technique called Singular Value Decomposition (SVD) to achieve a compression of the space.

used to create word vectors for the words in an utterance, including (for the sake of simplicity) the predicate P (indicating the source of the metaphor) and its argument A (indicating the target). The space is interrogated to find m neighboring predicates that are most similar to P, and from these m neighbors, the k most similar to the target A are selected. The ad-hoc category into which the metaphor places the target concept A is then constructed to be the centroid of the vectors for P, for A and the k vectors chosen from the m neighbors of P. The resulting vector represents a corrected version of the default (context-free) vector for P, one that has been corrected so that it can better represent the affordances of the concept A. For example, using the settings $m = 500$ and $k = 5$ for the metaphor "rumors are viruses," the resulting vector is very close in semantic space to that for *spread, contagion*, and *epidemic*. Utsumi [2011] further constructs a variant of this algorithm to perform metaphorical comparison rather than metaphorical categorization, by calculating the centroid of the vector for A and the vectors of the k common neighbors of A and P in the vector space (where the most apt common neighbors are found by varying a similarity threshold until the k commonalities are found). Utsumi [2011], following Bowdle and Gentner [2005], argues that categorization and comparison are not competing theories of metaphor but competing strategies, and both have a role to play in metaphor comprehension.

3.2   ANALOGICAL APPROACHES: MAPPING MEANINGS BETWEEN DOMAINS

A capacity for analogical reasoning has long been considered a hallmark of intelligence. This has made analogy a staple of IQ and scholastic aptitude tests, and made it a hardy perennial of AI research. Indeed, seminal early work by Evans [1964] described a computer program (ANAL-OGY) for solving precisely the kind of geometric analogies that are found on IQ tests. Long after Aristotle first described proportional analogy as just one kind of metaphor, or at least as just one possible conceptual/semantic motivation for projecting the name of one idea onto another, the exact cognitive and algorithmic relationship of metaphor to analogy continues to be a thoroughly vexing issue. Many researchers feel that analogy is the core mechanism against which the problem of metaphor interpretation should be defined (see e.g., Winston [1980]; Carbonell [1982]; Gentner et al. [1989]; Holyoak and Thagard [1989]), while others (such as Way [1991]; Veale and Keane [1992, 1994]) believe metaphor to be the central explanatory phenomenon, and yet others believe that both processes are related but ultimately distinct, so that one cannot be reduced to the other (e.g., Indurkhya [1992]). Those researchers that hold metaphor to be a class of analogical mappings adhere to the belief that metaphors are interpreted via some cross-domain transfer of semantic structure. This section surveys a number of analogical models that epitomize this view.

Winston [1980] focuses more on allegory than metaphor, and emphasizes the role of analogical transfer in the learning of solutions to new problems. He does so by describing how past experiences, or precedents, may be employed to obtain insights into novel situations, by using the causal structure of a precedent to make explicit what is otherwise implicit in a novel but analogous situation. To maximize the explanatory power of an analogy, Winston advocates that abstract causal relations among entities and actions, such as CAUSE, INFLUENCE, WANT, and PERSUADE, should be transferred invariant between domains, with the effect that this transfer of content imposes an explicit causal structure on an otherwise poorly understood target domain. (By way of comparison, Carbonell [1982] also argues that metaphor and analogy employ an *invariance hierarchy* of relations that are preserved in any figurative cross-domain transfer of meanings.) This transfer should also allow a system to generate additional hypotheses to further explain the unstated relationships between entities and events in the target domain. For instance, if a weak but career-wise man is married to an ambitious and domineering woman, an analogy to Shakespeare's *Macbeth* suggests that this wife might drive her hen-pecked husband to usurp, by foul means, his boss's position. In this sense, Winston's approach not only uses the analogical precedent to understand the causal dynamics of a particular situation, but also to learn from past experience how to anticipate future events arising from these power relations. It becomes a major question, then, to decide how much of an explicit match with a precedent is necessary before additional causal structure in the source/precedent can also be projected onto the target. Winston [1980] surmounts this problem by limiting the transfer of relationships to causal relations. His matching algorithm exhibits an in-built competence to vet causal relations and inferences for wellformedness, and is thus able to justify the inferences produced in a mapping by tracing through the resultant structure to determine whether conclusions are supported by existing causal links.

Most AI approaches to analogical matching are founded on the assumption that conceptual structures are represented as graphs, and that an analogical match captures a sub-graph isomorphism[4] between the graph representation of the source and target domains. All things being equal, the largest sub-graph isomorphism is to be preferred, as this wrings maximal semantic value from the analogy (see Veale and Keane [1997]). Nonetheless, not all parts of a source domain may be equally illuminating about the target, and so we generally also prefer for a sub-graph isomorphism to capture some causal insight into the workings of the target and source. Where Winston explicitly provides an inventory of the causal relations that are most likely to contribute to such an insight, Gentner [1983] instead offers a more general principle called the *systematicity principle*. The parts of the source domain that provide the most complete causal explanation of the target are those that are the most connected to the rest of the domain and show how the parts cohere into a whole. The most systematic mapping between target and source is not necessarily the one that establishes the most 1-to-1 mappings between elements of the source and target domains, but the one that aligns the most well-connected parts of the source to the target.

In her diaries, Virginia Woolf chides her own lack of productivity with the note "*What a disgraceful lapse! Nothing added to my disquisition, and life allowed to waste like a tap left running.*" To demonstrate the applicability of Gentner's structure mapping theory (SMT) to meta-

---

[4]An isomorphic mapping between two graphs will establish a one-to-one connection between the nodes of each graph, so that each node in one graph is connected to a distinct node in the other, and so that the edges that connect the nodes of each graph can also be mapped to each other in a 1-to-1 fashion. A sub-graph isomorphism is an isomorphic mapping between a part of one graph and a part of another. The largest sub-graph isomorphism will find the largest parts of two graphs that can be isomorphically mapped to each other.

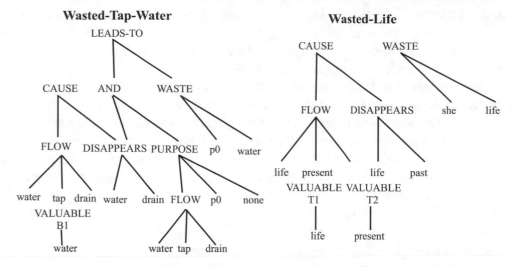

Figure 3.1: Structural representations of *Life* and *Water* argued to underpin Woolf's metaphor.

phor analysis—and by extension, the computational implementation of SMT, the structure mapping engine (SME), to computational metaphor interpretation—Gentner et al. [1989] argue that analogical mapping is the key to interpreting the metaphor "*She allowed life to waste away like a tap left running.*" Figure 3.1 illustrates the representation of the source and target domains as imagined by these authors.

Notice how the structure on the left explains what it means to *waste* water: not only must water be allowed to flow into a drain and disappear, it must be the express purpose of an agent for this to happen so that the disappearance can be considered *waste*. The structure on the right mirrors the explicit content of the metaphor, noting (rather philosophically) that the speaker is allowing their life to flow into the past and that they are wasting their life. Each structure also captures the beliefs, via a single predicate-subject attribution in each case, that water is valuable and that life is valuable too. Following the systematicity principle, this shared attribution does not anchor the mapping, but is included as an interesting corollary of the central part of the mapping. Instead, it is the dense cluster of isomorphic structures at the center of the mapping—involving FLOW, CAUSE, and DISAPPEAR—that anchors the analogy and the metaphor. Around this subgraph isomorphism, a process of analogical inference can now map additional structure from the source onto the target structure, and explain *how* the speaker is wasting her life, by purposely allowing it to disappear into the past.

If this example reveals the ambition of the *metaphor-as-analogy* view, it also highlights some profound issues. Any theory of analogy or metaphor that hitches itself to the structure of a domain will be remarkably sensitive to structural choices of the representations that are used to capture meaning. In effect, a structural theory of metaphor and analogy must also be a theory of knowledge representation. As a result, Winston's approach ties itself to specific causal predicates, and, although Gentner's SMT needs no such inventory, and aims for a more general criterion of interestingness with its systematicity principle, it, too, assumes an unrealistic symmetry in how different domains are represented. It seems unlikely that our mental representations of the flow of water and the passage of time would actually be quite so isomorphic as they appear in Figure 3.1, and more unlikely still that our model of LIFE would appeal to a FLOW metaphor in just the right part of the representation on the right (to say nothing of the fact that FLOW seems to be used literally on the left and figuratively on the right). There is undoubtedly a strong structural dimension to our perception of analogical similarity, and theories such as Winston's and Gentner's do clarify a number of pivotal mechanisms. Yet these theories can only be as computationally useful as their representational assumptions allow. The need for *just-so* representations dogs all structural theories of analogy, from Winston [1980], to Carbonell [1982], to Gentner [1983], to Holyoak and Thagard [1989] (who use a neural network to find systematic matches via constraint satisfaction in a model called ACME), to Veale and Keane [1997] (who use *spreading activation*[5] in a semantic network to find connections between the source and the target). Real examples and real knowledge are complex, and rarely as neat as our analyses assume.

Straightforward engineering decisions can also have profound consequences in any structure-sensitive approach. The SMT approach, as embodied in the SME computational model (see Falkenhainer et al. [1989]), assumes that domain structures are represented in LISP-like recursively nested lists. Nesting within predicate arguments allows SME to recognize high-order logical structure, and in turn to determine which predications contribute most to the systematicity of a mapping. Causal predications, for example, contain other predications as arguments, and are recognized as systematically central because they offer high-order connectivity, not because their predicates have special names such as CAUSE, INFLUENCE, LEADS-TO, or PURPOSE. ACME hinges on a similar structural intuition, even if it ultimately turns these nested lists into densely-linked constraint-solving localist neural networks. But the Sapper model of Veale and Keane [1997] and Veale and O'Donoghue [2000] hinges on a different representational assumption: all of its domain knowledge is stored not as separate lists of content, as though bundled for discrete access in a semantic dictionary, but as a single semantic network encompassing all domains. This network is a graph of labeled vertices connected by labeled directional arcs, in which concepts from different domains may be linked to each other by one or more relational arcs. Although a semantic network is essentially a set of flat triples, the nested representations of SME and ACME can be mapped onto such a network without loss of information, by reifying nesting structures as discrete vertices in their own right. Nonetheless, although they are essentially interchangeable, the choice of one representation or another has significant computational consequences for a metaphor system.

---

[5]*Spreading activation* [Collins and Loftus, 1975] is a quantitative form of marker passing [Norvig, 1987] in which a numeric activation measure rather than a symbolic marker is passed from node to node, or concept to concept, in a graph representation of meaning (such as a semantic network). This numeric measure attenuates as it passes from one node to the next, until it becomes so weak that it cannot spread any further. The activation of a concept node is the sum of the activation signals it receives from its neighbors in the network. Spreading activation thus allows a system to determine which concepts are ultimately reachable from another, and the extent to which one concept *primes* another.

Sapper applies an Aristotelian approach to a network representation of meaning. Between any two vertices T_1 and V_1 that are each connected to a third vertex G via arcs with the same relational label (such as *ISA* or *ATTRibute*) Sapper will automatically add a new bridging arc to allow spreading activation to flow directly between T_1 and V_1. In Sapper this strategy is called *triangulation*, although it is similar in character to Aristotle's strategy *(c)*, in which two species T and V are relatable because they share a common genus G. But Sapper will also automatically add a new bridging arc between any two vertices T_2 and V_2 if T_2 is connected to another vertex T_1 with the same relation that connects V_2 to another vertex V_1, and if T_1 and V_1 are already connected by a bridging arc. In Sapper this strategy is called *squaring*, since it allows the system to analogically build on the bridges laid down by triangulation, or by previous uses of squaring. Since Sapper exploits the proportion $T_2:V_2::T_1:V_1$ to derive a relationship between T_2 and V_2 based on a perceived similarity between T_1 and V_1, squaring is essentially the semantic network equivalent of Aristotle's strategy *(d)*. An interpretation of any copula metaphor of the form "*[T] is [V]*" is now constructed by Sapper by simultaneously spreading activation from the vertices for *[T]* and for *[V]*. The bridging arcs over which waves of competing activation intersect are recognized as possible entity-level matches between the domain of *[V]* and the domain of *[T]*. Sapper searches for the largest, structurally coherent subset of bridges that yield a 1-to-1 mapping between the *[V]* and *[T]* domains. This mapping—comprising a set of entities and their inter-relationships placed into analogical correspondence—is taken to be the interpretation of the metaphor "*[T] is [V]*."

Sapper searches for the same end-result as SME and ACME and other explicitly structural models of metaphor and analogy: a global mapping of entities and relations that puts the target/tenor and source/vehicle domains into a coherent, isomorphic correspondence. For instance, when analyzing the metaphor "*My surgeon is a butcher*," it finds an analogical correspondence between surgery and slaughter, scalpels and cleavers, operating theatres and abattoirs, patients and animals, etc. Sapper thus finds much the same interpretations as SME and ACME on the example problems for which those systems excel, such as the analogy of Figure 3.1, once their nested representations have been converted into the corresponding set of flat triples to define a semantic network. Sapper cannot operate directly on nested structures. Conversely, although SME and ACME can operate with Sapper's triples directly, they do not obtain anything like the results they get with hierarchically nested representations. Veale and Keane [1997] show that subtle representational choices are key to the operation of different models of analogy. Interchangeable representations that express the same information in different ways may give rise to vastly different mappings and qualities of mapping. As those authors show, a well-chosen representation can be the difference between achieving a densely connected mapping and one that is little more than a flat agglomeration of disparate elements.

As highlighted by the representation in Figure 3.1(right), it is not possible to cleanly separate structure from process when it comes to analogy, or to models of metaphor based on analogy. The operation of *all* computational models of analogy hinges on the representational choices of their designers, insofar as these choices shape the search-space in which the models will seek out structured isomorphisms between the source and target domains. Yet it is far from clear whether a single representational schema is suited to all possible analogies, and Sapper's simple system of flat triples is no more a universal representation than any other. Rather, just as researchers in different domains of endeavor may have good reasons for employing one system of representation over another, we can expect that challenging analogies may frequently require us (or our systems) to find mappings between domains that are represented using very different formats of varying complexity and expressive power.

For Hobbs [1981] and Hobbs et al. [1993], analogical alignment is less a matter of exact structural matching between source and target, and more a matter of selective inferencing in the target domain arising from a projection of logical content from the source. Those aspects of the source meaning that can logically take root in the target domain are deemed to form part of the interpretation, while those that cannot are instead selectively filtered. So alignment becomes less an issue of structure *mapping* and more an issue of structure *shifting*. Hobbs et al. [1993] use weighted abduction to determine which aspects of the source meaning can be sensibly shifted into the target domain and interpreted relative to what we know about the target. Abduction is an unsafe (yet very useful) mode of reasoning in which one works backward from observable effects to likely causes. Thus, if one possesses the logical implication $p(x) \rightarrow q(x)$ and then observes $q(a)$, it may be meaningful to infer $p(a)$ as the cause of $q(a)$. Of course, there may be many potential causes of $q(a)$, and so the more evidence we can observe to support our abductive hypothesis, the better. For instance, we may well feel safer hypothesizing $p(a)$ from the implication $p(x) \rightarrow q_1(x) \wedge q_2(x) \wedge q_3(x)$ and the observations $q_1(a), q_2(a)$ and $q_3(a)$. In cases where we can observe just some of the consequent clauses $q_i(a)$ we may assume the missing clauses to be true, but at a cost. Hobbs et al. [1993] describe how the clauses of a logical implication may be weighted by cost, with different clauses carrying different *assumption costs* so that assumptions that require a leap of faith by a cognitive agent come with a higher price tag. When deciding which aspects of the source meaning can be shifted to, and sensibly interpreted in, the target domain, the weighted abduction algorithm aims to minimize the assumption costs in its line of reasoning. As such, it chooses the target-domain interpretation that best fits what it already knows about the target and which least taxes the credulity of the agent.

Consider this example from Hobbs [1979, 1991]: "*We insist on serving up these veto pitches that come over the plate the size of a pumpkin.*" This metaphor, as quoted from the remarks of a U.S. congressman, complains about how congress is making life *too* easy for the President, by sending bills to the White House that can be vetoed by the President with no significant political cost. The source domain is that of baseball, as indicated by the words "plate" (the area over which the batter stands) and "pitches" (the hurling of a baseball toward the batter; from the pitcher's perspective, it is preferred that the ball fly over the plate and fly past the batter). In baseball parlance, "pitches that come over the plate the size of a pumpkin" are easy-to-hit pitches, which is to say, pitches that make the ball as easy to hit as a flying pumpkin. (Like Hobbs. we pass over the metonymy between balls and pitches of balls that allows pitches to be described as pumpkin-sized.) As argued in Hobbs [1979], the interpretation requires an analogical mapping from the source domain of baseball onto the target domain of U.S. politics, so that the pitcher is mapped to Congress, the ball(s) to bill(s), the batter to the President, the act of pitching a ball to the act of sending a bill, and the act of hitting the ball to the act of vetoing a bill. An important aspect of the analogy that must be assumed from our understanding of baseball is that the Congress and the President have an adversarial relationship, likely arising from the fact that they serve the interests of different parties, just as the pitcher and the batter play for different teams. Hobbs [1991] assumes that this knowledge of baseball and politics is formally axiomatized, e.g., by an axiomatic schema that encodes the logical relationships between pitchers, batters, balls, pitching, and hitting (the *baseball_schema*) and by a schema that encodes the relationships between Congress, the President, bills, signing, and vetoing (the *congress_schema*). An additional schema is needed to relate the act of sending a bill to the President to the act of pitching a ball to the batter; this is axiomatized in a generic fashion to abstract away from balls and bills and simply relate *sending (something)* to *pitching (something)*. With these axioms in play, the original metaphor can now be interpreted using abductive reasoning, by first assuming the *baseball_schema* to be relevant, and then using the clauses of this schema (at their specified costs) to find the lowest-cost interpretation that explains the use of baseball terminology in a statement about partisan politics.

But what is the justification for an axiom that conveniently relates *pitching* to *sending* and thereby makes the larger interpretation fall into place? One can argue that pitching really is a kind of sending, and so this is the kind of literal definition that we might expect to find in any NLP system. Nonetheless, if one were to say that a pitcher *"sent"* the ball to the batter, then this would strike many a reader as a metaphorical use of *"send."* So it seems more natural to assume that the axiom encodes a conventional metaphor that has made its way into our logical representations of human behavior. Indeed, Hobbs [1991] asserts that a metaphor is not conventional if it has not been codified in some way in our system of logical axioms. Or, as he puts it, "the existence of such an axiom in the knowledge-base is precisely what it means in this framework for a metaphor to be conventional." Hobbs's [1991] abductive approach derives a certain measure of robustness from its use of weighted clauses, its ability to assume unstated information at a cost, and its willingness to search for the lowest cost abductive interpretation that explains the metaphor. But it is also heavily reliant on the logical axioms and schemas that encode not just domain knowledge, but also the inter-domain knowledge that underpins conventional metaphors. As we shall see next, this makes Hobbs [1991]'s take on metaphor not just an analogical approach, but a schematic approach, too.

3.3 SCHEMATIC APPROACHES: FAMILIES OF METAPHOR

Every computational approach to metaphor must commit to specific choices of process and of representation. Nonetheless, it is useful to distinguish between those approaches that are primarily *process-centric* and those that are more *representation-centric*. The corrective approaches surveyed here offer an essentially process-centric view of metaphor, in which the question of whether an utterance should be considered a metaphor—a quality of an utterance we may call its *metaphoricity*—resides in the processes that operate on the semantic representation of the utterance rather than in the representation itself. Thus, Wilks and Fass each describe how special processes of diagnosis and repair might be applied to the same semantic structures that were designed to accommodate literally-expressed meanings. Russell, and Aarts and Calbert—who each store explicitly metaphorical meanings in the semantic dictionary—also leave no room for any explicitly metaphorical content in the semantic structures that are the ultimate products of metaphor interpretation. The structural approach of Winston, of Gentner and of other analogists likewise assumes that metaphoricity resides in how two structures are aligned, mapped, and used for subsequent transfer and inference, rather than in these structures themselves. Nonetheless, as shown in Figure 3.1, approaches that aim to be representation-neutral often end up being defined by the tacit assumptions they implicitly make about representation. Try as one might, it is hard to construct a representation that is entirely metaphor-free. For metaphor is not just parasitic on our representation of literal meaning; it is often parasitic on other metaphors too.

Consider again the notion that LIFE is something that flows from the present into the past, as expressed in the representation of Figure 3.1(right). This conception of LIFE is not very different from the metaphor LIFE IS A JOURNEY as analyzed in Lakoff and Johnson [1980], and appears to be founded on the very same SOURCE-PATH-GOAL schema (Johnson [1987]). Indeed, in comparing LIFE to WATER, the authors of Figure 3.1 appear to employ the metaphor LIFE IS A STREAM (of events, experiences, etc.), as found in the nursery rhyme *Row, Row, Row Your Boat, Gently Down the Stream*. However, the metaphor, which is used in the Woolf example (Figure 3.1) to make the source and target representations align, is evidently used here as though it were a literal construct. A more representation-centric approach would acknowledge that the notion of LIFE AS A STREAM (flowing from present to past) is just one way of representing the concept of LIFE, that this view is in fact a conceptual metaphor, and represent it as such in a way that would allow it to support the full range of corresponding figurative inferences. What is needed then is an explicit data structure that captures both the generality of a conceptual metaphor and its potential to support a delicately nuanced interpretation when it is rendered in a linguistic form that conveys aspect, attitude, affect, and/or intent [Narayanan, 1997].

Carbonell [1982] proposes an approach that is as representation-centric as it is process-centric. Inspired by Lakoff and Johnson [1980], Carbonell notes that *"there appear to be a small number of general metaphors (on the order of fifty) that pervade commonly spoken English,"* and describes a model that represents these general metaphors explicitly, so that a computational system might recognize them, reason about them, and derive target-domain inferences from them in the context of an utterance. Carbonell's system can be seen as an integration of Lakoff and Johnson's philosophy with Winston's computational view of analogy: thus, his system first recognizes which general metaphor in its collection of schemas (such as MORE IS UP, LESS IS DOWN, LIFE IS A JOURNEY, LANGUAGE IS A CONDUIT, etc.) is instantiated by a given figurative utterance, and then performs a cross-domain mapping under the guidance of the chosen metaphor schema. Carbonell generalizes Winston's approach to work not just with causal relations, but with an *invariance hierarchy* of relations that are typically mapped unchanged in any figurative transfer. This hierarchy opens up the spectrum of mapping-invariant relations to include goals, planning strategies, functional attributes, temporal orderings, tendencies, social roles, and structural relations. As Carbonell notes, the listener *"ought to know why a particular metaphor was chosen,"* especially when literal alternatives are available. In Carbonell's model, the motivation for using a metaphor is often to be found in the logic of the metaphor schema itself, and should be integrated whenever possible into the listener's interpretation of the utterance.

Essentially, a conceptual framework comprising the mapping-invariant parts of the source is transferred directly, and then imposed, upon the target domain. In contrast, those parts of the source that are not granted preservation status by the invariance hierarchy must be restructured by a special *transfer* mapping if they are to find a place in the target domain. For instance, in understanding the metaphor *"Inflation is soaring,"* the conceptual metaphor schema MORE IS UP is recognized and activated, allowing the system to reason that *soaring* indicates a rapid upward change in altitude in the source domain, and will thus indicate a rapid upward change in a comparable dimension in the target domain. As such, basic mapping information in the metaphor schema indicates that INFLATION will undergo a rapid upward increase, while a more elaborate transfer mapping will reason, in the specific domain of economics activated by the utterance, that it is prices that are undergoing rapid upward change, so that goods are quickly becoming more expensive.

By representing metaphor as a schematic source of conceptual knowledge, Carbonell's approach earns expected dividends in terms of reasoning and inference, but also derives a number of other processing benefits that are perhaps less obvious. First, although it only attempts to understand a statement as a metaphor when conventional literal processing yields an anomaly, the system does not view all anomalies as metaphors. Rather, it treats an anomalous utterance as a metaphor once it recognizes the utterance as an instance of a known metaphor schema. It is a metaphor system that processes metaphors and is guided by metaphors. Second, it can store conventional renderings of general metaphors in dictionary structures that make explicit the underlying metaphor. Third, it can learn these conventional renderings from repeated exposure to many different utterances. Fourth, Carbonell suggests that his approach might allow new species of a general metaphor to also be learned by a system, insofar as the analogical mappings that arise from the interpretation of related metaphors might be generalized and packaged to form a new metaphor schema.

James Martin's [1990] metaphor interpretation, denotation and acquisition system (MIDAS) offers a comparable representation-centric approach to metaphor. Martin focuses on conventional metaphors, those familiar forms that have become part of the furniture of language, yet which still have the power to surprise us, even if only to occasionally remind us of their metaphoricity, whenever they are given new life in a novel instantiation. MIDAS uses the KO-

DIAK knowledge-representation language to explicitly encode the metaphor schemas employed by the system, and applies these schemas in the domain of computer system dialogues (specifically, in the domain of operating-system concepts that underpins the Berkeley *Unix Consultant* (UC) NLP help system; see Wilensky et al. [1988]). Martin's approach combines elements of Lakoff and Johnson [1980], by whose philosophy it is inspired, as well as elements of Carbonell [1982] and Gentner [1983]. As in the latter work, metaphor is assumed to benefit from the systematicity of an analogical mapping between the source and target domains, a mapping which in turn preserves the central core of the source domain and transplants it onto the target/tenor. Martin uses the notion of *core relation*s to tie together the elements of each domain into a coherent whole, and formulates a *Metaphor Preservation Principle* to ensure that these core-relations are preserved in any mapping. For instance, *having*, *getting* and *giving* are all core-related terms that allow us to talk of possessions, while *entering*, *in*, *out* and *exiting* are all core-related terms when we speak of containment. If we can *enter* a metaphorical container, it makes sense to assume that when we are *in* that container we can choose to *exit* that container. Martin's *Metaphor Preservation Principle* thus states that the metaphorical use of core-related words in a target domain must hierarchically preserve the core-relationships established among the corresponding words in the source domain.

MIDAS thus approaches metaphor as a re-framing operation. We frame certain notions such as CONTAINMENT and POSSESSION in a particular way and with particular words in conventional language, and metaphor allows us to apply that framing to a target domain for which such a convenient frame does not yet exist. The *Metaphor Preservation Principle* ensures that the source frame is coherently transported to, and properly unpacked in, the target domain. Importantly, MIDAS also supports the extension of a metaphor schema by imposing a number of extension requirements: a *Subset* requirement, which ensures that the extended use of the metaphor preserves all the core relations of the original metaphor; a *Closeness* requirement, which ensures that the new ideas introduced in the extended use are obviously and naturally connected to the ideas in the original schema; and a *Coherence* requirement, which ensures that the source and target domains are extended in comparable ways that, if not identical, at least have identical abstractions. Metaphor extension is a productive mechanism in which even simple extensions can yield communicative benefits, as Martin shows with the extension CAUSING INFECTION IS TRANSFERRING POSSESSION of the more basic metaphor schema INFECTIONS ARE POSSESSIONS. This extension presumes a POSSESSOR of the INFECTION AS POSSESSION, just as in the core metaphor, and adds an act of transfer between the closely related ideas of GIVER and POSSESSOR. Moreover, it coherently mirrors the GIVING relationship in the source domain with a RESULTING-STATE relationship in the target domain.

Conventional metaphors are much more than frozen expressions and idioms: they offer productive, extensible ways of thinking about the world and of framing a discussion. To allow a computational system to fully exploit this productivity, the representation of each metaphor schema must be rich enough to support in-domain reasoning in the source domain, the results of which can then be transferred into the target domain (see Barnden and Lee [2002], Barnden

[2006]). Moreover, the representation must be flexible enough to support reasoning with multiple connected schemas at once. For instance, consider the possible interactions of the CONTAINER and ORIENTATION schemas. We may simultaneously represent a state such as COMA or TROUBLE or DEBT as an immersive CONTAINER (we can be in a coma, in trouble, or in debt) and as a DOWNWARD-ORIENTED-STATE (we fall into a coma, we get into trouble by tripping ourselves up or by digging our own grave, and we may try to climb out of debt). Entering a state such as COMA or TROUBLE or DEBT thus entails, figuratively, entering a container and assuming a downward orientation, while leaving such a state implies that we exit the container and resume an upward orientation. Veale and Keane [1992] take this need for schema-based reasoning and complex schema interactions as their starting point, but rather than represent these metaphorical schemas in a knowledge-representation language, they build a new representation language that uses these very schemas as its primitive operators. These operators include *enter* and *exit* (for containment metaphors), *up-state* and *down-state* and *push-up* and *push-down* (for orientation metaphors), and *connection* and *disconnection* and *cause-connection* and *cause-disconnection* (for spatial location metaphors). The lexico-semantic structures that are associated with words in a semantic dictionary can now be constructed from these operators, and these structures can, in a process not unlike that in Wilks [1975], be combined into a *Conceptual Scaffolding* that represents the entire utterance.

Veale and Keane [1992] show how a wide variety of actions, such as *rescue, collapse, destroy, trap, support, marry,* and *divorce* can be given a conceptual scaffolding representation. For instance, *rescue* is modeled as the caused movement of a patient from a container with a downward orientation (*Danger*) to a location of upward orientation (*Safety*). Whether this rescue is literal and physical, and entails the physical disconnection of a person from a dangerous place and a subsequent connection with a place of safety, or figurative, and entails a disconnection and connection that are entirely metaphorical (e.g., from a bad marriage to a state of emotional freedom, or from a state of near-bankruptcy to financial solvency), this distinction is not captured in the scaffolding itself, and so the same scaffolding is constructed for literal and figurative uses of the word "*rescue*." In either case, whether the usage is intended figuratively or literally, the scaffolding is ultimately replaced, operator by operator, with the domain-specific relationships that are most coherent with our knowledge of the target. Thus, the financial use of "*rescue*" may replace the downward-oriented start state with the state *Insolvent*, and the upwardly oriented end state with the state *Solvent*. Yet even when the scaffolding is elaborated and replaced in this way, it leaves behind an analogy: the state of *Insolvency* is seen as a kind of *Danger* and the state of *Solvency* is seen as a kind of *Safety*. The metaphor thus re-frames our understanding of finance using the language and ideas of a rescue operation.

Each of these schematic approaches emphasizes the necessity of in-domain reasoning in the target domain. Schematic approaches are, by their very nature, generic approaches: they apply general structures to specific utterances, and so a domain-specific reasoning process is required to anchor a generic interpretation in the specifics of the target domain (as in e.g., Hobbs [1991]). Although a metaphor may evoke a source in all its of richness, every figurative description is ultimately *about* its target. Nonetheless, in-domain reasoning in the source domain can also contribute to the meaning of a metaphor and convey valuable insights about the target. Indeed, as employed in the ATT-Meta computational model of Barnden and Lee [2002] and Barnden [2006], source-domain reasoning may contribute as much as any process grounded in the target domain, and may sometimes contribute even more to an interpretation. ATT-Meta, which offers a rule-based, goal-directed reasoning system for inferring and projecting propositional *ATTi-tudes in Metaphor-based reasoning*, principally concerns itself with schematic metaphors of mind. These metaphor schemas, which include the highly productive IDEAS ARE OBJECTS and IDEAS ARE POSSESSIONS, as well as MINDS ARE PHYSICAL SPACES and MINDS ARE CONTAINERS, allow ATT-Meta to reason about the differences in interpretation of "*John grasped the plan*" and "*John was dimly aware of a plan forming in the back of his mind.*" It is in-domain reasoning in the source domain that allows the system to infer that a graspable idea is one that one can hold firmly, see clearly and interrogate fully, while an idea at the back of one's mind (relative to a thinker's central position, figuratively speaking, in one's own mind) affords a much less rigorous evaluation of its qualities.

ATT-Meta, as in each of the previous approaches, posits an important role for analogical mapping in the metaphor interpretation process, for it is analogy that provides the 1-to-1 links that connect the source and target domains. However, most analogical approaches tacitly assume that the source's contribution to an interpretation is circumscribed by this mapping from the source onto the target. Under this assumption, an element in the source domain can only contribute to an interpretation if it can first be connected to a corresponding element of the target, and thereby influence any reasoning process that is anchored in the target domain. Barnden argues that this assumption, although rarely stated explicitly, is a fallacy. Metaphors project more than propositional structure from a source: they can also project a speaker's attitudes and feelings about the source, by encouraging listeners to evoke—and then project onto a target—those attitudes and feelings for themselves.

Consider the metaphor "*prices shot through the roof.*" The verb "*to shoot*" conveys a generic sense of speed, and in the context of "*roof*" (which, among other things, denotes an upwardly-oriented position) it also conveys a sense of rapid upward motion. So prices are *rocketing*, or *soaring*, or *rising quickly*. But what does the concept *roof* correspond to in the target domain of goods and their prices? Does it correspond to some expectation of a maximum price threshold, in the same way that *floor* might correspond to a minimum price threshold? (In the terminology of Martin [1990], *floor* and *roof* and *ceiling* are core-related terms.) It may, yet it may also correspond to nothing at all. Now consider this variation on the metaphor: "*prices crashed through the roof.*" Once again we have a rapid vertical increase in prices (let us put aside the question of whether prices are in fact soaring up or crashing back down to earth), but this time the verb "*to crash*" suggests *noise*, *shock*, *chaos*, and *surprise*. We might imagine falling debris, and a gaping hole in an imaginary roof. Prices must crash into something to yield this shock-inducing effect, and a roof is the standard upwardly-oriented obstacle into which something might vertically crash. But once again, there is no real need to map *roof* to anything in the target domain; it has served its purpose fully within the source domain, and is free to remain there, unmapped, while its affective contribution to the metaphor—feelings of *surprise* and *dismay*—are projected in its stead. Of course, one can also map *roof* if one wishes, especially if the notion of a maximum price threshold is a topical one. The point is that it is not always necessary to do so to grasp the intended meaning of a metaphor.

If CMT is rooted in a level of thought that is deeper than discrete symbols, in the level of feelings and bodily sensations, some theorists go further and argue that metaphor is directly anchored to the neural level of action and representation. In contrast to the corrective approach of Cottrell [1987], which exploits the connectionist properties of identity mapping networks to map metaphorical onto literal meanings without a mediating conceptual structure, Feldman and Narayanan [2004] and Feldman [2006] present a schematic CMT approach called the *Neural Theory of Language* (NTL). This NTL combines the conflation hypothesis of Johnson [1999] with the primary metaphors of Grady [1997] to show how high-level metaphorical mappings can be built from the bottom up, from low-level sensorimotor activations to high-level conceptual abstractions. In the NTL model, sustained simultaneous activation in different domains (e.g., the domains of *affection* and *warmth*, or *verticality* and *quantity*) ultimately leads to the establishment of permanent neural connections between the neuronal clusters that code for these domains. Once this linkage is established, activation of one domain can now cause activation in the other. Primary metaphors arise after this conflation stage, once the cognitive agent comes to understand that the conflated phenomena belong to distinct conceptual domains. This is necessary if the agent is to appreciate that some cross-activations suggest literal entailment (e.g., *physical_warmth* → *physical_closeness*) while others suggest metaphorical entailment (e.g., *physical_warmth* → *emotional_closeness*).

Anchored in this neuronal substrate are higher-level conceptual schemas, such as SOURCE-PATH-GOAL. As its name suggests, this schema is rooted in the schematic roles SOURCE, PATH, and GOAL, and represents an extension of the TL schema that codes for the movement of a TRAJECTOR relative to a LANDMARK. SPG is activated in utterances that speak of literal movement along a path (e.g., "*he flew from New York to Las Vegas and then drove the rest of the way to Los Angeles*") as well as those that suggest figurative movement (e.g., "*his career took him from the mail room to the board room*"). Just as one neuronal cluster may activate another, at the higher level of schemas, one conceptual schema may *evoke* another. In turn, each schema forms part of a tight pairing of linguistic form to conceptual/semantic meaning called a *construction*. A comprehensive system of form:meaning pairs, or constructions, is called a *construction grammar* [Goldberg, 1995], provided that sufficient constructions are available to support the piecemeal mapping of arbitrarily complex utterance forms to their meanings. Croft [2003] and Sullivan [2007, 2013] describe how constructions are key to successfully understanding linguistic metaphors. In the case of culturally entrenched metaphors and blends, constructions may inform us that the words of an utterance allude to something larger than themselves. Recall that, in the earlier example of

Figures 2.1 and 2.2, it was the construction "*painting in [the] attic*" that alerted us to a deliberate allusion to the plot of Oscar Wilde's *The Picture of Dorian Gray*. Croft [2003] and Sullivan [2007] explore the extent to which the structural properties of a construction (e.g., which element serves as the autonomous landmark, and which serves as the dependent trajector relative to this landmark?) can offer us important clues as to which elements mark out the source domain of a metaphor and which mark out the target. For instance, in the metaphor "*bright student*," it is more sensible to locate the autonomous element *student* in the target domain and to consider the dependent element *bright* as designating the source domain of the metaphor. Because the meaning component of NTL's constructions (i.e., its conceptual schemas) are anchored in a neural substrate that makes some claim to cognitive and neurological plausibility, NTL's construction grammar is called *Embodied Construction Grammar* (ECG) (Bergen and Chang [2002], Feldman and Narayanan [2004]). In this respect, NTL aims to offer a top-to-bottom implementation of CMT, although application-oriented researchers may choose to focus on models and CMT-inspired approaches with less theoretical ambition and greater computational simplicity.

3.4   COMMON THEMES AND FUTURE PROSPECTS

These various computational models exhibit a number of common themes that cut across, to varying degrees, all three types of approach. For instance, most assume the existence of a literal (or at least normative) meaning of words that can be given a coded, semantic form that a system can store in a semantic dictionary. Each assumes that some form of structural mapping is required to arrive at the interpretation of a metaphor, although some approaches are more explicit in the manner of this mapping. For the corrective approaches, the mapping offers a translation from an anomalous, literal representation of an utterance's source-domain meaning into a more apt representation of meaning in the target domain. For the analogical approaches, this mapping is itself a key part of the interpretation, for it establishes one of the speaker's goals in using a metaphor: to show how, deep down, two very different concepts are causally and relationally similar. For the schematic approaches, analogical mapping yields the blueprint that allows a schema to project the source domain onto that of the target, so that aspects of the source can spur plausible inferences about the target. Finally, each assumes that metaphor is itself a unit of conceptual representation, even if it is only the schematic approaches that openly embrace and exploit this conceptual aspect of metaphor. As shown in Figure 3.1, it is all too easy for a convenient metaphor or two to creep into a representation that purports to be wholly literal, while semantic markers—especially those that are chosen to convey the extensible qualities of a concept—are frequently little more than hard-coded metaphors. And, as Martin [1990] notes, the semantic primitives that underpin a literal semantics may themselves be hard-coded metaphors in disguise: he notes, for example, that the *mtrans* (*mental transfer*) primitive in conceptual dependency representations (used by Cater [1985], Russell [1992] and others) simply codifies the CONDUIT metaphor of communication as identified by Reddy [1979]. No matter what kind of approach is used, an NLP system must *already* contain and exploit metaphor at some level if it is to offer a robust response to novel metaphors. Our survey of the history of AI models suggests that it is better to make this prior knowledge of metaphor explicit and declarative rather than implicit, procedural, or unwittingly hard-coded.

As we saw in the introduction, in our analysis of the conventionalized "pulling strings" metaphor, seemingly innocuous examples of everyday metaphor are revealed to be considerably more complex—in terms of both their knowledge requirements and the complexity of the reasoning that they entail—when we peer under the surface to interrogate their inner workings. But as we also saw in our analysis of the blending example of Figure 2.2, we humans can handle this complexity effortlessly, often without missing a beat, never mind breaking a sweat. So what then are our prospects for a computational model of figurative language processing that can cope robustly with such demanding examples from such unassuming sources? As we have seen, the neurally inspired perspective of Feldman and Narayanan [2004] lends itself to a computational model that anchors its high-level schematic structures to an artificial neural network, and aims to explain not just metaphor (primary and complex), but also, to an extent, blending. However, although it is not without computational interest or explanatory power, this model cannot yet be considered as an engineering basis for robust computational systems, at least not ones that can be pressed into service for open-domain NLP duties. In contrast, the vector-space approaches of Kintsch [2001] and Utsumi [2011] offer a robust data-driven approach to metaphor that may be extensible to other figurative phenomena such as blending. Indeed, the use of word vectors to represent meanings, and the use of centroid vectors to represent a conceptual integration of multiple perspectives, goes some distance toward capturing the notion of a *middle space* that is intrinsic to conceptual blending (see e.g., Fauconnier and Turner [1994], which sketches an early version of their theory in which the blend space is considered to be a middle space between the inputs that project into it). However, as the example of Figures 2.1 and 2.2 demonstrates, blending is an inherently structured process; blended information is not simply pooled and averaged, but flows in a carefully orchestrated fashion to and from mental spaces. Veale and O'Donoghue [2000], Pereira [2007], Goguen and Harrell [2010], and Kutz et al. [2014] each present alternative, highly structured symbolic approaches to blending with their own special emphases, while placing analogical structure-mapping at the core of each. Nonetheless, these approaches are all equally dependent on structured representations, resulting in a time-consuming need for hand-coded knowledge. Veale [2012b] later turned to an automatic means of acquiring propositional knowledge from the Web, and of robustly combining these propositions into lightweight blends called *conceptual mash-ups*. Although the approach seems a promising one, its representations are a good deal flatter than those required to handle the example of Figure 2.2. At present, no computational approach to blending seems entirely satisfactory, and the field awaits a robust hybrid model that combines the scale and practicality of bottom-up statistical approaches with the top-down structured control of symbolic approaches.

CHAPTER 4

Metaphor Annotation

4.1 METAPHOR IDENTIFICATION IN CORPUS LINGUISTICS

The goal of studies in corpus linguistics is often to characterize metaphors used in particular corpora of interest, such as metaphors used by a certain political figure, metaphors used in public discourse about a certain topic in a certain period of time, or metaphors in texts in a certain professional field [Cameron, 2003, Charteris-Black, 2005, Koller, 2004, Musolff, 2000, Partington, 1995]. The operating definition of what constitutes a metaphor, as well as the granularity of analysis (e.g., word or phrase level) may differ across studies. This might not be a problem for any given study, as studies usually operate with aggregate figures, such as the totals or proportions of certain kinds of metaphors in the given corpus; thus, even if some of the specific instances of metaphors identified in the corpus are somewhat subjective, significant differences between corpora are still likely to hold up (given the particular definition of metaphor that is used in the study). Corpus-linguistic studies often address the interpretive and strategic aspects of metaphor use, and might therefore focus on certain culturally, politically, or pedagogically interesting metaphors, leaving open the possibility that other, less salient, metaphors in the same texts might be ignored. However, if one seeks an exhaustive characterization of metaphor in a given corpus, or a comparative characterization across different studies, then the lack of methodological consistency in identifying metaphors becomes problematic: "*Variability in intuitions, and lack of precision about what counts as a metaphor, makes it quite difficult to compare different empirical analyses*" [Pragglejaz Group, 2007, p. 2]. Thus, out of the multiplicity of approaches and techniques, a recognition has grown that the field needs "*principled solutions if an annotated corpus of metaphors in texts is to be produced for research purposes*" [Heywood et al., 2002, p. 51].

Consequently, researchers in the corpus linguistics tradition have sought a reliable method for identifying metaphors in any given text—an endeavor often referred to as the development of a reliable *annotation protocol* in the computational linguistics universe. This line of work culminated in a protocol called the *Metaphor Identification Procedure* (MIP) developed by a group of metaphor researchers publishing under the acronym of *Pragglejaz* (using the first letters of the first names of Peter Crips, Ray Gibbs, Alan Cienki, Graham Low, Gerard Steen, Lynne Cameron, Elena Semino, Joe Grady, Alice Deignan, and Zoltan Kovecses) [Pragglejaz Group, 2007]. According to the MIP protocol, a metaphor occurs when a word is used in a text in a way that (a) is different from its more basic contemporary meaning, and (b) can be understood in comparison with the basic meaning. The protocol provides a definition of a *basic meaning* as well as of a *contemporary meaning*, using reference dictionaries for sense inventories and for historical information about word senses. The method can be applied to all lexical items in natural discourse. Since, at this time, MIP can be regarded as the base protocol upon which most current studies build, we will present it in some detail, followed by a discussion of the variations that have been put forward in subsequent research.

4.2   THE MIP OVERALL

The MIP is explicated in Figure 4.1.

---

1. Read the entire text-discourse to establish a general understanding of its meaning.

2. Determine the lexical units in the text-discourse.

3. (a) For each lexical unit, establish its meaning in context, that is, how it applies to an entity, relation, or attribute in the situation evoked by the text (contextual meaning). Take into account what comes before and after the lexical unit.

    (b) For each lexical unit, determine if it has a more basic contemporary meaning in other contexts than the one in the given context. For our purposes, basic meanings tend to be:

        i. more concrete, insofar as what they evoke is easier to imagine, see, hear, feel, smell, and taste;

        ii. related to bodily action;

        iii. more precise (as opposed to vague); and

        iv. historically older.

    Basic meanings are not necessarily the most frequent meanings of the lexical unit.

    (c) If the lexical unit has a more basic current-contemporary meaning in other contexts that in the given context, decide whether the contextual meaning contrasts with the basic meaning but can be understood in comparison with it.

4. If yes, mark the lexical unit as a metaphor.

Figure 4.1: The MIP for identifying metaphors in text [Pragglejaz Group, 2007].

We note that criteria 3(b)i–3(b)iv have at least a partial order, with the historical constraint being weaker than the others. Thus, in the sentence *Sonia Gandhi struggled to convince Indians that she is fit to wear the mantle of the political dynasty into which she married*, the lexical item *fit* is deemed metaphorical, as it possesses the basic meaning "healthy and physically strong" and the contextual meaning "suitable to play a particular role due to personal qualities such as leadership, integrity, talent." According to historical precedence, the contextual meaning is actually older than the basic one; however, the historical ordering constraint is overridden by the embodiment constraint, as the "healthy" meaning is more directly physically experienced.[1]

The MIP is designed to be flexible and thus accommodate different definitions of the key notions used in the procedure, such as *lexical unit*, *contemporary meaning*, *concrete*, *precise*, *contrasts*, and *can be understood in comparison*. Clearly, the more of these notions that are left to the intuitions of the analyst, the more room that is created for potential disagreement between analysts. For example, if one analyst treats *eat up* in *"Eat up, and we'll go for a walk"* as a single lexical unit, it is likely to be identified as a non-metaphor,[2] while a decision to treat *eat up* as two lexical units would instead yield an annotation where *up* is identified as an instance of the MORE IS UP conceptual metaphor with the basic meaning of "high" and the contextual meaning of "a lot, all there is." Thus, different decisions regarding the identification of lexical units can lead to serious disagreement, which might otherwise be avoided if identification is performed independently and prior to the application of the MIP, by, for example, a specially-designed tokenizer—thus externalizing, as it were, the decision-making involved in the identification of lexical units. Such a strategy would also take the subjectivity out of step (2) of the protocol, potentially eliminating subsequent disagreements.

However, the downside of such a strategy is that it can lead to the introduction of a systematic bias into the results of the annotation—in particular, regarding the treatment of particles and possibly also the treatment of phrasal verbs.[3] Many phrasal verbs would be seen as metaphorical if their lexical parts were treated as separate units, and since phrasal verbs are fairly common in English, this strategy could have a significant impact on measurements of the metaphoricity of a given text or of the distributional properties of metaphors generally. We should also note that the usefulness of a corpus annotated using a particular operationalization of a vaguely defined notion might be limited by possible theoretical disagreements. For example, one could argue that treating phrasal verbs as single units while treating words that comprise commonplace idioms as separate lexical units is not especially parsimonious.

To address the impact of potentially different operationalizations of key notions, the Pragglejaz Group recommends that researchers applying the MIP provide a detailed record of whatever operational definitions they employ [Pragglejaz Group, 2007, p. 14], including definitions of what constitutes a lexical unit, any decisions regarding transcription, a complete list of the sense inventories that were used, as well as the identity and background of the annotators (for example, distinguishing metaphor researchers from lay people). If such decisions are systematically documented, there may gradually emerge an understanding of the effects of various decisions on the MIP's findings, and of their appropriateness to the specific goals pursued in an annotation project.

---

[1]This discussion is based on the analysis of "fit" in Pragglejaz Group [2007].

[2]Compare this to *"They drove on, eating up the distance between themselves and home"* (from the examples in the Macmillan dictionary definition of *"eat up"*).

[3]Consider *"He turned against me and voted for John instead."* If *turn against* is treated as a single lexical unit, it will not be identified as a metaphor, but if *turn* is considered a separate unit, then it has a basic meaning "change one's physical position" and a contextual meaning "change one's attitude toward someone," where the first is more concrete and anchored in the body, hence *turn* would be identified as a metaphor.

Using their own specifications of the vaguely defined key concepts (discussed in the following section), Pragglejaz Group [2007] reported $\kappa = 0.72$ for a news text and $\kappa = 0.62$ for a transcript of conversation, across 6 annotators, all highly experienced researchers of metaphor (the figures were 0.70 and 0.56, respectively, when using average pairwise Cohen's kappa[4] measures).

While the MIP is a general protocol designed to encompass a variety of considerations through specifications of the key concepts, there are additional aspects of metaphor in discourse that are not directly addressed in this framework, such as whether the author used the metaphor deliberately, whether the metaphor effectively helped the author achieve her communicative purpose, or whether a metaphor would be recognized by a non-expert reader [Beigman Klebanov and Flor, 2013, Steen, 2008]. The effect of these considerations remains to be explored, as well as the extent to which experiments with data annotated using MIP and alternative protocols would yield substantially different computational models.

4.3   SPECIFICATIONS OF AUXILIARY CONCEPTS

In their own specification of the protocol, the Pragglejaz Group generally take the externalization approach to the definition of lexical units, sense inventories, and historical etymologies, while leaving it to analysts to judge for themselves the concreteness/abstractness, precision/vagueness, and degree of embodiment for various meanings, as well as the notion of (sufficient) contrast and the possibility of understanding the two meanings by comparison. It must be noted, however, that externalization does not equate to automation; in the analysis of Pragglejaz Group [2007], dictionaries and definitions were consulted and adhered to as per the general guidelines, but such guidelines could be overruled. In this section, we discuss the definitions proposed by Pragglejaz Group [2007], as well as some alternative definitions.

4.3.1   SENSE INVENTORIES

Pragglejaz Group [2007] used the Macmillan English Dictionary for Advanced Learners[5] [Rundell and Fox, 2002] as their primary inventory of contemporary word senses and as an aid in identifying single- vs. multi-word lexical units. In addition, they looked to the Shorter Oxford English Dictionary on Historical Principles [Little et al., 1973] as an authority on etymology. Steen et al. [2010] also used the Longman Dictionary of Contemporary English[6] for a second opinion in cases where the Macmillan dictionary alone proved insufficient. Furthermore, they

---

[4]Cohen's kappa, or κ, is a statistic that measures the agreement between two annotators on a categorization task. Unlike the raw agreement measure, which simply measures the frequency with which the annotators are observed to agree with each other, κ estimates the amount of this agreement that is due to chance and scales its measure accordingly. A κ of 0.8 or higher may be considered a strong agreement, a kappa of 0.6–0.8—a substantial agreement, while a κ of 0.2 or less may be considered a weak agreement at best (see Landis and Koch [1977] for some commonly used benchmarks). However, there are no absolutes when it comes to interpreting kappa scores. Artstein and Poesio [2008] provide a comprehensive survey of kappa and kappa-like measures and their use in the evaluation of inter-annotator agreement in computational linguistics.

[5]Available online at http://www.macmillandictionary.com/.

[6]Available online at http://www.ldoceonline.com/.

used the Oxford English Dictionary[7] whenever the Macmillan and Longman dictionaries did not yield a clear classification, specifically in cases where an apparent distinction between the contextual and the basic senses of a lexical unit proved difficult to categorize. The OED may help to elucidate the connection between two senses through an obsolete common source, and thus help to determine that both senses are not sufficiently related to be understood in comparison with each other.

In a number of recent studies in computational linguistics that involved the annotation of metaphors [Beigman Klebanov and Flor, 2013, Hovy et al., 2013b, Jang et al., 2014, Shutova and Teufel, 2010, Tsvetkov et al., 2014], sense identification was viewed as a responsibility of the annotators that did *not* demand an adherence to external sense inventories. This decision allowed the annotation to capture the reader's intuitions about the senses that are available for a given expression, although such intuitions may differ from person to person and introduce an additional source of subjectivity and a concomitant drop in inter-annotator agreement. On the other hand, this approach has the advantage of capturing the senses that are commonly perceived rather than those that are theoretically available. For example, based on the definitions in the Macmillan dictionary, the use of *attitude* in *"His negative* attitude *toward the new employee surprised me"* would be considered metaphorical due to its basic meaning of "position of the body," yet the existence of this sense in contemporary usage often surprises annotators. Conversely, the fact that Macmillan lists only a single sense for *widespread* ("happening or existing in many places, or affecting many people") does not preclude annotators from seeing this as deriving metaphorically from the less abstract sense of *spread*: "to cover a surface with a thin layer of a soft food." Similarly, the Macmillan dictionary does not list physical senses for *basis, coverage, rely on, outweigh*, or *downfall*, yet annotators might perceive the physical basis behind the more common abstract meanings.

4.3.2   CRITERION FOR SENSE DISTINCTIVENESS

Pragglejaz Group [2007] do not explicitly address this issue, but Steen et al. [2010] propose a practical guideline whereby "separate, numbered senses" in a dictionary for the same lexical unit are sufficiently distinct. If there is only a single sense in the dictionary, that sense counts as basic, and any difference from that sense will count as a sufficient distinction. We note, however, that dictionary definitions do not always respect the distinctions in metaphoricity that one might want to make. For example, Macmillan lists "easy to see or understand" as one sense for the word *apparent*, while an annotator may want to consider the "easy to understand" sense as metaphorical and the "easy to see" sense as basic. Similarly, the first definition of *workings* is "the workings of something such as a system, organization, or piece of equipment are the parts that control it or make it work." This definition does not allow one to draw a distinction between mechanical operations (as in *"the inner workings of a computer"*) and a metaphorical conception of an organization or an institution as if it were a mechanical system (as in *"the workings of the stock market"*).

---

[7]Available online at http://www.oed.com/.

Shutova and Teufel [2010] asked annotators to provide the source-target domain mapping for every metaphorical usage of a verb that they identified, drawing from lists of source and target categories that were provided by the researchers. These lists of categories were based on the Master Metaphor List [Lakoff et al., 1991], augmented with additional categories occurring in the BNC data. Thus, the implicit criterion for sufficient difference is the ability to identify distinct source and target domains in the corpus-adjusted inventories of domains for the lexical item in question.

4.3.3   LEXICAL UNIT

Pragglejaz Group [2007] generally treat every word as a separate lexical unit.[8] The process of tokenization into words is not explicitly discussed in the Pragglejaz paper. Steen et al. [2010] rely on the tokenization and part-of-speech annotations in the British National Corpus (BNC) from which they draw their corpus; they consider all words provided with an independent part-of-speech (POS) tag as separate lexical units. The case where a sequence of space-separated words is given a single POS tag is that of *polywords*, that is, expressions that contain a space yet always appear as a continuous unit in a text, such as *"of course"* and *"all right."* These are each marked in the BNC with a single POS tag.

There are some exceptions to this general rule: cases where a space-delimited sequence of words, each with its own POS tag, is still treated as a single unit, and cases where a hyphenated word with a single POS tag is treated as two units. We discuss these exceptions below.

Compounds

Pragglejaz Group [2007] do not explicitly discuss compounds; presumably, the decision to treat a compound as a single lexical unit is made if the compound is a headword in the dictionary. Steen et al. [2010] remark that compounds have a tell-tale sign: the primary stress in the compound is on the first word, and the secondary stress—on the second (as in *power plant* or *ice cream*); their proposal is to accept a compound as a single lexical item if it both appears as a headword in the dictionary and has this stress pattern.[9] A question arises regarding compounds that are not listed in the dictionary, such as novel formations often spelled with a hyphen (for example, *under-five* and *honey-hunting*). Steen et al. [2010] propose treating those as two separate lexical units (even though they are given a single POS tag in the BNC), because the reader would actually need to actively construct the meaning of such a compound out of its two component parts. Acknowledging the possibility that the actual text under analysis could employ a spelling variant that differs from that in the dictionary, Steen et al. [2010] suggest going by the dictionary spelling, as the dictionary reflects the accepted spelling norms.

---

[8]According to Pragglejaz Group [2007], "all headwords in the dictionary" are lexical items, but this does not seem to exhaust the inventory. For example, neither *Sonia*, nor *Gandhi*, nor *Sonia Gandhi* are listed as headwords in the Macmillan online dictionary, yet *Sonia Gandhi* is treated as a lexical unit in the example annotation, so out-of-vocabulary items can also be considered lexical units.

[9]An item might be listed as a headword in a dictionary but not have the compound stress pattern, such as *nuclear power*; Steen et al. [2010] treat those as two separate units.

Proper names

The grouping together of proper names is not addressed explicitly in Pragglejaz Group [2007], although the example annotation considers the First-Name Last-Name sequence referring to a single individual as a single unit (as in *Sonia Gandhi*). Steen et al. [2010] differ by treating the individual parts of proper names as separate lexical units—thus, *New York* is comprised of two units, *New* and *York*. An exception to this separation practice is made for proper names that are listed in a dictionary and have a stress pattern that is typical of compound terms (i.e., a primary stress on the first word). Thus, *Labor Party* and *Pulitzer Prize* have the same stress pattern as the compound *power plant*, and will be treated as single units, whereas *Sonia Gandhi* and *New York* do not, and will be treated as two separate units.

Phrasal verbs

Phrasal verbs are treated as single units, since they *"are not the semantic sum of their parts"* [Pragglejaz Group, 2007]. The identification of a verb-particle sequence as a phrasal verb is done using the criterion that the sequence appears as a headword in the dictionary designated as the sense inventory for the annotation project. Steen et al. [2010] propose adding the criterion that the BNC provides the particle with the special AVP tag (adverbial particle), as opposed to the PRP tag for a preposition following a verb. A caveat to a dictionary-based procedure is that a sequence of words that can be used in a phrasal construction might not be used in the actual sentence in the corpus. For example, while *look up* is a phrasal verb meaning "to try to find a piece of information," this is not the correct sense for the use of these two words in *she looked up into the sky*; to find the correct contextual sense ("direct your eyes toward something or someone"), one would need to consult the entry for the verb *look*. The part-of-speech tags for the sentence at hand can sometimes help disambiguate these issues, but such tags, especially if produced automatically, may be erroneous. Thus, BNC gives the AVP tag to *up* in this sentence.

While the decision to treat the phrasal verb as a single unit seems unproblematic for a phrasal verb like *take off* (e.g., of an airplane) or *come up*, Pragglejaz Group [2007] note that there are other cases where the contributions of the verb and the particle are more transparent, as in the set of phrasal verbs that contain the particle *up*—such as *eat up*, *drink up* and *grow up*—where the verb has its usual meaning and the particle contributes the notion of *finishing*. Treating phrasal verbs as single units also introduces complications when a lexical unit becomes non-contiguous because there is intervening material between the verb and the particle, as in *turn* him *down* or *switch* it *off*.

Parts of speech

Pragglejaz Group [2007] consider words that share the same orthographic form as constituting the same lexical unit. Thus, *long* the adjective and *long* the adverb are considered to be the same lexical unit with, presumably, a combined dictionary entry, since in the Macmillan dictionary (as well as in many others) same-form words with different parts of speech are assigned different sense inventories. This decision, much like the decision to consider phrasal verbs as single units, has systematic implications for metaphor identification. One would thus find *more* metaphors using this approach than in one where different parts of speech were considered as different lexical items. Consider the words *long* and *hard* in *he fought long and hard in this campaign*.[10] The basic senses of the adjectival uses of these words have to do with space and materials, respectively, so their use in the sentence would be metaphorical. However, they are in fact used adverbially in the sentence. As their dictionary definitions as adverbs pertain only to *time* (for *long*) and to *difficulty* (for *hard*), no contrasting basic senses can be found and the words would thus be considered non-metaphorical. Conflating various parts of speech gives one access to more potential basic senses, thus increasing the chances of classifying an item as a metaphor. The MIP-VU[11] approach developed by Steen et al. [2010] takes an alternative approach, where word class is part of the identity of the lexical item.

Considerations pertaining to a computational linguistics context

In a computational linguistics context, one needs to consider the typical end-use of the annotated corpus. Such a corpus will likely serve as training data for a machine learning (or other computational) system so that a conditioned system could eventually be employed to find metaphors in unseen texts. Since we should not expect that any new text will come with special annotations regarding compounding or stress patterns, it is important to choose definitions that are amenable to practical automation with robust state-of-the-art techniques. For instance, the identification of proper names in a text (Named Entity Recognition, or NER) is reasonably within reach of the current NER systems [Cucerzan, 2007, Finkel et al., 2005, Ratinov and Roth, 2009], while the detection of phrasal verbs can be done (albeit imperfectly) using state-of-art POS taggers such as that of [Toutanova et al., 2003].[12] Alternatively, one might use software that is specifically designed to define an inventory of phrasal verbs [Pichotta and DeNero, 2013] in conjunction with a system for classifying an actual occurrence of a verb+particle sequence as phrasal or otherwise [Baldwin and Villavicencio, 2002, Tu and Roth, 2012]. Dou et al. [2009] and Arciuli and Thompson [2006] describe methods for automatic high-accuracy assignment of stress in English, while Bell and Plag [2012], Mishra and Bangalore [2011], and Sproat [1994] present models of stress assignment that are specific to English noun-noun compounds. The identification of compounds—and especially their differentiation from frequent but entirely compositional word sequences—is currently an active research endeavor in the computational linguistics community, with a dedicated annual workshop series on multiword expressions now in its second decade.[13]

---

[10]This example is due to Steen [2008].

[11]The MIP-VU protocol differs from the MIP in a number of ways. It is discussed further in Section 4.5.3.

[12]The Penn Treebank tagset of Marcus et al. [1993] contains the tag RP for particles, and it is usually used to indicate a phrasal verb, although not always, and not all phrasal verbs are thus marked; Baldwin and Villavicencio [2002] report an F-score of 0.774 (P = 0.834, R = 0.565) for extracting phrasal verbs out of the Penn Treebank annotations. They propose to use the output of a parser as well as of the POS tagger to improve the detection of phrasal verbs. PropBank—an annotated corpus that ties verbs and their arguments to specific propositions (see [Palmer et al., 2005]) can be used to correct for inconsistencies in phrasal verb annotations in the Penn Treebank [Babko-Malaya et al., 2006].

[13]http://multiword.sourceforge.net/PHITE.php?sitesig=MWE

Various techniques for identifying non-compositional sequences are presented in Tsvetkov and Wintner [2014], Boukobza and Rappoport [2009], Caseli et al. [2009], Zhang et al. [2006], Deane [2005], Melamed [1997].

4.4 THE MIP IN LANGUAGES OTHER THAN ENGLISH

Pasma [2012] reports on a study that applied the MIP to a 1,000,000-word corpus of Dutch news texts and conversations. The authors report a challenge in finding a Dutch dictionary that would be a close counterpart to the Macmillan dictionary used by Pragglejaz Group [2007]. In particular, although the Van Dale dictionary [den Boon and Geeraerts, 2005] is an authority in Dutch lexicography, it is not a corpus-based dictionary but a reference dictionary. Corpus-based dictionaries such as the Macmillan provide detailed explanations of uses in context. A reference dictionary often defines meanings using synonyms, that is, in terms of other words that themselves need to be interpreted; additionally, deverbal nouns are often defined simply as the action of the relevant verb, making it unclear whether this is the only (and therefore basic) sense of the noun, or whether the definition of the verb needs to be consulted. Another dictionary-related challenge is that nearly all polywords are described in the Van Dale dictionary under the headword only, and do not receive a separate entry; similarly, part-of-speech tags in the corpus provide separate tags to each of the members of the polyword construction. Following the MIP protocol, such cases would have to be analyzed as two different words. Specifics of Dutch word formation also need to be taken into account, such as the phenomenon of separable complex verbs (such as *ingaan* "in-go" and *opzoeken* "up-look") that are semantically similar to phrasal verbs in English yet exhibit systematic variation in spelling. The infinitival form is spelled as a single word (and listed in the dictionary that way) while in other syntactic environments the complex can be spelled as two words with intervening material (although the separate spelling is not listed in the dictionary). A spelling normalization step is thus needed to account for variations in a parsimonious manner.

Badryzlova et al. [2013a,b] reports on a study aimed at annotating Russian discourse for metaphor using the MIP-VU procedure. Three annotators with prior experience in conceptual metaphor analysis annotated four text excerpts (500–600 words each) representing four genres (news, speech, academic, fiction) drawn from the Russian National Corpus,[14] using two dictionaries. The authors report an inter-annotator agreement of $\kappa = 0.68$, significantly below the $\kappa = 0.84$ reported for the English annotation using MIP-VU. The author performed some adjustments to the protocol that allowed reaching a better agreement ($\kappa = 0.90$). Much like in the study on Dutch reviewed above, many of the challenges came from the specifics of the dictionary design. The Russian dictionaries used in the project tended to provide many more fine-grained senses for words than those observed in the Macmillan dictionary, and so annotators had difficulties singling out a particular basic sense from a plethora of related senses. To appreciate the problem, consider the definitions of the verb *open*—while WordNet [Fellbaum, 1998] lists 11 senses, Macmillan lists only 6, by, for example, collapsing transitivity distinctions into a single

---

[14]http://ruscorpora.ru/

numbered sense. These authors thus decided to require identification of a family of basic senses, rather than a specific basic sense. The Russian dictionaries used in the project were reference dictionaries, exhibiting the same issue as discussed in the earlier case of Dutch dictionaries. The Russian dictionary also provides a wide variety of stylistic markers for various word senses, and although it is clear that archaic senses are ruled out by the MIP and senses marked with the "spoken" style tag are acceptable, there is less clarity regarding various fine-grained register-related stylistic distinctions listed in the dictionary.

4.5 ANNOTATED DATASETS

In this section, we describe some of the existing metaphor-annotated datasets that can be licensed for research use. Table 4.1 summarizes these datasets, including information about language, data source, annotated categories, annotated lexical items, context provided during annotation, reliability, size, and licensing information. We also review several studies that resulted in annotated repositories for which no licensing information is currently available (see Section 4.5.5).

4.5.1 CATEGORIZED COLLECTIONS OF METAPHORS

Lakoff et al. [1991]: The Master Metaphor List

In our earlier discussion of Carbonell [1982], we noted his claim that *"there appear to be a small number of general metaphors (on the order of fifty) that pervade commonly spoken English."* The Master Metaphor List of Lakoff et al. [1991] sets out to create an inventory of these metaphors. It is a document that provides a relatively large inventory of conceptual metaphors: about 70 conceptual metaphors are listed (of the same order of magnitude then as Carbonell [1982]'s estimate), organized into four top-level classes—event metaphors, mental-state metaphors, emotion metaphors, and others. For a given conceptual metaphor, the resource provides source and target domains, linguistic examples, and conceptual mappings derived from the metaphor, and also shows more specialized cases that elaborate upon the general schema. For example, for the conceptual metaphor STATES ARE LOCATIONS, the following information is provided:

- *Source Domain:* locations

- *Target Domain:* states

- *Examples:* He is in love. What kind of a state was he in when you saw him? She can stay/remain silent for days. He is at rest/at play. He remained standing. He is at a certain stage in his studies. What state is the project in?

- *Purposes are Destinations*

- *Comparison of States is Comparison of Distance*

- *Special case 1*: Harm is Being in a Harmful Location

- *Special case 2*: Existence is a Location (Here)

- *Special case 3*: Opportunities are Open Paths

Barnden [1997]: ATT Metaphors of Mind

Barnden [1997] annotated about 1,200 text and speech excerpts containing instances of metaphors of mind, classified according to the conceptual metaphor they instantiate. The dataset is available for research and educational use.[15]

Rash [2006]: Metaphors in *Mein Kampf*

As a part of her study on the rhetoric of violence, Rash [2006] collected approximately 2,000 metaphors from Adolf Hitler's *Mein Kampf*.[16] The metaphors are categorized according to source domain. Sentences containing the metaphor are provided, in German and in their English translation, along with page references to the original and to its translation. Here is an example entry for the metaphor *Gottheit* (deity), p. 14:

> Da aber darf man sich auch nicht wundern, wenn unter einer solchen Gottheit wenig Sinn für Heroismus übrigbleibt. [= money] (MK, p. 292) [And we have no call for surprise if under such a deity little sense of heroism remains (Mh., p. 242)].

Pasanek [2006, 2015], Pasanek and Sculley [2008]: Metaphors of Mind in 18th century literature

Metaphors of Mind: An Eighteenth-Century Dictionary [Pasanek, 2015] documents metaphors of mind in (predominantly) British literature written between 1660 and 1819. The author created the database using a harvesting approach, by searching texts for occurrences of words that are indicative of the target domain of MIND (*mind, heart, soul, thought, idea, imagination, fancy, reason, passion, head, breast, bosom, brain*) and words from other semantic fields within 100 characters of the target. The author addressed in an in-depth fashion the source domains for *fetters, government, minerals, war,* and *writing*. Some additional domains covered in the database are *animals, architecture, garden, light, liquid, body, optics* and *weather*. The database, which is curated and continuously updated by Pasanek, contains approximately 15,000 excerpts with metaphors, and can be browsed and searched using a variety of selection criteria.[17] Searchable classifications include literary period, source domain, genre, gender and political affiliation of the author. The database is licensed under the Creative Commons Attribution-NonCommercial-ShareAlike 2.5 Generic (CC BY-NC-SA 2.5) license.

Cardillo et al. [2010]

Cardillo et al. [2010] performed three norming studies resulting in 280 pairs of closely matched metaphoric and literal English sentences that are characterized along 10 dimensions: length, fre-

---

[15] Available from http://www.cs.bham.ac.uk/~jab/ATT-Meta/Databank/table.html.
[16] The data is available from http://webspace.qmul.ac.uk/fjrash/metaphors_mein_kampf.pdf.
[17] See http://metaphors.iath.virginia.edu/metaphors.

quency, concreteness, familiarity, naturalness, imageability, figurativeness, interpretability, valence, and valence judgment reaction time. These stimuli are designed to address questions about the role of novelty, metaphor type, and sensory-motor grounding in metaphor comprehension. The sentences were created using seed sets of verbs and nouns that have salient motion and sound qualities.[18]

4.5.2   ANNOTATIONS OF SPECIFIC CONSTRUCTIONS OR TARGET EXPRESSIONS

Birke and Sarkar [2006]: TroFi

Birke and Sarkar [2006] annotated 50 English verbs with examples of literal and non-literal usage. The original set of 1,298 sentences (25 verbs with between 1–115 examples each) from the *Wall Street Journal* was annotated for literal/non-literal usage by one annotator (one of the authors of the paper), and a reliability sample of 200 sentences was annotated by the second author, yielding an inter-annotator agreement of $\kappa = 0.77$ between the two. Subsequently, 25 additional verbs were annotated, for a total of 3,736 sentences.[19]

Bambini et al. [2014]: Literary Metaphors in Italian

Bambini et al. [2014] present a dataset of 65 instances of the genitive "*X of Y*" metaphors drawn from literary sources in Italian, along with their sentential contexts, as well as 115 such instances out of context.[20] The data were selected by three linguists working independently, and all potentially problematic cases were excluded. In a psycho-linguistic experiment, the authors collected ratings of cloze probability, familiarity, concreteness, difficulty, and meaningfulness.

Tsvetkov et al. [2014]

Tsvetkov et al. [2014] made available sets of 884 adjective-noun metaphors and 884 adjective-noun pairs with a literal meaning; these were used to train the models described in their paper.[21] These authors additionally made the test data available for their evaluations, comprising 4 sets: adjective-noun and subject-verb-object sequences in their sentential context in English and in Russian, each set containing 200–250 instances, balanced between metaphorical and literal. A pool of test sentences was created by a moderator using seed lists of common verbs and adjectives and by extracting sentences containing words that frequently co-occur with seed words. Test sentences were then selected by the moderator so that no sentence contained more than one metaphor and no sentence contained a metaphor that was not an adjective-noun or a subject-verb-object metaphor. The remaining sentences were annotated by 5 native speakers for English,

---

[18]The data is available from: `http://link.springer.com/content/esm/art:10.3758/BRM.42.3.651/file/MediaObjects/Cardillo-BRM-2010.zip`.

[19]The data is available from `http://natlang.cs.sfu.ca/software/trofi.html`, distributed under the license specified in `http://www.cs.sfu.ca/~anoop/students/jbirke/LICENSE.html`.

[20]The data is available from `http://s3-eu-west-1.amazonaws.com/files.figshare.com/1685445/File_S1.xlsx`.

[21]This data set is available from `https://github.com/ytsvetko/metaphor/tree/master/resources/AdjN`.

and by 6 for Russian. The annotators were given these general instructions: *"Please, mark in bold all words that, in your opinion, are used non-literally in the following sentences. In many sentences, all the words may be used literally."* The reported inter-annotator agreement is $\kappa \geq 0.75$, for all test sets. The data, which is available online,[22] is distributed under the Open Database License.

Hovy et al. [2013b]

Hovy et al. [2013b] created a set of 3,872 metaphorical and non-metaphorical words in their sentential contexts (in which 1,749 were metaphorical) using a bootstrapping approach. The procedure was as follows. A list of 329 metaphor examples was downloaded[23] and, for each expression, sentences were extracted from the Brown corpus that contained the seed word. The sentences were then classified as having metaphorical/non-metaphorical/impossible-to-decide uses of the highlighted expression, by 7 annotators on Amazon's crowd-sourcing platform Mechanical Turk (AMT). The annotators were asked to consider whether the highlighted expression was used in its original meaning. Figure 4.2 presents some example sentences. The reported inter-annotator agreement is $\kappa = 0.57$. The final labels were assigned via a weighted voting of the annotators using MACE [Hovy et al., 2013a], an implementation of an unsupervised item-response model that down-weights the votes of less-reliable annotators.[24]

Sentence	Label
"Peter is the **bright**, sympathetic guy when you're doing a deal," says one agent.	yes
Below he could see the **bright** torches lighting the riverbank.	no
Her **bright** eyes were twinkling.	yes
Washed, they came out surprisingly clear and **bright**.	no

Figure 4.2: Examples of Brown corpus sentences extracted for the metaphor *a bright idea* using the seed *bright*, along with their annotations, from Hovy et al. [2013b].

4.5.3 FULL-TEXT ANNOTATIONS

Steen et al. [2010]: VUAmsterdam Corpus

Steen et al. [2010] annotated 187,570 lexical units across all parts of speech in a running text, in 115 fragments extracted from the BNC-Baby corpus, sampling across academic, conversation, fiction, and news genres. The data was annotated using the MIP-VU procedure. The data was annotated by 6 annotators, all researchers and researchers-in-training in the field of metaphor. Inter-annotator agreement was $\kappa = 0.84$. The dataset is available[25] under a Creative Commons Attribution ShareAlike 3.0 Unported License.

---

[22]https://github.com/ytsvetko/metaphor/tree/master/input/
[23]Examples were downloaded from http://www.metaphorlist.com and http://www.macmillandictionaryblog.com.
[24]The dataset is available from http://www.edvisees.cs.cmu.edu/Edvisees.html.
[25]http://www2.let.vu.nl/oz/metaphorlab/metcor/search/

The MIP-VU annotation protocol [Steen et al., 2010] differs somewhat from Pragglejaz Group [2007] in the specification of what is considered a lexical item. Namely, proper names and noun-noun sequences with a non-compound stress pattern are treated as separate units even if listed in the dictionary as a single entry. Secondly, the part-of-speech is now considered part of the lexical unit, so words sharing orthography but differing in part-of-speech will be treated as different units. Furthermore, Steen et al. [2010] adopt a strict criterion whereby transitive and intransitive meanings of the same verb cannot be used to form a basic-contextual meaning pair; similarly, count and mass senses of nouns cannot be compared. Steen et al. [2010] also remove any consideration of the historical precedence of meanings from their definition of basic meanings, and resort to diachronic considerations only when specific problems arise.

Perhaps the most significant departure from the MIP protocol is the treatment of so-called *direct* metaphors that would come out as non-metaphors according to MIP. A particular case in point is that of a simile, where the source term is actually used in its basic sense and hence is not metaphorical according to the MIP. For example, in *"Juliet is like the sun,"* the basic sense of sun—namely "the star in the sky that provides light and warmth to the Earth"—is used, and the sentence sets up a comparison that emphasizes the similarity between Juliet and this solar body. However, the comparison in question is not a literal comparison. One could not, for example, make a list of properties that are common to Juliet and the sun in the way one could for, say, Jupiter (the planet) and the sun, as the properties shared by Juliet and the sun—such as *bright*, *radiant*, and *attractive*—are themselves figurative, domain-incongruent properties in the sense of Tourangeau and Sternberg [1981]. Rather, the simile sets up a cross-domain comparison in which a person is compared to a celestial body that can be seen as an indirect discourse about the target (Juliet). MIP-VU differs from MIP in that the incongruity between the basic meaning and the contextual meaning is not referential (as it would have been in *Juliet is the sun*—here, the two descriptors refer to the same referent who happens to be a person, not a planet) but topical, i.e., the sun in *Juliet is like the sun* is used to indirectly talk about people, not about planets. Similes are marked as direct metaphors using a special tag.

MIP-VU also addresses the possibility of an incongruity when an expression becomes fully interpreted and resolved, thus treating referring expressions (such as pronouns) as implicitly metaphorical if their co-referents are metaphorical. For example, the pronoun *it* in *"Naturally, to embark on such a step is not necessarily to succeed immediately in realizing it"* is annotated as an implicit metaphor because its co-referent *step* is a metaphor.

Shutova and Teufel [2010]

Shutova and Teufel [2010] and Shutova et al. [2013] annotated the verbs in a set of texts (761 sentences in total) extracted from the BNC as metaphorical or non-metaphorical. The data were sampled across genres, including fiction, news, essays, and radio broadcasts (transcribed speech). Certain classes of verbs were excluded from annotation: auxiliary verbs, modal verbs, aspectual verbs (*begin*, *start*, *finish*), and light verbs (such as *take*, *give*, *put*, *get*, *make*). Phrasal verbs were treated as single units. The annotation was performed by three volunteers who were native speakers of English and had some background in linguistics. The annotators followed the MIP protocol, specifying the criterion that the contextual meaning "can be understood" using the basic meaning (in the original MIP protocol) by asking the annotators to identify the source-domain mapping that underlies the metaphoricity, using lists of source and target categories provided by the researchers. The lists of categories were based on the Master Metaphor List [Lakoff et al., 1991]. If none of the suggested categories matched their intuitions, annotators were also permitted to introduce source and target categories of their own. The annotators were not given any particular dictionary as an inventory of senses, but relied on their intuitive understanding and the lists of source and target categories. The reported inter-annotator agreement on metaphor/non-metaphor classification is $\kappa = 0.64$ [Siegel and Castellan, 1988]. The agreement on source and domain category assignment was $\kappa = 0.57$, and reached $\kappa = 0.61$ when some of the categories were collapsed together.

Shutova [2010] extracted metaphorical expressions from this corpus to create a dataset for her metaphor paraphrasing experiments. Human annotators were presented with a set of sentences containing the metaphorical expressions and were asked to write down all suitable literal paraphrases for the highlighted metaphorical verbs. Five volunteer subjects—all native speakers of English—were asked to perform this task. All annotations were then compiled into a paraphrasing gold standard. For instance, the verb *leak* in *to leak a report* could be paraphrased as *reveal, disseminate, publish, divulge,* or *disclose,* according to this gold standard. The data is available by request from the author.

Beigman Klebanov and Flor [2013] Essay Corpus
Beigman Klebanov and Flor [2013] annotated a set of argumentative essays written in response to a prompt question regarding the role of communication in modern society. The essays were written by test-takers in a high-stakes examination for graduate school entrance in the U.S., with a time limit of 45 minutes. The annotation was performed by 2 research assistants. The annotators were given guidelines that geared their annotations toward metaphors that were relevant to the author's arguments.

> Generally speaking, a metaphor is a linguistic expression whereby something is compared to something else that it is clearly literally not, in order to make a point. Thus, in Tony Blair's famous assertion that "*I haven't got a reverse gear,*" Blair is compared to a car in order to stress his unwillingness and/or inability to retract his statements or actions. We would say in this case that a metaphor from a vehicle domain is used. . . . [more examples] . . . The first task in our study of metaphor in essays is to read essays and underline words you think are used metaphorically. Think about the point that is being made by the metaphor, and write it down.

During training, the annotators applied these guidelines to 6 essays responding to a different prompt; then, sessions were held where the annotations were discussed, including the explication of the role played by the metaphor in the essay. During the actual annotation, the annotators were not required to explicitly interpret the metaphor or its argumentative contribution. The annotation set includes 116 essays with the total of 29,207 content word tokens, out of which 3,211 were marked as metaphors. The reported inter-annotator agreement was $\kappa = 0.58$. The dataset is not available for distribution, but access can be requested for research purposes by an individual researcher under a non-disclosure agreement, and interested parties should contact the authors of the paper.

4.5.4 SUMMARY OF ANNOTATED DATA AVAILABLE FOR PUBLIC OR LICENSE-BASED USE

Table 4.1 summarizes the annotated datasets reviewed above, according to the language involved (English, German, Italian, Russian), the annotation labels used (Metaphor, Literal, Non-metaphor, Non-literal, Personification, Source domain, Target domain, etc.), the kind of items that were annotated (all words, verbs, nouns, etc.), the context of annotation (excerpts of roughly sentence length, whole texts, phrases), sources of the data, the size of each dataset, the reliability of the annotation, and the relevant licensing conditions.

4.5.5 ADDITIONAL ANNOTATED MATERIALS

Jang et al. [2014]

As a first step in a study aimed at understanding the social and discursive functions of metaphor in online forums, Jang et al. [2014] annotated data from three web discussion forums including a breast cancer support group, a Massive Open Online Course, and a forum for street gang members. Two graduate students with linguistic knowledge served as annotators and were instructed to annotate non-literal, conventionalized, and literal language in sentences in randomly sampled posts to these forums; about 100 sentences per forum were included. The annotation protocol was based loosely on MIP, requiring that (a) an expression has an original established meaning; (b) the expression needs to be used in context to mean something significantly different from that original meaning; (c) the difference in meaning should not be hyperbole, understatement, sarcasm, or metonymy. Similes and idioms with a metaphorical basis are included in the non-literal class. No prior unitization into lexical units was performed. The inter-annotator agreement at word level excluding stop words was $\kappa = 0.49$ for the binary classification of literal vs. non-literal and conventionlized language. The authors observed substantial variation between the forums in terms of inter-annotator agreement, with the breast cancer forum yielding the highest agreement of $\kappa = 0.63$ and the gang forum data yielding the lowest, with $\kappa = 0.39$. The authors observed that the gang forum data was particularly challenging due to extensive use of slang and non-standard grammar and spelling, as well as references specific to this sub-culture that were more familiar to one annotator than to the other. The authors also experimented with annotation using Amazon's crowd-sourcing platform *Mechanical Turk*, with generally lower agreement scores.

Table 4.1: Metaphor-annotated datasets. Language: E (English), G (German), I (Italian), R (Russian). Annotated Categories: M (Metaphor), L (Literal), $\bar{L}$ (Non-Literal), $\bar{M}$ (Non-Metaphor), P (Personification), S (Source Domain), T (Target Domain), U (Uncertain), I (implicit non-metaphor annotation—all metaphors in text are marked explicitly, the remainder of the words are non-metaphors). Annotated Items: A (all words in running text), M (mixed - words of various POS, phrases), V (verbs), N (nouns), J (adjectives), R (adverbs). Context during Annotation: S (excerpts of roughly sentence length), T (whole text), P (phrase, such as adj-n or v-obj). License: F (free), R (free for research/education), C₁ (CC BY-NC-SA 2.5), C₂ (CC BY-SA 3), D (Open Database License), I (individual license under non-disclosure agreement), A (available from author by request).

Author	Lang.	Data Source	Anno. Cat.	Anno. Items	Context during anno.	Reliability	Size	License
Lakoff	E	—	ST	M	S	—	?	F
Barnden	E	Text, Speech	MS T=mind	M	S	—	1,200	R
Rash	GE	Hitler's *Mein Kampf*	MPS	M	S	—	~2,000	F
Pasanek	E	18-th century literature	M.S. T=mind	M	S	—	~15,000	C₁
Birke	E	WSJ	L$\bar{L}$	V	S	κ=.77	3,736	R
Steen	E	BNC	MP$\bar{M}$U	A	T	κ=.84	187,570	C₂
Cardillo	E	Constructed	ML	NV	S	—	280	F
Shutova	E	BNC	$\bar{M}$MST	V	T	κ=.57-.64	761	A
Beigman	E	argumentative student essays	MI	NVJR	T	κ=.58	29,207	I
Hovy	E	Brown Corpus	M$\bar{M}$U	M	S	κ=.57	3,872	F
Bambini	I	Literary	M	genitive X of Y	SP	—	180	F
Tsvetkov	ER	—	ML	JV	SP	$\kappa \geq$.75	~2,700	D

Shaikh et al. [2014]

Shaikh et al. [2014] semi-automatically constructed a repository of human-validated metaphors about Governance and Economy in American English, Mexican Spanish, Iranian Farsi, and Russian. The repository lists examples of metaphorical language, classified by source and target domains, as well as by affect (positive or negative) and semantic relationship (*patient*, *property*, or *agent*). The repository contains approximately 100,000 instances of metaphors in English, and 1,500–3,000 in other languages.

CHAPTER 5

Knowledge Acquisition and Metaphor

Even the laziest use of metaphor involves a calculated use of knowledge. A high-level, simplified explication of this calculation might look as follows.

1. Speaker S wants to convey a specific viewpoint on a topic T to a listener L.

2. Specifically, S wants to highlight the aspects A, B, and C of topic T.

3. S believes that A, B, and C are also aspects of a vehicle V.

4. Moreover, S believes that L will strongly associate V with A, B, and C.

5. S thus describes T to L in terms of V.

6. L unpacks V to arrive at an understanding of T that emphasizes A, B, and C.

This script is simplified in a number of ways. For instance, S may not actually believe that A, B, or C are aspects of V: it is enough for S to believe that L (and/or everyone else) believes that A, B, and C are salient aspects of V. So, even if S dissents from the common view of V, it is necessary for S to know that this is the consensus view, and to exploit it accordingly. The above script also does not consider the perlocutionary effects of the metaphor "$[T]$ is $[V]$," since V may also evoke unwanted associations X, Y, or Z in the listener L (e.g., "*Juliet is the sun*" might be taken to mean that one should not make direct eye contact with Juliet; see Veale and Keane [1994]). Ultimately, it is not enough for S to use S's knowledge of V; S must use what S believes to be common knowledge of V that is shared by S and L and any other potential listener. An NLP system for generating metaphors will assume the role of S, and so must possess the same knowledge of T and V as a human S, while an NLP system for interpreting metaphors must possess the same knowledge of V as a human L.

This knowledge has an uncertain epistemological status. It is not encyclopedic knowledge, and is often little more than folk wisdom. No single computational resource provides all of the knowledge necessary for metaphor processing. Lexical resources such as WordNet [Fellbaum, 1998] can be used to provide a categorical view of T and V, although WordNet is unlikely to provide the hierarchical richness that is needed for category-centric views of metaphor, whether for that of Aristotle, Glucksberg, Way, or for any of the corrective approaches. (However, automatically-enriched versions of WordNet, such as the more divergent version constructed by Veale and Li [2015] that is automatically augmented with categorizations from the Web, have been shown to offer a markedly more effective set of categories for use in metaphorical processing.) Hand-coded resources like WordNet also typically lack the density and diversity of relational connections that are needed to support analogical approaches to metaphor, and no WordNet-like resource with the scale of WordNet currently contains the explicit knowledge of conceptual metaphors that is needed to support a schematic approach. Nonetheless, free large-scale resources like WordNet are a useful starting point for computationally modeling the detection and/or interpretation of metaphor in text.

This book considers two alternate sources of knowledge for metaphor processing in an NLP system. These sources are not mutually exclusive, and a robust metaphor-processing system may conceivably use a hybrid of both sources. The first of these sources is WordNet, and comparable lexical resources for languages other than English (such as the HowNet system for Chinese of Dong and Dong [2006]). The second is the World-Wide-Web, or any large source of free text from which lexico-semantic knowledge can be automatically extracted for use in metaphor processing. The Web, as a vast repository of real language usage and real metaphors, is also an implicit repository of the folk knowledge needed to understand these metaphors. As explored in the next chapter, the texts of the Web can be used to drive a statistical approach to metaphor processing. In this chapter we focus on the Web as a locus for knowledge extraction via symbolic, pattern-matching techniques.

5.1   WORDNET AND OTHER LEXICAL ONTOLOGIES

WordNet is the lexico-semantic resource most prominently used by metaphor processing research at present.[1] WordNet is a broad-coverage lexical ontology, where lexical entries are organized into sets of synonyms, or *synsets*, that are connected via a network of semantic relationships. Each synset represents a specific, shared sense of the words included in it. For instance, the verb synset "(interpret, construe, see)" encodes a meaning which may be glossed as *"make sense of; assign a meaning to"* and which is evident in the example sentence "How do you interpret his behavior?" Each synset is also assigned a lexicographic definition, or a *gloss*, of the kind that one finds in a conventional print dictionary. Each synset is linked to other synsets by semantic relations such as *hyponymy* (a subsumption relationship between more specific and more general noun senses), *meronymy* (part-to-whole relationships between noun senses), and *antonymy* (an oppositional relationship between adjective senses). An extract from a representative sub-network of WordNet is shown in Figure 5.1, which illustrates a portion of the synset hierarchy describing the concepts of *reading* and *understanding*. Note how it also includes a number of metaphorical senses, e.g., the *comprehension* sense of *grasp*, defined in WordNet as "get the meaning of something," and the *reading* sense of *skim*, defined in WordNet as "read superficially."

---

[1]http://wordnet.princeton.edu/

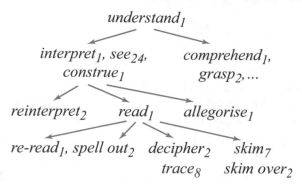

Figure 5.1: An example of synset hierarchy in WordNet.

However, a great many metaphorical senses are absent from the current version of Word-Net, leading a number of researchers to advocate the necessity of systematic inclusion and mark-up of metaphorical senses in such general-domain lexical resources [Alonge and Castelli, 2003, Lönneker and Eilts, 2004] and to further claim that this effort would be beneficial for the computational modeling of metaphor. Metaphor processing systems could then either use this knowledge or be evaluated against it. Lönneker [2004] mapped the senses from EuroWordNet[2] to the Hamburg Metaphor Database [Lönneker, 2004, Reining and Lönneker-Rodman, 2007], which contains examples of metaphorical expressions in German and French. However, currently no explicit information about metaphor is integrated into WordNet for English.

Driven by this lack of explicit annotation, computational approaches such as [Peters and Peters, 2000, Wilks et al., 2013] have focused on detecting metaphor directly in lexico-semantic resources. Peters and Peters [2000] mine WordNet for examples of systematic polysemy, which allows them to capture metonymic and metaphorical relations. Their system searches for general synsets that are relatively high in the WordNet hierarchy and that share a number of common domain-spanning words among their descendants. Peters and Peters found that such synsets often happen to be in a metonymic (e.g., *publisher—publication*) or a metaphorical (e.g., *theory—supporting structure*) relationship. Wilks et al. [2013] uses WordNet glosses to acquire the selectional preferences of verbs, which can then be used to annotate specific word senses as literal or metaphorical. Their approach is based on the selectional preference violation view of metaphor that dates back to the work of Wilks [1978] and which was later built upon by Fass [1991]. According to Wilks, metaphors provoke a violation of selectional preferences in a given context. Recall that selectional preferences are the *soft* semantic constraints that a predicate places onto its arguments. Consider again this earlier example:

---

[2]EuroWordNet is a multilingual database containing WordNets for several European languages (Dutch, Italian, Spanish, German, French, Czech, and Estonian). The WordNets are structured in the same way as the Princeton WordNet for English. http://www.illc.uva.nl/EuroWordNet/.

1. My car *drinks* gasoline. [Wilks, 1978]

The verb *drink* normally requires a subject that is an *animate* being and a direct object that is a potable *liquid*. Therefore, *drink* taking a *car* as a subject in (1) is an anomaly, which, according to Wilks, suggests the metaphorical use of *drink*. Wilks et al. [2013] focused on the conventionalized metaphors that are included as word-senses in WordNet. The main hypothesis guiding their approach is that if the first (main) WordNet sense of a word does not satisfy the preferences of its context in a given sentence, and there is a lower-ranked (less frequent) sense in WordNet that does satisfy the preference, then that use of the word in that WordNet sense is very likely to be metaphorical. For instance, in the example "Mary married a real *brick*," the first sense of *brick* is glossed as "a physical object," thus violating the preference of *marry* that selects for a *person*; however, the second sense of *brick* which can be glossed as "a reliable person" satisfies this preference.

To implement this approach, Wilks and his colleagues acquire typical preferences for specific verb senses from their WordNet glosses. They use a semantic parser [Allen et al., 2008] to identify the nominal arguments of the verbs in these glosses and their semantic roles; and then—in shades of Aristotle—generalize from their specific senses to higher-level hypernyms in WordNet. These higher-level generalizations are then used to define preference classes. The performance of their system was compared to a baseline using hand-coded verb preferences from VerbNet[3] [Kipper-Schuler, 2005]. The evaluation was carried out on a set of 122 sentences from the domain of *governance*, manually annotated for metaphoricity and selected so that the dataset contains 50% metaphorical instances and 50% literal instances. They report an F-score[4] of 0.49 for the VerbNet-based system and 0.67 for the WordNet-based one, the latter showing higher recall and the former higher precision. This approach of Wilks and his colleagues rests on the assumption that WordNet's ranking of senses correlates well with the literal-to-metaphorical scale, with literal senses being more frequent, and thus higher ranked, than figurative senses. It also makes the simplifying assumption that there is only one literal sense for any given word. While this may be true for many words, it is relatively easy to find counter examples. For instance, the first WordNet sense of the verb *erase* is metaphorical, glossed as "remove from memory or existence," as in the example sentence "The Turks *erased* the Armenians in 1915." The conventional, literal sense is ranked second. The reliance on WordNet sense numbering is thus a limitation of the approach in Wilks et al. [2013]. Another issue, one that those authors themselves point out,

---

[3]Verb classes are groupings of semantically-related verbs that share the same argument structures (or the potential to take the same kind of arguments), and which assign much the same interpretation to these arguments. The Levin classes [Levin, 1993] are the most well-known verb classes that have been described for English. VerbNet is an annotated corpus in the vein of PropBank [Palmer et al., 2005], in which Levin classes are used to annotate verbs.

[4]The balanced F-score of a test is calculated to be the harmonic mean of its *precision* and its *recall*. Variants of the F-score measure can be created to give more or less weight to *precision* or *recall*, but such variants will be denoted F_β where $\beta \neq 1$. Unless otherwise stated, "F-score" here denotes the balanced F-score, also known as the F_1-score.

is that this approach is likely to detect metonymic uses along with metaphor, and conflate the two, and so a method to discriminate between these two figurative phenomena is still needed.

Krishnakumaran and Zhu [2007] used the hyponymy relation in WordNet to detect semantic violations. Their method deals with verbal, nominal, and adjectival metaphors, but annotates them at the sentence level. Given a copula (or *IS-A*) metaphor (e.g., "The world is a *stage*") they verify if the two nouns involved (i.e., *world* and *stage*) have senses for which a hyponymy relation holds in WordNet. If they do not, then this sentence is tagged as containing a metaphor. For verbal and adjectival metaphors (e.g., "He *planted* good ideas in their minds" or "He has a *fertile* imagination"), they calculate bigram probabilities of verb-noun and adjective-noun pairs (including the hyponyms/hypernyms of the senses of the noun in question). If the combination is not observed in the data with sufficient frequency, it is considered metaphorical. This idea is a modification of the selectional preference view of Wilks. However, by using simple bigram counts over verb-noun pairs, Krishnakumaran and Zhu [2007] lose a great deal of information compared to a system extracting verb-object relations from parsed text. When the authors evaluated their system on a set of example sentences compiled from the Master Metaphor List, whereby highly conventionalized metaphors (or *dead* metaphors) are taken to be negative examples, they reported an accuracy of 0.58. They do not deal with literal examples as such: essentially, the distinction they are making is between the senses included in WordNet—even if they are conventionalized metaphors—and the senses that are not included in WordNet.

WordNet has also been used as a component in largely statistical approaches to metaphor. For instance, Shutova [2010, 2013] used the hierarchical structure of WordNet to identify senses that share common features (defined as sharing a common hypernym within three levels of the WordNet verb-sense hierarchy). WordNet synsets have also been employed: to form selectional preference classes [Mason, 2004]; to detect semantically related concepts [Gandy et al., 2013, Mohler et al., 2013, Strzalkowski et al., 2013]; and to identify high-level properties of concepts, most notably WordNet super-senses, that can serve as features for classification [Hovy et al., 2013b, Tsvetkov et al., 2013]. These approaches are discussed in detail in the next chapter, as their reliance on WordNet is minimal, and the statistical component is at the heart of each method. Other lexical resources employed for metaphor processing include *FrameNet*[5] [Fillmore et al., 2003] and the *SUMO* ontology[6] [Niles and Pease, 2001, 2003]. Gedigian et al. [2006] extracted the verbs of MOTION and CURE from FrameNet and used FrameNet-style annotation of semantic

---

[5]Recall our earlier discussion of Hobbs [1991] and his use of axiomatic schemata such as that for congress sending a bill to the president or for pitchers throwing balls at batters in baseball. These schematic structures, which relate events to their various participants, are also commonly called *frames* in the context of lexical-semantics. FrameNet is the result of a WordNet-like endeavor to construct a large database of the common frames in the English language, allowing a computer to understand e.g., that X buying a book from Y is an alternate frame perspective on Y selling a book to X. The same events may be structured by different frames that reflect differing perspectives on the event.

[6]SUMO, the *Suggested Upper Merged Ontology* is an upper-level, domain-general foundational ontology that can be used to support a variety of domain-specific ontologies (such as for technology, warfare, terrorism, art, etc.).

roles in the PropBank[7] corpus as features in their classification experiments. Dunn [2013a,b] extracted the high-level properties of concepts from SUMO, such as domain type (e.g., ABSTRACT, PHYSICAL, SOCIAL, MENTAL) and event status (e.g., PROCESS, STATE, OBJECT), which were then used as features in statistical classification.

WordNet is essentially a discriminatory knowledge source: it discriminates word senses from each other by placing them into different synsets, and further discriminates these senses and synsets by placing them in different parts of its various network structures, such as its IS-A hierarchy of noun-senses. But nowhere does WordNet explicitly and formally express the semantic *differentia* on which these discriminations are based, either with the aid of logical formulae or with *markerese*. In contrast, the *HowNet* system of Dong and Dong [2006] is a constructive knowledge-source: it expresses, in explicit logical terms, the semantic qualities that differentiate alternate senses of the same word, while also giving logical form to the qualities that make any two lexical concepts either similar or dissimilar. Although HowNet was originally designed to capture the lexico-semantic organization of Chinese, in much the same way that Princeton WordNet was originally designed to capture the lexico-semantic organization of English, it has since evolved into a bilingual system that maps Chinese and English lexical labels onto the same word senses and explicit logical definitions. Chinese words that have no direct English equivalent are associated with a paraphrasing English gloss instead [Dong and Dong, 2006]. Thus, the HowNet entry for the Chinese word *Mang Ren* (glossed as "*blind man*" in English) is a conceptual graph that defines a blind person as a *human* who is the *experiencer* of a *disability* that affects that *part* that is its *eye* and whose *scope* is the ability to *look* (the lexico-semantic terms that are used as semantic components of the concept graph are italicized in this paraphrase).

Veale [2005] observes that many of HowNet's conceptual graphs for different words and concepts have the same schematic structure, and rely on the same logical connectives and case roles (such as *experiencer* and *scope* for "*blind man*"). For instance, the HowNet entries for "*lame person*" and "*cripple*" have a structure that is isomorphic to that for "*blind man*," while "*surgeon*" and "*repairman*" or "*assassin*" and "*virus*" have structures that can be made isomorphic with the application of simple generalization rules. Veale [2005] presents an algorithm for generating structural hashes for each of HowNet's conceptual definitions, allowing a system to quickly find isomorphisms—and thus the analogical mappings that support metaphors—between distant pairs of lexical concepts. Veale reports that an isomorphic analogue can be retrieved for more than 60% of HowNet's conceptual graph definitions, yielding an average of 2.5 entity-to-entity mappings for each one (such as *eye = leg* and *look = walk* for *blindman = cripple*). More specifically, two thirds of analogies generated using structure hashing/mapping yield two entity-level mappings, one quarter yield three entity-level mappings, and one tenth imply four or more. Veale [2006a] further observes that HowNet's semantic structures may yield more possibilities for analogy and metaphor if they are pre-processed first, using not just generalization rules but also figure-ground-

---

[7]PropBank, or *proposition bank*, is an annotated corpus in which verbs and their arguments have been tagged so as to tie them to the same propositions. Such a resource provides empirical evidence for how ideas cluster in an utterance to form propositional content, and for how nouns relate to verbs.

reversal rules, so that, e.g., the subsidiary term in one definition—such as *treasure* in the definition of *treasure chest*—can be focalized in a new formulation (e.g., to redefine *treasure* as anything that happens to be stored in a *treasure chest*, whether a trove of gold coins or a stash of love letters). Overall, Veale [2006a] concludes that WordNet is better suited to category-centric computational models of metaphor, owing to its richer IS-A hierarchy for noun-senses (which is considerably richer than HowNet's), while HowNet is better suited to analogical models of metaphor, owing to its explicit logical definitions that facilitate structure-mapping processes. Inevitably, Veale concludes that a tight integration of both resources should offer a more comprehensive basis for computationally modeling metaphor than either alone.

5.2   EXTRACTING KNOWLEDGE FROM FREE TEXT

Text is an artifact that is constructed from knowledge to communicate knowledge, and a computer can automatically extract both kinds of knowledge—that which has shaped an utterance, and that which an utterance is designed to convey—with varying degrees of ambition or success. A useful proxy for the former kind of knowledge is a statistical model built from the frequencies of words and their associations in a corpus of relevant co-texts. For instance, Bollegala and Shutova [2013] describe a system that uses the texts of the Web (as accessed by sending targeted queries to a web search engine) to extract co-occurrence statistics for the verbs and nouns in an utterance. These statistics can then be used by an automated system to generate a set of candidate paraphrases for metaphorical uses of verbs that employ more literal alternatives instead. So given a verb-noun metaphor where the verb is used metaphorically—for example, "*to **mend** a marriage*"—their system first automatically extracts a set of lexico-syntactic patterns that capture the typical linguistic variations on the verb phrase (e.g., "to VERB (mend) their NOUN (marriage)") before dispatching the highest scoring patterns (e.g., "*to * their marriage*") to a web search engine to harvest alternate paraphrases for the verb. Their system then filters and re-ranks the extracted paraphrases using automatically acquired verb preferences [Shutova, 2010], as described in Chapter 6. Although clearly useful and relatively straightforward to construct, one might argue that a statistical model of this kind does not constitute knowledge in the AI sense, at least in the classical AI sense of the metaphor systems surveyed in Chapter 3. Such knowledge is not to be found in statistical generalizations, as useful as these might be, but in the specific contents of specific utterances.

Speakers rarely use language for the interchange of bald facts. Or rather, the transmission of explicit factual content is rarely the only (or most interesting) thing that is happening in a linguistic utterance. The most interesting knowledge in an utterance is the set of presuppositions on which the utterance is built but which the utterance does not explicitly articulate. When a speaker says "*It is an oven in here*," the term *oven* is used metaphorically to describe the unnatural and uncomfortably high temperature of a room. Ovens, when turned on at least, produce high temperatures and this unspoken knowledge, shared by speaker and listener, is used to convey the desired meaning (e.g., paraphrased thusly: "*it is too hot in here—this is a room, not an oven*").

Fortunately, because metaphors can often be ambiguous, speakers sometimes use a more explicit form of figurative comparison, such as *"it is **as** hot **as** an oven in here."* In such cases, the shared presupposition (that ovens are containers that get uncomfortably hot) is made partially explicit. From such examples, a machine can learn to associate terms with the properties they convey whenever they are used figuratively. Given a stable construction like the *as*-simile frame, from which an agent can extract the underlying presuppositions with relative ease and accuracy across a large number of instances, a machine can harvest this large number of instances from a text corpus like the Web and acquire the desired knowledge using simple extraction patterns [Hearst, 1992]. We consider a number of such patterns in this section: simile patterns (for *as*-similes and *like*-similes); categorization patterns; and question patterns. Each kind of pattern offers a different window onto the knowledge that underpins metaphor, and allows a machine to acquire different kinds of knowledge in turn, ranging from properties to behaviors to category structures and arbitrary relationships.

5.2.1   SIMILE PATTERNS

A metaphor is more than an implicit simile [Glucksberg and Haught, 2006], although, as noted in Section 2.4, it is convenient to assume that both hinge on the same kinds of knowledge and pivot on the same kinds of conceptual distinctions. Similes come in varying shapes and sizes, only some of which are amenable to the extraction of practical, reusable knowledge for a metaphor system. For instance, Fishelov [1992] distinguishes between *poetic (P)* and *non-poetic (NP)* similes. For Fishelov, a non-poetic simile is one that employs a simple unadorned vehicle term, as in *"as black as ink"* or *"as dry as sand."* NP similes are often hackneyed, insofar as they employ (and reinforce) a stereotypical view of a familiar vehicle. A poetic simile, in contrast, will construct an elaborate vehicle for a comparison, as Raymond Chandler did in *Farewell My Lovely* to describe the hulking "Moose" Molloy: *"he was about as inconspicuous as a tarantula on a slice of angel food."* Not only does this particular P simile offer an ironic description (the simile tells us that Molloy is anything but inconspicuous), there is little reuse value for an NLP system in extracting the qualities of a vehicle that is so elaborate that it is unlikely to occur as part of any other comparison. As such, an NLP system should limit itself to simple NP similes when looking to extract the qualities of familiar vehicles. Fishelov notes that P similes do not draw upon different concepts or qualities from NP similes; rather, P similes use the same familiar concepts to evoke much the same stereotypical qualities, but use them in elaborate, fanciful, and novel combinations. The vehicles and salient qualities of NP similes are thus likely to prove useful in the understanding (or generation) of future P similes and novel metaphors.

To acquire the stereotypical properties of familiar concepts, such as *cute* for *babies* and *tough* for *cowboys*, the pattern *"as [P] as a [V]"* can be used to form web queries, where *[P]* denotes a single adjectival property, *[V]* denotes a single noun (or lexicalized compound), and either or both can be replaced with a wildcard operator. Such patterns are commonly called "Hearst" patterns after Hearst [1992], who demonstrated the usefulness of simple lexical patterns for knowledge extraction from corpora. Note that we need no slot for a tenor *[T]* in our simile constructions, as we do not wish to learn how arbitrary tenors have been described by others on the Web, as such viewpoints on a tenor are very likely to be idiosyncratic and context-sensitive. We only wish to learn a mapping from *[V]*s to their *[P]*s, and vice versa. Likewise, to acquire the stereotypical behaviors of familiar concepts, such as *crying* for *babies* and *swaggering* for *cowboys*, the Hearst pattern ""*[B+ing] like a [V]*" can be used to form a set of web queries, where *[B]* denotes a single verb like *cry*, *[B+ing]* denotes its present continuous form (e.g., *crying*) and *[V]* again denotes a single noun vehicle. The web queries we construct from these patterns can range from the unfocused to the tightly specific. For instance, the unfocused query "*as * as a ***" will aim to extract as many *as*-similes as it can via a search engine such as Google (for which * is a wildcard operator), but a query with two wildcards and no content words will exercise no sway over the texts that a search engine will match to it, the diversity of these texts, or the words that are bound to its wildcards. To focus a search engine on the kind of NP similes and familiar vehicles a metaphor system can best use, web queries should be anchored to an explicit property, behavior or vehicle noun. Veale and Hao [2007] thus use WordNet to generate a large number of focused instantiations of the general "*as [P] as a [V]*" pattern: Wordnet's adjective list is used to generate instantiations of *[P]*, one instance per adjective such as *tall*, *dark*, or *handsome*. Specifically, Veale and Hao use only those adjectives for which WordNet suggests an antonym (such as *short* for *tall*), as this focuses the extraction process on a manageable set of 2,000 or so properties that suggest a scale of possibilities (on which an *as*-simile marks out a specific point). The mapping of *[V]*s to *[P]*s that is extracted from the retrieved similes is then used to identify a pool of *[V]*s that should be elaborated further. A second cycle of queries is thus generated using every noun in this pool to instantiate the *[V]* slot of the query, while a wildcard is used for *[P]*. For example, the first-cycle simile "*as brave as a Viking*" leads to the second-cycle query "*as * as a Viking*," which allows the system to extract adjectival qualities such as *blond* and *fierce* for *Viking*.

Veale [2013a] uses a hypothesis-driven approach to simile retrieval that binds *both* of the wildcards in each simile pattern. The intuition is simple, and allows a retrieval/extraction system to search the long-tail of infrequent similes that can be found on the Web, rather than just those that occur in the most highly ranked web documents. (It is important to note that a search engine's ranking of a web page has little bearing on the quality or otherwise of any similes found on that page.) If the property *P* is hypothesized to be stereotypical of a vehicle *V*, we can expect someone on the Web to have already used the simile "*as P as a V*." Likewise, if the behavior *B* is generally held to be stereotypical of *V*, we can expect the simile "*B+ing like a V*" to be used somewhere on the Web. Veale [2013a] uses the Google n-grams database of short web fragments [Brants and Franz, 2006] to provide these hypotheses. Specifically, a Google 3-gram of the form "*a [P] [V]*" (such as "*a wild gypsy*") suggests the hypothesis that P is stereotypical of V, while a 3-gram of the form "*a [B+ing] V*" (such as "*a shambling zombie*") suggests that behavior B is typical of *V*. For the former, the query "*as P as a V*" (where P is an adjective and V is a noun) is generated, and for the latter the query "*B+ing like a V*" is generated. These queries are sent to a web search engine, and if any matching documents at all are found, we consider the hypothesis validated. In this way, Veale [2013a] builds a lexicon of stereotype representations that contains over 75,000 validated associations of vehicles to properties or behaviors.

Mappings of this kind are of particular value to a metaphor interpretation and/or generation system. Veale and Hao [2007] describe how their *Aristotle* system uses these mappings to find the most likely interpretations of copula metaphors of the form "*[T] is [V]*," such as "*terrorists are wolves*." The system works in two modes: stand-alone mode, which uses the Google n-grams as a corpus to validate its interpretation hypotheses; and dynamic mode, which uses real-time web search for this purpose. Consider the example "*terrorists are wolves*:" *Aristotle* hypothesizes that any stereotypical property or behavior of *wolf* can be projected onto *terrorist* if there is corpus evidence to suggest that it is also apt for that topic. This evidence is sought in the Google n-grams in stand-alone mode; thus, the 2-gram "*ferocious terrorists*" validates the hypothesis that terrorists, like wolves, can be ferocious (as well as *hungry*, *nasty*, and *cruel*). In dynamic mode, such hypotheses are validated by sending a variety of alternate queries to a web search engine in real time, allowing the system to reason about trending topics from pop-culture, such as proper-named entities. For instance, the metaphor "*Kate Moss is a pencil*" is interpreted to mean *thin (Kate Moss)*, rather than *sharp (Kate Moss)*, because pencils are stereotypically thin and because Kate Moss is frequently described as thin on the Web. These validating queries can identify whether a projected property is also stereotypical of a tenor, by looking for the corresponding simile on the Web. Thus, the simile "*as thin as Kate Moss*," which finds over 1,000 matches via Google, suggests that *thinness* is a very salient pencil-like property of this particular tenor.

5.2.2   CATEGORIZATION PATTERNS

The *such-as* construction "*Xs such as Ys [and Zs]*" offers a more conventional example of a Hearst pattern, one that is typically used to acquire category knowledge for the understanding of literal language. Yet all AI models of metaphor are, to some extent, also dependent on this kind of knowledge. Taxonomic generalizations offer a means of bridging one specific concept to another, allowing corrective approaches to apply type constraints or to translate between semantic frames, allowing analogical approaches to map between isomorphic structures with non-identical relationships, and allowing schematic approaches to reduce a specific metaphor to a generic schema. But, as argued by Way [1991], a category system for metaphor processing must also be a dynamic system, one that cross-categorizes familiar concepts in diverse ways, and one that continuously learns to categorize in new ways. Metaphor is a divergent process that demands a divergent palette of categorization options, many more than narrowly convergent systems such as WordNet (Fellbaum [1998]) or HowNet (Dong and Dong [2006]) can offer. Where a convergent category system encodes a single "valid" way of viewing every topic—for instance, WordNet provides just one parent category for almost all of its word senses—a divergent system embraces many competing viewpoints, any of which may be valid in the context of a novel metaphor.

A Hearst pattern is a superficial approximation to a linguistic construction. This superficiality makes Hearst patterns easy to implement and apply, but it also makes them *leak*, since a pattern will often match texts that do not actually instantiate the corresponding construction. The *as*-simile pattern, for instance, matches texts such as "*as well as a [V]*" that are not similes ("*as well as*" can mean the same as "*comparable to*" and "*also*"). But a hypothesis-driven use of Hearst patterns, as in Veale [2013a], reduces leakage by using patterns to simultaneously confirm and flesh out the relationships that a system already has sound reasons to assert. Much as in metaphor and analogy, the hypothesis-driven use of Hearst patterns leverages the knowledge that a system already possesses, to expand this knowledge with relationships that are coherent with what the system already knows. Veale et al. [2009] and Veale and Li [2013] use the simile-derived mapping of vehicles to their stereotypical properties (*[V]*s to *[P]*s) to formulate hypotheses that allow it to instantiate the categorization pattern "*Xs such as Ys [and Zs]*". For every V to P mapping, Veale and Li instantiate the pattern to form the queries "*P * such as Vs*" and "*P * such as * and Vs.*" The first query allows the system to acquire a general category C for V (via the wildcard), and in the process, acquire a fine-grained category C_P for V. The second pattern does much the same, but also allows the system to identify another member V_2 of C_P (via the second wildcard). The additional member V_2 can now be used as the basis of another hypothesis and another round of queries, to acquire additional new members of this category, or of new fine-grained categories, for which new members can be found using subsequent queries. In short, Veale et al. [2009] and Veale and Li [2013] present an iterative bootstrapping process that grows a large, fine-grained category system from web content, one that exhibits enough divergence and cross-categorization to support metaphor processing.

For example, after learning from a web simile that *champagne* is *expensive*, Veale and Li's system generates the queries "*expensive * such as champagne*" and "*expensive * such as * and champagne.*" Dispatching these queries to Google, the system acquires a set of fine-grained categories C_P, containing e.g., *expensive victuals, expensive wines, expensive drinks, expensive foods*, and *expensive products*. The first of these also contains *caviar* as a member, the second also contains *Bordeaux, Burgundy*, and *Barolo*, the third *whiskey* and *vodka*, the fourth *salmon*, and the fifth *cognac*. The categories acquired for a given vehicle/source can be expansive enough to link diverse concepts that one would expect to find in very different parts of the WordNet noun-sense taxonomy, as illustrated by a snippet that is retrieved for the first query: "*expensive tastes such as champagne, shellfish, private jets, and sports cars.*" A category system that unites *champagne* and *sports cars* under the same fine-grained genus, rather than a trivial generalization such as *Physical Thing*, is one that can support metaphor interpretation and generation. Veale and Li [2013] thus show how their bootstrapped category system, named *Thesaurus Rex*, can be used in a computational model of metaphor. They first use the system to implement a numeric measure of semantic similarity that accords well with human intuitions, and argue that a good metaphor—such as "*tobacco is poison*" or "*divorce is war*"—must be understood in terms of how it affects the perceived similarity of the source and target. Before a metaphor, the semantic similarity of *divorce* and *war* will be low; that

Shared Category for *divorce and war*

adverse_event, bad_event, bad_thing, catastrophic_event, changing_event, critical_event, destructive_thing,

devastating_event, disruptive_event, distressing_event, domestic_conflict, domestic_event,

dramatic_event,

economic_event, emotional_event, environmental_event, experienced_event, external_event,

extraordinary_event, financial_event, identifiable_event, immoral_act, important_event, legal_event,

major_conflict, major_event, negative_event, ordinary_event, outside_event, painful_event, past_event,

rare_event, recent_event, severe_conflict,

severe_event,

significant_event, single_event, social_event, social_occurrence, stressful_event,

sudden_event, traumatic_event, unanticipated_event, unavoidable_event, uncontrollable_event, undesirable_event,

unexpected_event, unexpected_occurrence, unforeseeable_event,

unforeseen_event, unfortunate_event, unpleasant_event,

unpleasant_thing, untoward_event, unusual_event,

Figure 5.2: Divorce is war: shared categorizations in *Thesaurus Rex*.

both are *events* is as informative as a convergent resource like WordNet can be on the subject. After the metaphor, when a diverse set of unifying categories has been identified (such as *traumatic event* and *severe conflict*; see Figure 5.2) the perceived similarity will increase significantly. To enable other metaphor researchers to employ *Thesaurus Rex*'s fine-grained categories in their own systems, Veale and Li present a public web service[8] through which they can be obtained on demand by 3rd-party systems.

The *such-as* construction "*Xs such as Ys*" has additional value for researchers of figurative language. Whereas the *as-simile* pattern is frequently subverted for ironic purposes—recall Chandler's simile "*he was about as inconspicuous as a tarantula on a slice of angel food*"—the *such-as* pattern is almost never used ironically. Veale and Hao [2007] estimate that 15–20% of web similes are ironic, and must be carefully filtered if the knowledge-base that is extracted from them is not to be corrupted with significant amounts of noise. For, despite what a naive reading of commonplace similes might suggest, cue balls are not hairy, bricks are not intelligent, and sledgehammers are far from subtle. However, any web texts that are retrieved for the *such-as* reformulation of a specific pairing of *P* and *V* derived from the simile "*As [P] as a [V]*" offer support for the belief

---

[8]Accessible at: http://ngrams.ucd.ie/therex2/.

that this simile is *not* ironic. Hao and Veale [2010] use this web-attested support as the basis of an algorithm for automatically determining whether a simile is ironic or otherwise. (Another key feature of the algorithm is the number of times the simile is found on the Web prefixed by the hedge "*about*," and whether the "*about*" form is the most frequent form of the simile on the Web.) Veale and Hao's algorithm identifies 87% of its 2,795 ironic test cases with 0.63 precision, and 89% of its 12,261 non-ironic test cases with 0.97 precision. The reported F-score for irony detection is 0.73; for non-irony detection it is 0.93; and for overall classification of both ironic and non-ironic test cases it is 0.88. In contrast, because irony is still relatively rare, a baseline system that classifies everything as non-ironic achieves an overall F-score of 0.81 without recognizing a single use of irony.

5.2.3   ARBITRARY RELATIONS

Depending on where one puts the wildcards, a Hearst pattern can be used either to instantiate a pre-determined relationship (by providing an explicit verb and/or preposition, and using wildcards in the noun positions; see e.g., Hearst [1992]), or to find the linking relationships that connect a specific set of nouns (by using a wildcard in the verb position between specific nouns; see e.g., Nakov and Hearst [2006] and Bollegala and Shutova [2013]). But Hearst patterns are only as effective as the terms that anchor them and that allow meaningful instantiations to be retrieved from a corpus or from the Web. Lacking concrete anchor terms, Veale and Li [2011] and Veale and Li [2014] go directly to the *Google n-grams* [Brants and Franz, 2006], a large, local database of short text fragments from the Web (of between 1–5 tokens in length) that have a web frequency of 40 or higher (at the time they were first collated). Veale and Li's system scans through every Google 3-gram looking for grammatical instances of the pattern "N_1 V N_2" such as "*dogs chase cars*" or "*cats hate water*." However, for every useful fact like "*bats have wings*" (frequency 87) and "*bats have pouches*" (frequency 2), or esoteric yet still interesting facts like "*bats carry rabies*," the Google n-grams contain a good deal of noise, not to say factual errors such as "*bats lay eggs*" (frequency 41). Veale and Li thus view web n-grams as a source of candidate relationships that must be manually filtered by a knowledge-engineer. To expedite this filtering process, they propose an *analogical principle* for ranking candidate facts: a candidate fact $rel(N_i, N_j)$ is ranked according to the number of potential analogies it can form with other facts $rel(N_x, N_y)$ already in the knowledge-base; two facts $rel(N_i, N_j)$ and $rel(N_x, N_y)$ may form an analogy if they share the same relation rel and if N_i is semantically similar to N_x (using a WordNet-based measure, say) and N_j is also semantically similar to N_y. Veale and Li [2014] show that the facts that are ultimately validated by a human judge are much more likely to be analogically similar to other validated facts than not. While good knowledge bases support analogy and metaphor, analogy and metaphor also facilitate the construction of good knowledge bases.

   Google n-grams are shorn of their larger context, so one can never be sure that even a well-formed n-gram is actually a complete phrase. Veale and Li [2011] eschew web n-grams, and thus avoid the need for manual filtering, by using an especially revealing Hearst pattern over the query logs of web search engines rather than the web documents returned by these engines. The pattern is the WH-question pattern "*Why do [X]s [VP]*" (or "*How do [Xs] [VP]*"). Questions of this form, such as "*Why do dogs chase cars?*" hinge on a belief that a speaker presupposes is shared by all yet is still sufficiently interesting enough to explore on the Web. Although query logs are jealously guarded by search engine companies, the most popular web queries (and WH-questions on the Web) can be accessed in the form of query completions, whereby a search engine like Google will offer predictions as to the final form of a partial query as it is entered. Veale and Li [2011] present an algorithm for *milking* completions from Google that acquires query completions[9] for WH-questions about a given topic $[N_i]$ and then extracts facts of the form $rel(N_i, N_j)$ from those that are syntactically simple enough to shallow parse. Facts that are extracted in this way for a topic N_i serve as informative features of N_i that allow N_i to be accurately classified into the correct WordNet category. Veale and Li also describe how, when few or no facts can be extracted for a topic N_x, a *conceptual mash-up* of the facts extracted for semantically similar terms N_y and N_z can be usefully employed as a proxy representation for N_x. Pattern matching over web content allows an NLP system to build a rich representation of the topics that are well-addressed on the Web, but knowledge acquisition processes for metaphor must also provide a means of filling the gaps for topics that are not so well served.

5.3   CONCEPTUAL METAPHORS

Schematic approaches view conceptual metaphors as more than useful generalizations of past figurative experiences, but as foundational knowledge structures that are key to the interpretation of novel metaphors. While schematic approaches have typically relied on manual efforts to encode this knowledge (recall, e.g., Martin [1990]; Barnden and Lee [2002]; and Barnden [2006]), the regularity with which conceptual metaphors are described in language may allow many of these schematic mappings to be extracted from corpus or web texts using variations on the ""*[X]s are [Y]s*" Hearst pattern. For instance, the Google n-grams contain many 3- and 4-grams that may be considered the linguistic expression of conceptual metaphors—such as "*Time is Money*," "*Argument is War*," and "*Politics is a Game*"—not least because theorists discuss these schemas in articles that appear on the Web. To realize practical utility from these extraction efforts, it is not necessary to extract metaphor-theoretic associations with great precision or with complete recall. It is sufficient that the extracted associations prove useful in the interpretation or generation of more novel metaphors, regardless of whether these associations conform to what cognitive theorists consider to be core conceptual metaphors. Veale et al. [2015] thus mine likely conceptual metaphors from the Google n-grams to drive the generation process in the metaphor-generating Twitterbot *@MetaphorMagnet*.

Li et al. [2013] queried the Web using lexico-syntactic patterns to acquire a set of potential conceptual metaphors. They automatically created two probabilistic "IS-A" knowledge bases: the

---

[9]Özbal and Strapparava [2012] alternatively use a third-party service to provide completions. A currently active service is: http://ubersuggest.org.

first contained hypernym-hyponym relations and was acquired by querying the Web using Hearst patterns [Hearst, 1992]; the second contained metaphors of the form *<target is a source>* that were acquired using the simile pattern "* BE/VB like *." The second knowledge-base was then filtered by removing the hypernym-hyponym relations present in the first database, to construct a metaphor knowledge base. The authors applied the resulting metaphor knowledge base to recognize and explain metaphors in text. They experimented with nominal metaphors (e.g., "Juliet is the *sun*") and verbal metaphors (e.g., "My car *drinks* gasoline"). In the case of nominal metaphors the database was queried directly and the corresponding metaphor was either retrieved or not. In the case of verb metaphors, where the noun denoting the source concept was not explicitly present in the sentence, the conceptual metaphor was derived from the selectional preferences of the verbs. The authors computed the selectional preferences of the given verb for the nouns present in the knowledge base, and "explained" the given metaphor in terms of the noun exhibiting the highest association with the metaphorical verb. For example, the system outputs an explanation "car is a horse" for the metaphor "my car *drinks* gasoline," since the conceptual metaphor CAR IS A HORSE is present in the knowledge base and *horse* satisfies the subject preference of *drink*. The authors evaluated their approach on a manually constructed dataset of 200 randomly-sampled sentences containing "is-a" constructions and 1,000 sentences containing metaphorical and literal uses of verbs. The annotation was carried out at the sentence level, i.e., complete sentences were annotated as metaphorical or not. The authors report an F-score of 0.69 for the recognition of "is-a" metaphors and 0.58 for the recognition of the verbal ones. Metaphor explanation performance (i.e., the source—target domain mappings generated for each recognized metaphor) was evaluated separately and the top-rank precision of 0.43 is reported.

5.4   SUMMARY

Information retrieval (IR) and extraction (IE) tools offer more than semantics-free simplicity and ease of use: they also boast an especially wide coverage when applied to web content. Indeed, the Web is not just vast but constantly growing and continuously topical. Metaphor systems that look for some or most of their knowledge on the Web can choose to focus on the most recent content, or the most authoritiative content (e.g., by exploiting Google's page-ranking mechanism), or the most frequent and oft-repeated (and thus confidence-inspiring) content. But they are also free to explore the long-tail of web content, of texts and phrases that are only found once or twice but which cohere with what a system already knows. Since metaphor is a productive and dynamic phenomenon, in which new metaphors arise as new events take place, the scale and ongoing expansion of the Web make it an attractive corpus—and knowledge-source—for metaphor research.

CHAPTER 6

Statistical Approaches to Metaphor

Recent years have witnessed a growing interest in statistical and machine learning approaches to the computational treatment of metaphor. As the field of computational semantics—in particular robust parsing and lexical acquisition techniques—has progressed to the point where it is possible to accurately acquire lexical, domain, and relational information from corpora, statistical approaches have opened new avenues for robust, large-scale metaphor processing models. Approaches based on distributional association measures, vector space models, supervised learning, clustering, and LDA topic modeling[1] have been proposed, bringing metaphor into the arena of statistical NLP. The parameters of these models are often estimated using the properties of large (and frequently unannotated) corpora, thus reducing their reliance on curated lexical resources and other sources of hand-coded knowledge. This allows statistical models to be more easily ported to new domains, fresh languages, and different tasks, and thus brings them a step closer to integration within commercial NLP systems.

6.1 ASSOCIATION MEASURES AND SELECTIONAL PREFERENCES

Semantic association measures [Baldwin and Kim, 2010, Hoang et al., 2009] quantify the strength of association between concepts (usually represented as individual words), providing useful information about relationships between the concepts and their "typical" properties to metaphor processing systems. Selectional preferences (SPs) can be viewed as a type of semantic association, where a predicate exhibits varying levels of association with different argument classes. SP models typically comprise a set of SP classes (automatically induced or extracted from manually created lexica and resources) and an association measure quantifying the relation between the predicate and each argument class. Verb preferences, in particular, have long been established as a central pillar of metaphor processing systems. The selectional-preference violation view of metaphor (Wilks [1978]) has been highly influential, and has inspired many subsequent approaches to metaphor identification. In its earliest guises, this preference-based approach viewed metaphor

---

[1]LDA, or *Latent Dirichlet allocation* [Blei et al., 2003], is a statistical means of creating a model of the implicit topics that guide the construction of a set of documents. LDA assumes that documents may contain a mix of multiple topics, and it is the presence of these topics that explains the use of specific words in each document. The approach takes its name from its assumption that topics are distributed across documents according to a Dirichlet prior.

as presenting a listener with a semantic anomaly, and used hand-coded descriptions of SPs to allow anomalous violations to be detected [Fass, 1991, Martin, 1990]. This early work was later bolstered by automatic approaches to the acquisition of SPs from lexical resources [Wilks et al., 2013]. Other approaches [Hovy et al., 2013b, Krishnakumaran and Zhu, 2007, Li and Sporleder, 2009, 2010] treated metaphor as a violation of semantic norms construed more broadly. Krishnakumaran and Zhu [2007] compute bi-gram probabilities of adjective-noun and verb-noun pairs and, if a given pair is not observed in the data with sufficient frequency, it is tagged as a metaphor. Li and Sporleder [2009, 2010] detect idiomatic language by computing the overall cohesion of a sentence (based on the semantic similarity of its elements to each other) and by identifying units that disrupt this cohesion. Hovy et al. [2013b] used a classifier with compositional features to identify metaphor as an unusual pattern in the compositional behavior of words.

Generally speaking, SP violation is a property of the surface realization of metaphor rather than its underlying conceptual structure, and one needs to bear this in mind when using SP violation as a detection heuristic. On one hand, SP violation can indicate various kinds of non-literalness and semantic anomaly in language, and so the approach is likely to over-generate. On the other hand, in the case of frequent conventional metaphors, no statistically significant violation can be detected in the data, and the approach would overlook many of these metaphors. Shutova [2013] conducted a data-driven study, where verb SPs were automatically acquired from corpora and all the nominal arguments below a certain selectional association threshold were considered to represent a violation and thus tagged as metaphorical. This approach attained a precision of 0.17 and a recall of 0.55, suggesting that the SP violation hypothesis does not scale well from approaches based on hand-crafted descriptions to large-scale, data-driven approaches.

In contrast, other, "non-violation" applications of SP have been found useful to the computational treatment of metaphor. Mason [2004] automatically acquired domain-specific SPs of verbs, and then, by mapping their common nominal arguments in different domains, arrived at the corresponding metaphorical mappings. For example, the verb *pour* has a strong SP for *liquids* in the LAB domain, and for *money* in the FINANCE domain. From these preferences Mason's system infers the domain mapping FINANCE—LAB and the concept mapping *money—liquid*. The domain-specific corpora were obtained by searching the Web for specific terms of interest. Mason used WordNet for the acquisition of SP classes and so the source and target domain categories are represented as clusters of WordNet synsets. He then applied the selectional association measure of Resnik [1993] to quantify verb preferences in the domains of interest. Mason evaluated his system against the Master Metaphor List (MML) [Lakoff et al., 1991], manually mapping his output (WordNet synsets) to concrete concepts described in the MML (13 mappings in total) and obtaining an accuracy of 77% (note that a mapping discovered by CorMet was considered correct if sub-mappings specified in the MML were mostly present with high salience and if incorrect sub-mappings were present with relatively low salience). Baumer et al. [2009] re-implemented the approach of Mason [2004] in the framework of a computational metaphor identification (CMI) procedure, and applied it to two types of corpora: student essays and political blogs. The authors present some interesting examples of conceptual metaphors that the system was able to extract, and which they claim may foster critical thinking in social science. However, they did not carry out any quantitative evaluation. Both CorMet and CMI require strong supervision in terms of manual pairing of the domains to compare. This means that their systems are only applicable within a limited-domain setting and this is likely to be a source of some difficulty when scaling to real-world, big-data tasks.

Shutova [2010] also uses automatically acquired SPs, but to address a different problem— that of metaphor interpretation. She defines metaphor interpretation as a paraphrasing task, where literal paraphrases for metaphorical expressions are derived from corpus data using a set of statistical measures. For instance, for the metaphors in "All of this *stirred* an unfathomable excitement in her" or "a carelessly *leaked* report" this system produces the paraphrases "All of this *provoked* an unfathomable excitement in her" and "a carelessly *disclosed* report" respectively. Shutova's experiments focused on paraphrasing metaphorical verbs. She first applies a maximum likelihood model to extract and rank candidate paraphrases, i.e., linguistically-rendered interpre- tations, for the metaphorical verb given its context. The likelihood of a particular interpretation i is computed as a joint probability of its co-occurrence with the words in the context $(w_1, \ldots, w_N)$ in their respective grammatical relations $(r_1, \ldots, r_N)$ with the metaphorical verb:

$$P(i, (w_1, r_1), (w_2, r_2), ..., (w_N, r_N)) = \frac{\prod_{n-1}^{N} f(w_n, r_n, i)}{(f(i))^{N-1} \cdot \sum_k f(i_k)}, \tag{6.1}$$

where $(f(i))$ is the frequency of the interpretation i on its own, $\sum_k f(i_k)$ is the number of times this part of speech is attested in the corpus, and $f(w_n, r_n, i)$ is the frequency of the co-occurrence of the interpretation with the context word w_n in the relation r_n. This model favors paraphrases that best match the given context. The candidates produced by the model are then filtered based on the presence of shared features with the metaphorical verb, as defined by their location and relative distance in the WordNet hierarchy. The output of the maximum likelihood model filtered by WordNet is shown in Figure 6.1 (left).[2] The system then re-ranks these candidates using their SPs to discriminate between figurative and literal paraphrases. Shutova treats a strong SP fit as a good indicator of literalness or conventionality. The SP distribution is defined in terms of the selectional association measure introduced by Resnik [1993] over the noun classes automatically produced using the noun clustering method of Sun and Korhonen [2009]. Selectional association quantifies how well a particular noun class fits the verb, as follows:

$$A_R(v, c) = \frac{1}{S_R(v)} P(c|v) \log \frac{P(c|v)}{P(c)} \tag{6.2}$$

where $P(c)$ is the prior probability of the noun class, $P(c|v)$ is the posterior probability of the noun class given the verb, R is the grammatical relation in question, and $S_R(v)$ is the overall SP strength of the verb measured as a Kullback-Leibler divergence [Kullback and Leibler, 1951]

---

[2]Shutova reports log-likelihood numbers for better readability.

Log-likelihood	Paraphrase		Sel. association	Paraphrase
hold back truth:			hold back truth:	
-13.09	contain		0.1161	conceal
-14.15	conceal		0.0214	keep
-14.62	suppress		0.0070	suppress
-15.13	hold		0.0022	contain
-16.23	keep		0.0018	defend
-16.24	defend		0.0006	hold
stir excitement:			stir excitement:	
-14.28	create		0.0696	provoke
-14.84	provoke		0.0245	elicit
-15.53	make		0.0194	arouse
-15.53	elicit		0.0061	conjure
-15.53	arouse		0.0028	create
-16.23	stimulate		0.0001	stimulate
-16.23	raise		≈ 0	raise
-16.23	excite		≈ 0	make
-16.23	conjure		≈ 0	excite

Figure 6.1: Output of the system of Shutova [2010].

between the probability distributions $P(c|v)$ and $P(c)$. The paraphrases re-ranked by this model are shown in Figure 6.1 (right). Shutova [2010] tested her system on a dataset of 62 metaphors expressed by a verb and reports a high accuracy of 0.81, as evaluated on top-rank paraphrases produced by the system. However, she uses WordNet for supervision, which limits the number and range of paraphrases that can be identified by her method. Shutova et al. [2012] and Bollegala and Shutova [2013] expanded on this work, applying the metaphor paraphrasing task in an unsupervised setting and extending its coverage. The method of Shutova et al. [2012] first computes candidate paraphrases according to the context in which the metaphor appears, using a vector space model. It then uses a SP model to measure the degree of literalness of the paraphrases. The authors evaluated their method on the metaphor paraphrasing dataset of Shutova [2010] and report a top-rank precision of 0.52 (which is high for a fully unsupervised lexical substitution system). Bollegala and Shutova [2013] used a similar experimental setup, although their method extracted a set of candidate paraphrases from the Web and ranked them based on search engine hits, attaining a precision of 0.42.

While the majority of metaphor processing systems treat metaphor identification and interpretation as two separate tasks and address them individually, Shutova [2013] presents a method that performs these two tasks simultaneously, as a holistic metaphor comprehension process. She again treats metaphor interpretation as paraphrasing and introduces the concept of *symmetric reverse paraphrasing* as a criterion for metaphor identification. The hypothesis behind the method is that the literal paraphrases of literally used words should yield the original phrase when paraphrased in reverse. For example, when the expression "clean the house" is paraphrased as "tidy the house," the reverse paraphrasing of *tidy* would generate *clean*. Shutova's expectation is that such

FYT Gorbachev **inherited** a Soviet state which was, in a celebrated Stalinist formulation, "national in form but socialist in content."
Paraphrase: Gorbachev <u>received</u> a Soviet state which was, in a celebrated Stalinist formulation, "national in form but socialist in content."

CEK The Clinton campaign **surged** again and he easily won the Democratic nomination.
Paraphrase: The Clinton campaign <u>improved</u> again and he easily won the Democratic nomination.

CEK Their views **reflect** a lack of enthusiasm among the British people at large for John Major's idea of European unity.
Paraphrase: Their views <u>show</u> a lack of enthusiasm among the British people at large for John Major's idea of European unity.

J85 [..] the reasons for this superiority are never **spelled out**.
Paraphrase [..] the reasons for this superiority are never <u>specified</u>.

J85 Anyone who has introduced speech act theory to students will know that these technical terms are not at all easy to **grasp**.
Paraphrase: Anyone who has introduced speech act theory to students will know that these technical terms are not at all easy to <u>understand</u>.

G0N The man's voice **cut in** .
Paraphrase: The man's voice <u>interrupted</u>.

Figure 6.2: Metaphors tagged by the system of Shutova [2013] (in bold) and their paraphrases.

symmetry in paraphrasing is indicative of literal use. The metaphorically-used words are unlikely to exhibit this symmetry property when paraphrased in reverse. For example, the literal paraphrasing of the verb *stir* in "*stir* excitement" would yield "provoke excitement," but the reverse paraphrasing of *provoke* would not retrieve *stir*, indicating the non-literal use of *stir*. Shutova experimentally verified this hypothesis in a setting involving single-word metaphors expressed by a verb in verb-subject and verb-direct object relations. She applied the SP-based metaphor paraphrasing method of Shutova [2010] to retrieve literal paraphrases of all input verbs and extended the method to perform metaphor identification by reverse paraphrasing. Shutova evaluated the performance of the system on verb-subject and verb-object relations using the manually annotated metaphor corpus of Shutova and Teufel [2010], containing 164 verbal metaphors. Shutova reported a precision of 0.68 and a recall of 0.66. The system outperforms a baseline using SP violation as an indicator of metaphor; this baseline approach attains a precision of just 0.17 and a recall of 0.55. Some examples of metaphorical expressions identified by the system and their literal paraphrases are shown in Figure 6.2.

SPs have also been used as additional components or filters in other approaches to metaphor. In their metaphor identification system, Shutova et al. [2010] filtered out verbs that have weak SPs, i.e., that are equally strongly associated with many argument classes (e.g., *choose* or *remember*), as having a lower metaphorical potential. Li et al. [2013] used SPs to assign the corresponding conceptual metaphor to metaphorical expressions. Given a metaphorically used verb, they acquired its SPs in a data-driven fashion and then searched their knowledge base of conceptual metaphors for a mapping between the target noun and the highly ranked preferences of the metaphorical verb. While the idea of violation (i.e., treating metaphor as a context outlier) is controversial and should be employed with care, the SPs themselves are an important source of semantic information about the properties of concepts that can be successfully exploited in metaphor processing in a variety of ways.

6.2   SUPERVISED CLASSIFICATION

A number of supervised approaches have trained classifiers on manually annotated data to recognize metaphors. Supervised classification is a machine learning task, in which a system learns to discriminate between classes of examples given relevant training data. To facilitate learning, the data is represented in the form of features that encode the properties of labeled examples and their contexts. The goal of the learning process is then to infer a function that maps the features to classes, ideally in a way that the system can generalize to unseen examples. In metaphor research, classifiers are typically trained to discriminate between two classes—literal vs. metaphorical language—and use a corpus annotated for literal and metaphorical examples as training data. The key question that supervised classification poses for metaphor research regards the features that are most indicative of metaphor and how best to abstract from individual linguistic expressions to their higher-level properties. The metaphor community has experimented with a variety of features, ranging from lexical and syntactic information to higher-level features such as semantic roles, WordNet super-senses, and domain-types extracted from specialist ontologies.

Gedigian et al. [2006] focused on metaphorical verbs related to MOTION and CURE within a limited domain of financial discourse. They used a maximum entropy classifier [Berger et al., 1996] to discriminate between literal and metaphorical language. The authors obtained their data by extracting the lexical items related to the MOTION and CURE frames in *FrameNet* [Fillmore et al., 2003]. They extracted the sentences containing these lexical items from PropBank and annotated them for metaphorical and literal usages. They then used the nominal arguments of the verbs and their semantic roles (as annotated in PropBank) as features to train the classifier and reported an encouraging accuracy of 95.12%. This result is, however, only a little higher than the performance of a naive baseline that assigns the majority class to all instances (92.90%), since 92% of the verbs of MOTION and CURE in the *Wall Street Journal* corpus are used metaphorically, making the dataset very unbalanced indeed. It should also be noted that the narrow focus on specific lexical items makes it possible for the system to learn a model for individual words without achieving the desirable level of generalization.

In contrast, Dunn [2013a,b] experimented with a wide range of metaphorical expressions from the VU Amsterdam Metaphor Corpus. A logistic regression classifier [Cox, 1958] was trained to annotate word uses as metaphorical or literal, using high-level properties of concepts as extracted from the SUMO ontology [Niles and Pease, 2001, 2003] as features. Dunn's system first maps the lexical items in the given utterance to concepts from SUMO, assuming that each lexical item is used in its default sense, i.e., no sense disambiguation is performed. The system then extracts the properties of concepts from the ontology, such as their domain type (ABSTRACT, PHYSICAL, SOCIAL, MENTAL) and event status (PROCESS, STATE, OBJECT). Those properties are then combined into feature-vector representations of the utterances over which the classification is performed. Dunn then applies a logistic regression classifier, implemented in Weka [Witten and Frank, 2005], using these features to perform metaphor identification. Dunn [2013b] evaluated his approach against the VU Amsterdam Metaphor Corpus [Steen et al., 2010], attaining an F-measure of 0.58. Although such an F-measure appears low compared to other approaches described in this section, it should be noted that the VU Amsterdam Metaphor Corpus is considerably larger than the datasets used in the majority of supervised classification approaches, suggesting that this evaluation is all the more objective. In addition, the corpus is not domain-specific, which makes it more difficult for the system to attain a high recall and precision. We thus believe that Dunn's approach may still be competitive with other approaches described in this section, which report higher performance results but which were evaluated on small (and for the most part, domain-specific) datasets. It is also worth pointing out that the VU Amsterdam Corpus is different from other datasets insofar as its annotation reflects a wider interest in the historical aspects of metaphor that extends beyond the metaphors of contemporary English. The corpus therefore includes a large number of highly conventional, lexicalized, and dead metaphors. This historical richness is likely to impact on system evaluation results, inasmuch as the corpus is more suited to the evaluation of systems that define metaphor solely in terms of source—target domain mappings and that do not consider conventionality or novelty as a factor.

Much like Dunn, Tsvetkov et al. [2013] also use a logistic regression classifier and a set of high-level, coarse semantic features to identify metaphorical language. They experiment with metaphor identification in English and Russian, first training a classifier on English data only, and then projecting the trained model to Russian using a dictionary. They abstract from the words in English data to their higher-level features, such as concreteness, animateness, named entity labels, and coarse-grained WordNet categories (corresponding to WN lexicographer files,[3] e.g., *noun.artifact, noun.body, verb.motion, verb.cognition,* etc.) They focus on subject-verb-object constructions and annotate metaphor at the sentence level. They evaluated their model on the TroFi dataset [Birke and Sarkar, 2006] for English (1,298 sentences containing metaphorical and literal uses of 25 verbs) and a bespoke dataset of 140 sentences for Russian, attaining F-scores of 0.78 and 0.76 respectively. The results show that porting coarse-grained semantic knowledge across languages is feasible in principle. However, several cross-linguistic studies [Charteris-Black and Ennis, 2001, Diaz-Vera and Caballero, 2013, Kovecses, 2005] suggest that there is considerable variation in metaphorical language across cultures. This means that training a model on one language before porting it to another is unlikely to achieve a complete coverage of metaphors in the target language, but limits its coverage to those metaphors that are either cross-cultural or

---

[3]http://wordnet.princeton.edu/man/lexnames.5WN.html

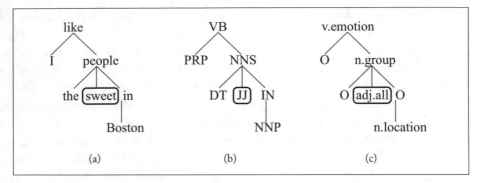

Figure 6.3: Dependency trees with lexical, part-of-speech, and WordNet super-sense features from Hovy et al. [2013a].

strongly embodied and conceptually primary (see Grady [1997, 2005] for a discussion of what makes a metaphor *primary*).

The work of Hovy et al. [2013b] is notable among the supervised learning approaches to metaphor, in that it focuses on compositional rather than lexical features. These researchers trained a Support Vector Machines (SVM) classifier [Cortes and Vapnik, 1995] with tree kernels [Moschitti et al., 2006] to capture the compositional properties of metaphorical language. Their hypothesis echoes the SP violation view in that unusual semantic compositions in the data are assumed to be indicative of the use of metaphor. As earlier described in Section 4.5.2, the model was trained on labeled examples of literal and metaphorical uses of 329 words (3,872 sentences in total), and was expected to learn the differences in the compositional behavior of these words in the given lexico-syntactic contexts. The choice of dependency-tree[4] kernels helps to capture such compositional properties. Hovy et al. [2013b] used word vectors, as well as lexical, part-of-speech tag, and WordNet super-sense representations of sentence trees as features, as shown in Figure 6.3. The authors constructed their dataset by extracting sentences from the Brown corpus [Francis and Kucera, 1979] that contained the words of interest, and annotating them for metaphoricity using Amazon Mechanical Turk. (Recall that Figure 4.2 in Section 4.5.2 presents example entries for the adjective "bright.") 80% of the data was used for training purposes, 10% for parameter tuning and 10% for the evaluation. The authors report encouraging results, an F-score of 0.75, which is an indication of the importance of syntactic information and compositionality for metaphor identification.

The approach of Li and Sporleder [2009, 2010], who detected idioms by measuring semantic similarity within and between the literal and non-literal parts of an utterance, is somewhat close in spirit to that of Hovy. The non-literal language considered by Li and Sporleder's model

---

[4]Dependency trees arise from parsing a sentence with a Dependency grammar, which—unlike a standard phrase-structure grammar—aims to capture the functional dependencies between words, such as between the verb and its arguments. As such, it prefers to designate verbs as the roots of trees and sub-trees, above the nouns that depend upon them.

captures metaphors, as well as other figures of speech. Their main hypothesis is that uses of a figurative word disrupt the cohesion of a sentence, which can be quantified by an inter-word similarity measure. This idea also harks back to Wilks' SP-violation approach to metaphor, although combinations of word usages with larger sentential contexts are also considered in determining the extent of a mismatch (or violation). Li and Sporleder used Normalized Google Distance [Cilibrasi and Vitanyi, 2007] as a similarity measure and a combination of classifiers (Support Vector Machines and Gaussian Mixture Models (GMM)) with sentence cohesion information as features to learn idiomaticity scores. They evaluated their system on a small dataset of 17 idioms and their literal and non-literal contexts of use. For each expression, its occurrences were extracted from the Gigaword corpus along with five paragraphs of context. These examples were then annotated for literalness with an inter-annotator agreement of $\kappa = 0.7$. There were 3,964 examples in total, with approximately 80% of them non-literal. The authors evaluated their method using 10-fold cross-validation and report an F-score of 0.75. However, they did not independently evaluate their system on metaphorical language. The general criticism of the SP violation approach to metaphor identification applies to Li and Sporleder's method. Namely, the system is likely to both over-generate (as a number of phenomena other than metaphor may cause a context mismatch) and under-generate (insofar as a high proportion of metaphors are both conventionalized and frequently used, and therefore their distributional properties are unlikely to capture any mismatch with metaphorical use-contexts). In addition, the annotation was performed at the sentence level, rather than at the word or relation level, which makes a higher F-score easier to achieve.

In contrast to other approaches, Mohler et al. [2013] focused on modeling conceptual information through rich semantic features. Their method relies on the notion of a semantic signature of a text. The authors define semantic signatures as sets of highly related and interlinked WordNet senses. They induce domain-sensitive semantic signatures of texts and then train a set of classifiers to detect metaphoricity by comparing the signature of a given text to the signatures of known metaphors. The key intuition behind this approach is that the texts whose semantic signatures closely match the signature of a known metaphor are likely to contain instances of the same conceptual metaphor. Mohler and colleagues conducted their experiments within a limited domain (the target domain of *governance*) and manually constructed an index of known metaphors for this domain. They then automatically created the target domain signature and a signature for each source domain among the known metaphors in the index. This was done by means of semantic expansion of domain terms using WordNet, Wikipedia links, and corpus co-occurrence statistics. Given an input text, the method first identifies all target domain terms using the target domain signature, then disambiguates the remaining terms using sense clustering, and classifies them according to their proximity to the source domains listed in the index. For the latter, the authors experimented with a set of classifiers, including a maximum entropy classifier, an unpruned decision tree classifier, support vector machines, and a random forest classifier, as well as combinations thereof. They annotated metaphor at the sentence level and evaluated their system on a balanced dataset containing 241 metaphorical and 241 literal examples. The authors obtained their highest F-score, 0.70, using the decision tree classifier. Their results demonstrate that rich semantic information is likely to be a successful feature in metaphor recognition. Nonetheless, Mohler and colleagues experimented within a limited domain and it is yet unclear how well such features scale to new domains and to real-world data.

Beigman Klebanov et al. [2014] used logistic regression to detect metaphors at the word level in a corpus of essays written for a graduate school admission test [Beigman Klebanov and Flor, 2013], as well as in the VU Amsterdam Corpus [Steen et al., 2010]. Metaphors of all content-word parts of speech were considered. The authors found that a baseline unigram model was surprisingly successful, especially for topically homogeneous sets of essays, where it attained F-scores of up to 0.64, with precision of 0.79 and recall of 0.54, suggesting that many of the writers responded to the same essay question with similar metaphors. For example, writers of essays addressing electronic vs. face-to-face communication often used distance-based metaphors to argue both for the anti-electronics position (e.g., electronic communication "drives people apart") and the pro-electronics position (e.g., electronic communication "brings people together"). However, even for data that is topically heterogeneous, such as news articles from the BNC, the unigram model attained a non-trivial F-score of 0.51, with a precision of 0.61 and a recall of 0.43. The authors suggest that consistently metaphorical use of some words is akin to the phenomenon of a domain-specific dominant sense, where the dominant sense of a polysemous word is observed in about 70% of usages [Koeling et al., 2005]. Going beyond the unigram baseline, Beigman Klebanov et al. [2014] used part-of-speech features and mean concreteness ratings from data collected by Brysbaert et al. [2013], as well as features based on topic models. These topic models were built using LDA from a corpus of *NYT (New York Times)* articles [Sandhaus, 2008], and the value of the feature for topic t for an instance w was $\log \frac{P(w|t)}{P(w)}$. The authors found that the topic features were effective not only for topically homogeneous sets of essays, but also for the News partition of the VU Amsterdam Corpus as well. The topic features improved recall by identifying words belonging to *NYT* topics that are often used metaphorically. For example, in the News data, a topic that deals with hurricane Katrina had a positive weight in metaphor classification, as words associated with suffering and recovery in disaster stories are often used metaphorically, such as *awash*, *damaged*, *relief*, *victim*, *distress*, and *swept*.

Research on metaphor that employs supervised learning suggests that rich syntactic, lexical, and semantic features allow us to induce generalizations about the use of metaphor in large datasets, even if these are domain-specific. However, in order to reliably capture the mechanisms that govern the production and comprehension of metaphorical language at a large scale, it is likely that one needs to address the deep conceptual properties of metaphor along with its surface qualities. Thus, models making generalizations at the level of metaphorical mappings and coarse-grained classes of concepts, in essence representing different domains (such as *politics* or *machines*), appear very promising. Yet, supervised learning methods face a significant challenge, that of the lack of manually labeled data for most domains. While the experiments described here have demonstrated the feasibility of machine learning within a small number of domains, scaling the associated methods would require extensive and costly annotation efforts. The metaphor community has thus also investigated minimally supervised models, based on clustering, LDA topic modeling, and heuristic features such as concreteness and imageability. We discuss such methods in the following sections.

6.3   CLUSTERING

Clustering refers to a class of machine learning techniques whose goal is to partition a large set of objects into smaller and meaningful clusters, such that the objects within a cluster are more similar to each other (given a definition of similarity) than to objects in different clusters. That is, clustering techniques set out to maximize intra-cluster similarity and to minimize inter-cluster similarity, relative to a given similarity function. Word clustering in particular is commonly used in NLP to identify words with similar meanings. For example, *apple, grape*, and *avocado* might belong to one cluster while *car, bike*, and *motorcycle* belong to another, in effect capturing (but not labeling) the distinction between fruits and vehicles. As in the case of supervised classification, clustering algorithms generalize over the properties of concepts and calculate their similarity to each other using feature representations that are derived from text data. The features typically used in word clustering experiments include the lexico-syntactic contexts in which the words appear, as well as information about sub-categorization frames and semantic roles. But, in contrast to supervised classification, unsupervised clusters are constructed without manually labeled training data.

Metaphor research exploits clustering techniques in a variety of ways. Some approaches use clustering to identify concepts whose meanings are similar or related to each other. For instance, Mason [2004] performed WordNet sense clustering to obtain SP classes, while Mohler et al. [2013] used clustering to determine inter-word similarity and to link words in semantic signatures of domains. Strzalkowski et al. [2013] and Gandy et al. [2013] clustered metaphorically used terms to form potential source domains, also by estimating the similarity of their meanings. Another line of research uses clustering to investigate how metaphor partitions the linguistic feature space. Shutova et al. [2010] points out that the metaphorical uses of words constitute a large portion of the co-occurrence features extracted for abstract concepts from text data, noting, for example, that the feature vector for *politics* contains GAME and MECHANISM terms as its frequent features. As a result, distributional clustering of abstract nouns with such features identifies groups of diverse concepts metaphorically associated with the same source domain (or sets of source domains). Shutova and her colleagues refer to this as "clustering by association." Shutova et al. [2010] exploit this property of co-occurrence vectors to identify new metaphorical mappings starting from a set of examples. Based on the same observation, Shutova and Sun [2013] used hierarchical clustering to derive a network of concepts in which metaphorical associations are exhibited at different levels of granularity.

The method of Shutova et al. [2010] focuses on identification of metaphorical expressions in verb-subject and verb-direct object constructions. It uses a small seed set of metaphorical expressions as examples, from which it implicitly learns the underlying metaphorical mappings and extends the set of mappings by means of verb and noun clustering. Based on clustering by association, Shutova and her colleagues derive clusters of concepts metaphorically associated with the same source domain. For instance, *democracy* and *marriage* will be clustered together, as both are viewed as social *mechanisms*, and, as such, appear with the *mechanism* terminology in the corpus. This allows the system to discover previously unseen conceptual and linguistic metaphors. For instance, having seen the seed metaphor "*repair* marriage," the system infers that "the *functioning* of democracy" is also used metaphorically. In this way the system expands from its initial seed set to embrace new concepts. These authors used the spectral clustering algorithm of Meila and Shi [2001] and derived their clusters using the grammatical relations of words as features. Once the clusters are obtained and linked using the seed expressions as a starting point, the system then searches a text corpus for verb-subject and verb-direct object expressions containing vocabulary from the metaphorically connected clusters. Shutova et al. [2010] applied their system to general-domain text (the whole BNC) and evaluated its performance by subjecting a random sample of the extracted metaphors to human judgment. They report a precision of 0.79 with an inter-judge agreement of $k = 0.63$ among five annotators. Their data-driven system favorably compares to a WordNet-based baseline, where synsets are used in place of automatically derived clusters. Shutova and colleagues have shown that a clustering-based solution has a significantly wider coverage, capturing new metaphors rather than merely synonymous ones, as well as yielding a 35% increase in precision. Although clustering itself is unsupervised, the approach still relies on a small number of seed expressions for supervision (62 seed expressions in total were employed in Shutova et al.'s experiments). However, it requires considerably fewer labeled examples compared to supervised classification methods that typically rely on thousands of labeled instances for training. In addition, since the system precision was measured on the output for individual seed expressions, it may be reasonably expected that the addition of new seeds would increase the recall of the system without any significant loss in precision.

Shutova and Sun [2013] took this work further by learning metaphorical associations between concepts directly from the data in an unsupervised fashion. They use hierarchical graph factorization clustering [Yu et al., 2006] of nouns with lexico-syntactic features to create a graph of concepts and to quantify the strength of association between concepts in this graph. While concrete concepts exhibit well-defined association patterns based mainly on subsumption within a single domain, abstract concepts tend to have both within-domain and cross-domain associates: that is, literal associates and metaphorical associates. For example, the abstract concept of DEMOCRACY is literally associated with a more general concept of POLITICAL SYSTEM, as well as metaphorically associated with the concept of MECHANISM. The system of Shutova and Sun [2013] automatically discovers these association patterns within the graph and uses them to identify metaphorical mappings. The mappings are represented in their system as cross-level,

---

source: fire

TARGET 1: sense hatred emotion passion enthusiasm sentiment hope interest feeling resentment optimism hostility excitement anger

TARGET 2: coup violence fight resistance clash rebellion battle drive fighting riot revolt war confrontation volcano row revolution struggle

TARGET 3: alien immigrant

TARGET 4: prisoner hostage inmate

---

source: disease

TARGET 1: fraud outbreak offense connection leak count crime violation abuse conspiracy corruption terrorism suicide

TARGET 2: opponent critic rival

TARGET 3: execution destruction signing

TARGET 4: refusal absence fact failure lack delay

Figure 6.4: Metaphorical associations discovered by the system of Shutova and Sun [2013].

uni-directional connections between clusters in the hierarchical graph (e.g., the FEELING cluster is strongly associated with FIRE). Example target concepts identified for the source concepts of FIRE and DISEASE are shown in Figure 6.4. To identify metaphorical expressions representing a given mapping, Shutova and Sun use the features that resulted in strong metaphorical associations between the clusters in question (e.g., "passion *flared*" for FEELING IS FIRE), as shown in Figure 6.5. The authors evaluated the quality of metaphorical mappings and metaphorical expressions identified by the system against human judgments and report a precision of 0.69 for metaphorical associations and 0.65 for metaphorical expressions (measured on a random sample of 200 expressions). To measure the recall of metaphorical associations, Shutova and Sun have created a gold standard, by asking human annotators to write down all of the target concepts that they associated with a given source. They report a recall of 0.61, as evaluated against this gold standard. While the performance of this system is lower than that of a semi-supervised method of Shutova et al. [2010] and a number of supervised classification methods described above, we should emphasize that this method is fully unsupervised and that it is generally more difficult to obtain a higher performance than a supervised or semi-supervised system when operating in an unsupervised setting. In turn, since the method of Shutova and Sun [2013] does not rely on manually labeled examples of metaphor, it can more easily be ported to new domains and datasets, and therefore has a significantly wider applicability than a comparable supervised system.

Besides word clustering, sentence clustering has also been employed in metaphor research. Birke and Sarkar [2006] clustered sentences containing metaphorical and literal uses of verbs. Their core hypothesis is that all instances of a particular verb in semantically similar sentences will have the same general sense, whether a literal sense or a metaphorical sense. This idea originates from a similarity-based word sense disambiguation method developed by Karov and Edelman [1998]. The method employs a set of seed sentences in which words are annotated with their senses, and computes similarity between the sentence containing the word to be disambiguated

---

feeling is fire

hope *lit* (Subj), anger *blazed* (Subj), optimism *raged* (Subj), enthusiasm *engulfed* them (Subj), hatred *flared* (Subj), passion *flared* (Subj), interest *lit* (Subj), *fuel* resentment (Dobj), anger *crackled* (Subj), feelings *roared* (Subj), hostility *blazed* (Subj), *light* with hope (Iobj)

---

crime is a disease

cure crime (Dobj), abuse *transmitted* (Subj), *eradicate* terrorism (Dobj), *suffer from* corruption (Iobj), *diagnose* abuse (Dobj), *combat* fraud (Dobj), *cope with* crime (Iobj), *cure* abuse (Dobj), *eradicate* corruption

---

Figure 6.5: Shutova and Sun [2013]: metaphorical expressions identified for the mappings FEELING IS FIRE and CRIME IS A DISEASE.

---

pour

nonliteral cluster

wsj04:7878 N As manufacturers get bigger, they are likely to pour more money into the battle for shelf space, raising the ante for new players.

wsj25:3283 N Salsa and rap music pour out of the windows.

wsj06:300 U Investors hungering for safety and high yields are pouring record sums into single-premium, interest-earning annuities.

literal cluster

wsj59:3286 L Custom demands that cognac be poured from a freshly opened bottle.

Figure 6.6: An example of the data of Birke and Sarkar [2006].

and all of the seed sentences. It then selects the sense that is used to annotate this word in the most similar seed sentences. In their TroFi system (Trope[5] Finder), Birke and Sarkar [2006] adapt this algorithm to perform general two-way classification, literal vs. non-literal, without further specifying the types of tropes they aim to discover. They evaluated their system on a set of 25 verbs (such as *absorb, die, touch, knock, strike, pour,* and others), for which they extracted a set of sentences containing literal and figurative uses of each one, 1,298 in total, from the Wall Street Journal Corpus. An example for the verb *pour* in their dataset is shown in Figure 6.6. Two annotators annotated the sentences for literalness, achieving an agreement of $\kappa = 0.77$. Birke and Sarkar report an F-score of 0.538 for their system on this dataset, which puts their method into a low performance range, as compared to more recent methods evaluated on the same dataset.

6.4   THE TOPICAL STRUCTURE OF TEXT

Two other approaches [Heintz et al., 2013, Strzalkowski et al., 2013] focused on modeling the topic structure of a text or set of texts to identify metaphors. The main hypothesis behind these methods is that the metaphorical language of a source domain should represent atypical vocabulary within the topical structure of a text (associated with a target domain). In order to identify

---

[5]A trope is a species of figurative language. As such, metaphor, irony, metonymy, and synecdoche can all be considered tropes.

such atypical vocabulary, Strzalkowski et al. [2013] acquire a set of topic chains by linking semantically related words in a given text. They experimented within a limited domain, the target domain of *governance*. Their method first identifies sentences containing target domain vocabulary and extracts the surrounding five-sentence passage. Topic chains are then identified in this passage by linking the occurrences of nouns and verbs, including repetition, lexical variants, pronominal references, and WordNet synonyms and hyponyms. Considering only the words outside this topic chain that are syntactically connected to a term in the chain, Strzalkowski and colleagues then compute the imageability[6] scores of these words and retain the highest-scoring ones as candidate metaphors. These authors then extract the common contexts in which the candidates are used in text corpora and cluster these contexts in order to identify potential source domains, or what they call "proto-sources." Strzalkowski et al. [2013] evaluated the performance of their method on four languages, English, Spanish, Russian, and Farsi, by eliciting human judgments of the system's outputs using Amazon's Mechanical Turk. Small datasets of 50 examples per language were annotated by around 30 annotators. The authors report a metaphor identification accuracy of 71% for English, 80% for Spanish, 69% for Russian, and 78% for Farsi. While the system performance is high within the domain of *governance*, it is possible that the approach may neither score so highly in other domains nor be easily ported to these domains. Due to its reliance on imageability scores, the method can delineate metaphorical language for abstract target domains, but should find more concrete[7] target domains harder to work with. For, in concrete domains, target domain words may also exhibit high imageability, forcing the system to rely solely on topic chain extraction to differentiate between literal and metaphorical usages.

Heintz et al. [2013] use LDA topic modeling [Blei et al., 2003] to identify sets of source and target domain vocabulary. In their system, the acquired topics represented source and target domains, and sentences containing vocabulary from both were tagged as metaphorical. Their goal was to create a minimally supervised metaphor processing system that is, in principle at least, portable to low-resource languages. The authors focused on the target domain of *governance* in experiments in English and Spanish, manually compiling a set of source concepts with which governance can be associated. The topics were learned from Wikipedia and then aligned to source and target concepts using sets of human-created seed words. When metaphorical sentences are retrieved, the source topics that are common in the document are excluded, thus ensuring that the source domain vocabulary is transferred from a new domain. While allowing the authors to filter out (some) literal uses, this strategy may also lead it to discard cases of extended metaphor. The authors collected the data for their experiments from news websites and governance-related blogs in English and Spanish, and applied their system to this data to generate a ranked set of metaphorical examples. They carried out two types of evaluation: (1) on the top five examples for each conceptual metaphor, as judged by two annotators to yield an F-score of 0.59 for English; and (2) on the 250 top-ranked examples of system output that were annotated for metaphoricity

---

[6]Imageability is an estimate of the ease with which a mental image can be created for a given word.
[7]Concreteness estimates the degree to which a word denotes an actual substance or tangible thing, as opposed to an abstract quality. Concreteness and abstractness may be taken to be opposite ends of the same scale.

using Amazon's Mechanical Turk, yielding a mean metaphoricity of 0.41 in English and 0.33 in Spanish. One of the assumptions behind this method is that the same source—target domain mappings manifest themselves across languages. However, this assumption may not extend beyond primary metaphors [Grady, 1997], leading to false positives and to limited coverage in some languages.

Exploiting the topical structure of text is a promising approach for metaphor identification. However, one needs to keep in mind that distributional similarity-based methods risk assigning frequent metaphors to the target rather than the source domain. For instance, *cut* may appear more frequently within the domain of economics and finance than in its home domain of knives and physical incisions. The choice of data for training such a model thus becomes crucial, and so an appropriately balanced dataset is required. Yet, if done carefully, modeling the topical structure of a text can be an important step toward achieving a robust model of extended metaphor in discourse.

6.5   VECTOR SPACE MODELS

Vector space models (VSMs) are a proven tool for modeling word meaning, term similarity, and semantic compositionality, in which the meanings of words, concepts, and phrases are represented as vectors in a high-dimensional semantic space. These vectors typically contain information about the lexico-syntactic contexts of use for a word or phrase in a large text corpus, so that terms that are relatively interchangeable will have very similar vectors and occupy nearby points in vector space. Large context windows allow vector representations to capture the topics to which a term contributes, and thus allows a VSM to capture the topical similarity of two terms. VSMs of word meaning have been used widely and successfully in NLP [Erk and Padó, 2008, 2009, 2010, Mitchell and Lapata, 2008, Thater et al., 2009, 2010, Van de Cruys et al., 2011] and underpin two recent approaches to metaphor interpretation [Mohler et al., 2014, Shutova et al., 2012].

Shutova et al. [2012] applied a VSM to find paraphrases for metaphorical expressions. Their method first uses a VSM to compute candidate paraphrases according to the context in which the metaphorical word appears. The meaning of a word instance in context is computed by adapting its original vector representation according to the dependency relations in which it participates. For this purpose, Shutova et al. [2012] built a factorization model in which words, together with the other words with which they share a context *window* and their dependency relations, are linked to latent dimensions [Van de Cruys et al., 2011]. These dimensions combine both types of contexts so as to induce broad, topic-capturing factors as well as tight, synonym-capturing factors. The factorization model determines which dimensions are important for a particular context, and adapts the dependency-based feature vector of the word accordingly. After the candidate paraphrases for the metaphorical word have been generated using this model, the system applies an SP model [Shutova, 2010] to measure their degree of literalness. The authors evaluated their approach on the dataset of metaphorical verbs of Shutova [2010], achieving a top-rank precision of 0.52, a promising result for a fully unsupervised method.

Mohler et al. [2014] used VSMs to assign conceptual metaphors to metaphorical expressions. Given linguistic metaphors identified by a supervised classifier [Bracewell et al., 2014, Mohler et al., 2013], this work focuses on analyzing the source and target words in the metaphor and their distributional properties so as to identify the domains that they belong to. Mohler and colleagues experiment with metaphors within the target domains of POVERTY, WEALTH, and TAXATION and compile a predefined set of source domains with which these targets are typically associated (51 in total). The source domains include, for instance, ABYSS and DISEASE for the target concept of POVERTY. The authors then extracted context vectors for source domain words in the metaphors and the given source concepts, and estimated their similarity as objects in a vector space. They experimented with three types of models: (1) dependency vectors, capturing immediate lexico-syntactic contexts of words; (2) latent semantic analysis (LSA) [Landauer and Dumais, 1997], capturing topical information from larger context windows; and (3) a continuous skip-gram[8] model (Word2Vector) [Mikolov et al., 2013], learning distributional representations for words using a neural network and providing a trade-off between dependency and topical information. Mohler et al. [2014] compared the three models against a human-annotated gold standard of source domain assignments and report the highest accuracy for LSA in English (54.9%) and Word2Vector in Spanish (58.6%), Russian (48.8%), and Farsi (48.4%).

6.6   CONCRETENESS

A number of approaches use the psycho-linguistic properties of concepts to derive heuristics for metaphor identification. Turney et al. [2011] introduced the idea of measuring the concreteness of concepts to predict metaphorical uses. Key to this approach is the intuition that metaphor is commonly used to describe abstract concepts in terms of more concrete or more physical experiences, and so we can expect to observe a discernible difference in the concreteness of source and target terms in a metaphor. Turney et al. [2011] thus developed a method to automatically estimate the concreteness of words for use in the identification of verbal and adjectival metaphors. The method works by learning from an initial set of examples to automatically rank words by concreteness, and then searches for expressions where a concrete adjective or verb is used with an abstract noun; for example, "*dark* humor" is tagged as a metaphor but "dark hair" is not. The dataset of Birke and Sarkar [2006] was used to evaluate the verbal metaphors, achieving an F-score of 0.68 that compares favorably to that reported by Birke and Sarkar. To evaluate adjectival metaphors, those researchers created a bespoke dataset of adjective-noun pairs for five adjectives, *dark, deep, hard, sweet*, and *warm*, and annotated 100 of these phrases for metaphoricity. When compared to these annotations, the accuracy of automated adjective classification is 0.79. However, as the adjective

---

[8]An n-gram is a sequence of *n* contiguous tokens in a text, without any intervening gaps. For instance, the Google n-grams [Brants and Franz, 2006] are n-grams from web content where *n* is 1,2,3,4 or 5. A skip-gram is an n-gram that is allowed to skip over tokens so that the selected sequence may contain gaps. A 1-skip n-gram is an n-gram where we are allowed gaps of at most one-token, that is, to skip at most 1 token between elements of the n-gram; a *k*-skip *n*-gram is allowed to skip at most *k* tokens in the text when constructing a window of *n* tokens.

dataset was constructed with concreteness in mind, the results reported for verb metaphors are likely to be more objective and more reliable.

Neuman et al. [2013] and Gandy et al. [2013] built upon Turney's approach to identify metaphorical expressions in a similar fashion. Neuman et al. [2013] incorporated the concept of SPs into their concreteness-based model to improve upon the performance of Turney's algorithm, by covering metaphors formed from concrete concepts only (as in, e.g., "*broken* heart") by detecting SP violations. The authors address three types of metaphor introduced by Krishnakumaran and Zhu [2007]—IS-A noun metaphors and metaphorical uses of verbs and adjectives—and claim to have carried out a more comprehensive evaluation of the abstractness-concreteness algorithm than that of Turney et al. However, the evaluation was performed against just five target concepts, namely *governance, government, God, mother*, and *father*, for which sentences describing these concepts were extracted from the Reuters [Lewis et al., 2004] and *New York Times (NYT)* [Sandhaus, 2008] corpora and annotated for metaphoricity. The authors report an average precision of 0.72 for their system on this limited-domain dataset, and report an average recall of 0.80. However, as the scope of the experiment is limited to the above five concepts, it is not clear how well the method would generalize to other concepts.

The system of Gandy et al. [2013] first discovers metaphorical expressions using the concreteness algorithm of Turney et al. [2011], and then assigns the corresponding metaphorical mappings with the help of lexical resources and context clustering. These researchers also focused on the three types of metaphor defined by Krishnakumaran and Zhu [2007]. Once the metaphorical expressions have been identified, Gandy et al. [2013] extract those nouns that tend to co-occur in a large corpus with metaphorical words, or what they call *facets* (e.g., the nominal arguments of "open" in "*open* government"). The goal of this process is to form candidate *nominal analogies* between the target noun in the metaphor and the extracted nouns. For example, the expression "*open* government" suggests the analogy "government ∼ door." Figure 6.7 shows how nominal analogies are formed based on a collection of metaphorical expressions. The individual (related) nominal analogies are then clustered together to identify conceptual metaphors, as shown in Figure 6.8. The authors evaluated their system by annotating metaphorical expressions for the five target concepts *government, governance, god, father*, and *mother* in selected sentences from the Reuters corpus [Lewis et al., 2004]. They report very encouraging results: $P = 0.76$, $R = 0.82$ for verb metaphors; $P = 0.54$, $R = 0.43$ for adjectival metaphors; and $P = 0.84$, $R = 0.97$ for copula constructions. The authors also evaluated the quality of conceptual metaphors produced by their system by eliciting human judgments, and report a precision of 0.65. Although the approach of Gandy et al. [2013] appears promising, its viability as a general method will only be established by a comprehensive evaluation on open-domain corpus data.

Two of the statistical approaches discussed earlier also investigated lexical concreteness as part of a more complex approach. For instance, Tsvetkov et al. [2013] used a coarse measure of concreteness as just one of multiple semantic features to train their classifier; a similar use was reported in Beigman Klebanov et al. [2014]. Other researchers have also explored the relevance

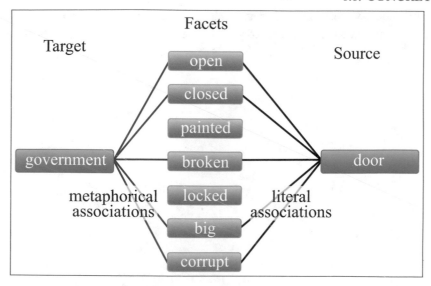

Figure 6.7: Nominal analogy induction from Gandy et al. [2013].

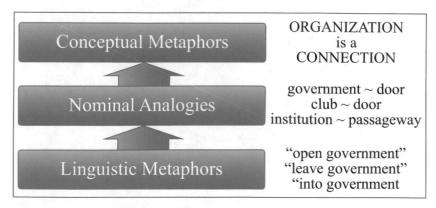

Figure 6.8: Gandy et al. [2013]: Three levels of analysis.

of concrete imageability—a measure of the ease with which a word's meaning can be mentally visualized—to metaphor identification (see Strzalkowski et al. [2013]). Based on the results of these experiments, concreteness has shown itself to be a practical feature for metaphor identification. However, it should be noted that the hypothesis of Turney et al. [2011]—that target words tend to be abstract and source words tend to be more concrete—explains only a fraction of metaphors and does not always hold. For example, one can use concrete-concrete metaphors (e.g., "*broken* heart"), abstract-abstract metaphors ("*diagnose* corruption"), and even abstract-concrete metaphors ("*invent* a soup"). However, the experiments conducted so far show that, within the concrete-abstract class of metaphor, the general method supports an encouraging level of performance. While concreteness may thus serve as a useful feature of more complex systems that take multiple factors into account, it is unlikely to be a reliable indicator of metaphor on its own.

CHAPTER 7

Applications of Metaphor Processing

In this chapter, we begin by surveying a variety of domains of application of metaphor detection and analysis. Due to the lack of availability of general-purpose automated metaphor detection tools until very recently, many of the studies surveyed in Section 7.1 rely on the manual or computer-assisted identification of metaphor. With the advent of effective tools to automate the detection and interpretation of metaphors, research questions raised in these studies can now be addressed at scale and in a more comprehensive manner. We then consider possible applications where metaphor processing would not only help human users to be more systematic, comprehensive, and efficient in obtaining data to satisfy their information needs, but would also help to augment the creative reach and expressiveness of the user (Section 7.2).

7.1 METAPHOR IN CULTURE, COMMUNICATION, AND EDUCATION

Like every word in an utterance or a text, a metaphor is a matter of choice. The choice could be more or less restricted (depending on the availability of an alternative phrase in the language), more or less personal (some words might be chosen due to the requirements of the specific situational context of text production, such as the venue and the occasion where the text would be delivered), more or less predictable, more or less sophisticated, or more or less effective. In general, choices, when systematically observed, might give rise to certain inferences about the authors and the contexts of language use, suggesting, for example, the following questions.

- Studying metaphors that occur in a similar discourse context across different authors, one could ask: What are the common background metaphors in a given discourse?

- Studying metaphors that are preferentially chosen by a certain author in a certain situation, one could ask: Why has this person chosen this metaphor? Is the choice effective?

- Observing trends in the kinds of writers that tend to choose or not to choose metaphors, one could ask: What characteristics of writers correlate with choosing to use metaphors?

7.1.1   COMMON METAPHORS IN CULTURES AND DISCOURSE COMMUNITIES

Automatic detection and classification of metaphors was the focus of a recent large-scale initiative funded by the U.S. government, using metaphor as a window into the thought processes of a given cultural, linguistic, or political community.[1] For example, Levin et al. [2014] describe a system for the detection of conventionalized metaphors dealing with conceptualizing the notions of taxation, wealth, and poverty, in English, Spanish, Russian, and Farsi. They found the conceptual metaphors to be quite different: In English, poverty is often framed as a disease, while in Russian, the predominant metaphor is that of an abyss. Shaikh et al. [2014] likewise found that disease was a common source of English metaphors of poverty, while certain other source domains were uncommon in English, yet used in Spanish data (poverty as a physical burden) or in Russian data (poverty as darkness). These papers join a long tradition of using metaphor analysis to identify and study cultural differences and similarities, in the contexts of cultural studies, media, politics, design, marketing, and education, among others [Charteris-Black, 2003, de Castro Salgado et al., 2011, Deignan, 2003, Deignan and Potter, 2004, Diaz-Vera and Caballero, 2013, Emanatian, 1995, Kövecses, 2003, 2008, Littlemore, 2003, Luodonpää-Manni and Viimaranta, 2010, Maalej, 2004, Matsuki, 1995, Musacchio, 2011, Musolff, 2000, Stefanowitsch, 2004, Yu, 1995, Zaltman and Zaltman, 2008].

When considering the discourse of a specific professional community (such as educators or business professionals) or a community built around a common experience (patients suffering from certain medical conditions), identification of its common metaphors can teach one about the perceptions of various stake-holders as well as about the dominant theories of a domain, which are often metaphorically structured [Bibik, 1997, Cameron, 2003, Cannice and Bell, 2010, Casonato, 2003, Charteris-Black and Ennis, 2001, Clarken, 1997, Eynon, 2002, Hunt and Menon, 1995, Izwaini, 2003, Jang et al., 2014, Kaviani and Hamedi, 2011, Koller, 2004, Lee, 2006, Leino and Drakenberg, 1993, Morgan, 1997, Nikitina and Furuoka, 2008, Partington, 1995, Semino et al., 2004, Skorczynska and Deignan, 2006].

7.1.2   METAPHOR AS A FRAMING DEVICE IN POLITICAL COMMUNICATION

The issue of understanding why certain individuals or groups use certain metaphors is intimately related to metaphor's function as a framing device. Framing can be defined as "selecting and highlighting some facets of events or issues, and making connections among them in order to promote a particular interpretation, evaluation, or solution" [Entman, 2003]. Metaphors are notorious for allowing subliminal framing, where the metaphor seems so natural that the aspects of the phenomenon in question that do not align with the metaphor are seamlessly concealed. For example, the metaphor WAR IS A COMPETITIVE GAME emphasizes the glory of winning and the shame of defeat, but hides the death-and-suffering aspect of the war, which makes sports metaphors

---

[1]See: http://www.iarpa.gov/index.php/research-programs/metaphor.

a strategic choice when wishing to arouse a pro-war sentiment in the audience [Lakoff, 1991]. It is therefore possible to gain a better understanding of political ideologies by identifying and explicating metaphors commonly used by their proponents [Beigman Klebanov and Beigman, 2010, Beigman Klebanov et al., 2008, Bosman, 1987, Charteris-Black, 2005, Fairclough, 2003, Lakoff, 2002, Landau et al., 2009, Lu and Ahrens, 2008, Moreno, 2008, Rash, 2006, Robins and Mayer, 2000, Thibodeau and Boroditsky, 2011]. For example, Lakoff [2002] identifies alternative emphases in the function of the family toward children—nurture vs. discipline—as a defining metaphor providing coherence to the Liberal vs. Conservative outlook in American politics. Consistent with this worldview, Barack Obama, a Democrat, construed the American people as being "hungry for this message of unity" (a feeding motif, related to nurture) [Beigman Klebanov et al., 2010], whereas Margaret Thatcher, a conservative British prime minister who broadly shared the U.S. Republican worldview, spoke about Britain "taking out a mortgage" (in reference to a loan from the IMF) and thus touched upon the motif of obligation, a related notion to discipline [Beigman Klebanov et al., 2008]. We can thus expect computational techniques to automate the identification of metaphorical motifs in large text collections, such as transcripts of political speeches or party manifestos.

7.1.3 METAPHOR COMPREHENSION AND USE AS A SKILL

Metaphor has many functions in communication, including evaluation, the management of agendas, and the explication of unfamiliar concepts, among others [Cameron, 2003]. An ability to comprehend and use metaphor appropriately is an important contributing factor to the overall communicative competence of a language learner [Littlemore and Low, 2006], and is thus a potential indicator of a learner's language proficiency. These observations open various possibilities for using metaphor processing in educational applications.

Littlemore et al. [2014] found that the use of metaphor in the writing of learners of English as a second language increases in line with general proficiency, both in terms of the proportion of metaphors used and in terms of the number of metaphor clusters in a text. Similarly, Beigman Klebanov and Flor [2013] found that a higher proportion of content words in the essays written by higher-proficiency writers are metaphorical. All essays were written in response to the same prompt question and in the same setting (i.e., a high-stakes college-level examination). In an earlier study, Danesi [1993] found that Spanish language learners produced texts with lower metaphorical density than native speakers. Automatic assessment of the overall metaphoricity, or of the metaphorical density, of a text, as well as other indicators such as the use of metaphor clusters, could potentially augment the capabilities of automatic language assessment technologies, with the obvious caveat that one needs to pay attention not only to the volume of the language learner's metaphoric production, but also to its quality [Kathpalia and Carmel, 2011, MacArthur, 2010].

Additionally, the culture-specific nature of metaphors and idioms make them a source of difficulty for second language learners. Thus, several studies showed that if a conceptual metaphor in the second language is not shared with the student's native language, the student is likely to have trouble interpreting it [Boers and Demecheleer, 2001, Deignan et al., 1997, Littlemore, 2003]. In a pioneering application of natural language processing to support teacher development, Burstein et al. [2013] designed a tool that highlights areas in the text where language learners might have comprehension difficulties to raise the awareness of teachers to such constructions; figurative uses are among those highlighted.

7.2   CREATIVITY APPLICATIONS IN NLP

Although the accurate representation of meaning is the ultimate goal of any deep NLP system, the choice of linguistic expression can often be just as important as the meaning it is used to convey. Any NLP system that aims to measure, predict, and optimize the stickiness,[2] virality,[3] persuasiveness, and/or affect of a message must thus be aware of how and why metaphors are used (and abused) in a text. A non-reductive metaphor-enabled NLP system must be able to do more than recognize and interpret metaphors: it should be able to truly evaluate metaphors as communicative gambits that may hit or miss, illuminate or complicate. We now consider a variety of applications of NLP technologies that exhibit a competence for metaphor at both the expressive and the meaning levels.

7.2.1   CREATIVE WRITING TOOLS

Productivity-enhancing software constitutes a major component of the commercial software market. Ranging from *Microsoft Office* to *Final Draft* (a screenwriting tool for film professionals) to *Adobe PhotoShop*, these tools make it easier for creative people to express themselves and to achieve their creative goals. Despite the market penetration of tools like *Microsoft Word*, and to a lesser extent *Final Draft*, it is fair to say that tools for creatively constructing and manipulating images and sounds are far more successful, and more richly featured, than the equivalent tools for language. There are good reasons for the language/image gap: One can manipulate an image with a wide range of continuous local transformations at a pixel level, and still obtain a valid image as output. Language, however, is a complex system of cultural symbols and rules—some explicit, many tacit—and simple manipulation of texts often yields a broken text (ungrammatical, unintelligible, meaningless) as output. Productivity tools for writers have made little headway beyond digitalized versions of old reliables, such as the thesaurus, the style guide, and the grammar book. These tools suggest simple word substitutions or word-order changes (e.g., use the passive voice in formal documents). These tools cannot help us to be more creative, by suggesting changes that would make our texts wittier, or more persuasive, or more memorable. To be sure, software like

---

[2]Stickiness is the degree to which a message is memorable and actually remembered by its audience. Some messages, such as advertising jingles and political slogans, are crafted to be sticky, while others, such as classic movie quotes (e.g., *these are not the droids you're looking for*) are often only accidentally sticky.

[3]Virality is the degree to which a message is considered interesting enough to pass along to others and thereby reach a large audience by word-of-mouth.

PhotoShop is equally uncreative, yet it offers such a wide range of features that it encourages creative experimentation by its users. By comparison, current productivity software for text creation offers a much-impoverished suite of features. Metaphor-enabled NLP systems may foster a new market for language-related productivity software, both for power-users (e.g., within advertising agencies, for speech-writers, etc.) and for casual users (e.g., users of smartphones who just want to compose a witty tweet or a catchy subject line for an email, or a funny caption for a photo), and for the broad swathe of experimental, playful, and mischievous language users that reside at many points along the casual/professional spectrum.

Samuel Goldwyn, the co-founder of MGM studios, famously summed up Hollywood's attitude to creativity with the line "Let's have some new clichés." On the face of it, this is both a shocking indictment of the Hollywood "factory" and yet another of Goldwyn's many memorable misstatements (such as "include me *out!*" and "the atom bomb, it's *dynamite!*"): after all, it's hard to think of clichés as new, or as something that can be invented on demand. Yet, on closer analysis, one can find real insight about creativity in Goldwyn's remark. Clichés are considered anathema to the creative process because they represent everything that is conventional and jaded about the status quo. However, clichés become tired through overwork, and are overworked precisely because they prove themselves so useful in so many different contexts. One productive form of new cliché is the humorously figurative comparison, as in "*as durable as a chocolate teapot*" or "*as useful as a screen door on a submarine.*" Speakers recognize a memorable comparison when they hear one, and re-use the best as eagerly as one retells a favorite joke. The most frequently reused comparisons can, in this way, acquire the clichéd status of a proverb. When the folklorist Archer Taylor collected his corpus of proverbial similes in 1954 (Taylor [1954]), he observed not just a wide variety of figurative comparisons in American speech, but a wide variety of humorous forms for the same descriptive qualities, such as "*durable*" and "*useful.*" Speakers are clearly drawn to popular comparisons of proven value, but are equally fond of coining their own, in the hope that their witty new descriptions will be widely reused by others in turn. This constant churn of figurative re-invention keeps our language fresh, and ensures that comparisons retain their ability to challenge and to entertain, even as others—such as "*crazy like a fox!*" or "*as clear as mud!*" – acquire an idiomatic status which makes them effortlessly understood. Although few writers set out to create a new cliché, most would like their efforts to become as much a part of the fabric of our linguistic culture as the most tenacious of clichés. So metaphor-enabled creative writing tools should—and will—be able to do more than suggest forms of expression that are already clichéd, but actually invent and suggest novel expressions of their own to suit the writer's current need, and do this so well that some of these new forms may eventually become clichés in their own right.

7.2.2   CREATIVE INFORMATION RETRIEVAL OF FIGURATIVE POSSIBILITIES

The invention of resonant new names—for businesses, products, services etc.—is a creative process that often involves metaphor in ways that are sometimes explicit but more often implicit. There is both a science and an art to creative naming (see Keller [2003]), for, although we want our new names to seem effortlessly apt, their creation often requires considerable amounts of search, filtering, evaluation, and refinement. So, while inspiration can arise from almost any source, a small number of reliable figurative strategies dominate. Punning, for instance, is popular as a naming strategy for non-essential services or products that exude informality. Puns thus proliferate in the names of pet shops and pet services (e.g., *Indiana Bones and the Temple of Groom*, *Hairy Pop-Ins*), hair salons (*Curl Up and Dye*), casual food emporia (*Thai Me Up*, *Jurassic Pork*, *I Feel Like Crêpe*, *Custard's Last Stand*, *Tequila Mockingbird*) or any small business that relies on a memorable hook to direct future footfall (*Lawn Order*, *Sew It Seams*, *Sofa So Good*). As innovations, punning names are optimal in the sense of Giora et al. [2004], insofar as they ground themselves in the familiar source domain of a cozy idiom ("*so far, so good*") or a popular TV show ("*Law and Order*") or a film ("*Indiana Jones and the Temple of Doom*") and give their audience a tiny thrill of recognition when first they encounter them. Such puns place greater emphasize on sound similarity than on semantic similarity, yet they best sit on a metaphorical chassis that allows properties of a source domain (e.g., the certainty and dependability offered by officers of the law in *Law and Order*, or the excitement of an action movie) to be projected onto the desired target domain (e.g., lawn work). Computational approaches to punning have yielded notable successes (e.g., Binsted and Ritchie [1997], Hempelmann [2008]), leading Özbal and Strapparava [2012] to obtain promising results for a pun-based automated naming system. With tongue placed firmly in anesthetized cheek, these authors suggest that the punning name "*Fatal Extraction*" might be used to imbue a dentist's advertisement with humor. To appreciate why intelligent punning is a figurative process that requires much the same insight into the relationship between the source and target ideas as a metaphor, consider another example: Özbal and Strapparava suggest that a vendor of cruise holidays might find use for the slogan "*Tomorrow is Another Bay*." But of course, the slogan only works because it projects appropriate associations (from *Gone With The Wind*) into the domain of holidays. The pun "*Die Another Bay*," although similar in structure and just as humorous, has no place in an advert for vacation cruises.

Another strategy for linguistic invention—the portmanteau word or formal blend—is also commonly used in branding, and is one that, like punning, makes frequent use of implicit metaphors. Özbal and Strapparava [2012] thus use a portmanteau strategy to propose apt new names for products and their salient qualities, and their system proposes e.g., "Televi*sun*" as a name for an extra-bright television. Names such as these, in which a given product (e.g., *television*) is identified with a stereotype (e.g., *sun*) for a particular property (e.g., *bright*), effectively compress the source and target of a metaphor into a single word. As noted in Veale [2006b], many of the most provocative (as opposed to merely concise) portmanteaux exploit a compressed metaphor, and thus require a figurative competence to intelligently generate and understand. For instance, the portmanteau *"Feminazi"* is a formal blend of "feminist" and "Nazi" which certain political pundits (such as Rush Limbaugh) employ to describe women who seem *too* strident in their fight for sexual equality. So just as "Televi*sun*" implies that the TV sits at the center of its owner's living room and perhaps even its owner's life, *"Feminazi"* suggests the proportional analogy *Feminist:Feminism::Nazi:Totalitarianism.*

Veale [2011] presents a computational paradigm named *CIR*, or *Creative Information Retrieval*, that is based on the observation that much of what is deemed creative in language is either a wholesale reuse of existing linguistic forms—linguistic *readymades*—or a coherent patchwork of modified readymades. CIR provides a non-literal query language to permit creative systems to retrieve suitable readymades with appropriate meanings from a corpus of text fragments such as the Google n-grams. In the CIR query language, *@Noun* matches any adjective that denotes a stereotypical property of *Noun* (so, e.g., *@knife* matches *sharp, pointy,* etc.) while *@Adj* matches any noun for which *Adj* is stereotypical (e.g., *@sharp* matches *sword, laser, razor,* etc.). In addition, *?Adj* matches any property or behavior that co-occurs with, and reinforces, the property denoted by *Adj* in similes; thus, *?hot* matches *humid, sultry,* and *spicy.* Likewise, *?Noun* matches any noun that denotes a pragmatic neighbor of *Noun,* where two words are neighbors if a corpus attests to the fact that they are often coordinated in language as comparable ideas, as in the Google 3-grams *"lawyers and doctors"* or *"pirates and thieves."* Thus, the query *"@cold @cold"* will retrieve bi-gram phrases whose first and second words denote a stereotype of coldness, such as *"robot fish"* or *"January snow."* The retrieved phrases may never have been used figuratively in their original contexts of use, but they can now be re-used to evocatively convey coldness in novel witticisms, similes, and epithets. Veale [2011] uses CIR as a flexible middleware layer in a robust model of affective metaphor interpretation and generation that also combines metaphors to generate poetry, while Veale [2012a] uses CIR in a generative model of irony, to coin ironic descriptions such as *"as threatening as a wet whisper"* and *"as strong as a cardboard tank."* A key advantage of using linguistic readymades for automated invention—perhaps the single biggest reason to exploit readymades—is that, as phrases, their syntactic and semantic wellformedness is attested by the outputs of human authors. Veale [2013b] outlines how a CIR middleware layer facilitates the robust engineering of a variety of existing figurative language applications, and suggests how a range of others that rely on related forms of linguistic appropriation might also become a practical reality using CIR.

7.2.3 NARRATIVE POSSIBILITIES: FROM METAPHOR TO METAMORPHOSIS

The imagination often takes flight on the wings of metaphor, allowing manufacturers to sell an appealing vision of a product to potential buyers, and allowing landmark television shows such as *Breaking Bad* to showcase imaginative story-telling at its most dramatic and its most transformational. *Breaking Bad* tells the tale of put-upon family man Walter White, a scientist with a brilliant mind who is trapped in the colorless life of a high-school chemistry teacher. When Walter is diagnosed with terminal lung cancer, he throws suburban caution to the wind and embraces a life of crime, first as a drug chemist of blue crystal *meth*, and later as the ruthless drug baron *Heisenberg*. Walter's transformation, "*from Mister Chips to Scarface*" (in the words of the show's creator Vince Gilligan) is psychologically compelling because it is so unexpected yet so strongly rooted in our common-sense notions of similarity: for a drug chemist and a chemistry teacher share many of the same skills, while a drug baron embodies many of the same moral flaws as a drug chemist. Like the best metaphorical juxtapositions, it suggests a creative transformation that seems so very obvious *after* the fact.

Literary transformations are often freighted with metaphorical meaning. Just think of the transformations of people into apt animals or plants in Ovid's *Metamorphoses*, or of Gregor Samsa's sudden, shame-driven transformation into a "*gigantic vermin*" in Franz Kafka's *Metamorphosis*. In *Breaking Bad*, where Walter's central transformation is slow-burning rather than magically immediate, a literal transformation is explained by the same kind of similarity judgments that motivate many of the most imaginative metaphors. A system capable of producing apt metaphors, rooted in meaningful similarities, might thus be re-purposed to propose unexpected-but-plausible character arcs for psychologically compelling stories. For, although Walter's journey from chemistry teacher to drug baron is made believable by similarity, it is made stimulating by *dis*similarity. Like the best metaphors, a thought-provoking character transformation marries states that are both similar and incongruously dissimilar, and so a transformation—or what we might call a *character arc*—from *A* to *B* is all the more surprising if our stereotype of *A* has properties that conflict with those in our stereotype of *B*. Thus, the metaphorical tension inherent in describing a scientist as a priest (of science) suggests the dramatic transformation of a scientist into a priest, while a healthy sense of irony can suggest the transformation of a nun into a prostitute (or vice versa), or a king into a slave, or a fool into a philosopher. Each metaphor-inspired transformation capitalizes on the dramatic possibilities of the oppositions that give the corresponding metaphors their semantic tension.

Veale [2014] presents a metaphor-driven system named *The Flux Capacitor* that serves as a simple generator of thought-provoking narrative arcs for use in automated story-generation. The system generates arcs of the form *what if an instance of class A became an instance of class B*, where its stereotypical representation of class *A* and class *B* suggest an obvious but interesting semantic opposition. *The Flux Capacitor* provides its transformations to an autonomous Twitterbot named *@MetaphorMagnet* (see Veale et al. [2015]), which packages these high-tension changes in the form of pithy, eye-catching tweets. The following tweets are representative of its outputs:

> *To arrange and throw a party: This can turn annoying wasps into entertaining hosts.*
> *#Wasp = #Host*

> *To join and travel in a pack: This can turn pretty girls into ugly coyotes. #Girl = #Coyote*

> *To believe in and enforce discipline: This can turn humble subordinates into haughty disciplinarians.*
> *#Subordinate = #Disciplinarian*

To incite and lead a mob: This can turn shy youngsters into outspoken rabble rousers.
#Youngster = #Rabble_rouser

If we accept that metaphorical conceits need not always be rendered as *metaphors* at the linguistic level, then our metaphor-generating tools can be used in diverse and unexpected ways to meet diverse creative needs in language.

CHAPTER 8

Conclusions

One of most profoundly useful lessons that software engineers learn in the course of their careers is this: the users of our software have minds of their own. Users do not always share the same mental model of a problem as a system's designers, nor do they always approach a system's interface with the same expectations. So when a system asks a user to enter a number, a user may prefer to enter a string like "*forty two*" rather than the integer *42*. A user's preferred format for dates may be different to that anticipated by a system's data structures, or a system may not anticipate all the ways in which a user can be exceptional and thereby fall into the cracks in its representations. Some users, for instance, may prefer to tick both the *male* and *female* checkboxes, while others may want to tick neither. Or a user may simply enter the right information in the right format into the wrong field. Real users are the best testers, and some can test our systems in surprising ways that show up the deep limitations in our designs. Many such problems can be mitigated by good interface design, but short of making its users employ an artificial sub-language, a robust NLP system that is expected to work with free text—including metaphor—must be ready for anything. While an NLP engineer cannot anticipate everything, a good engineer will build a degree of robustness into a system to allow it to deal gracefully with the unexpected, especially when the user is actually right.

This is the most important application of computational metaphor processing: it adds robustness to our NLP systems and makes their treatment of meaning and speaker intent more expansive and less brittle. As early as Hobbs [1981], computational researchers have argued that metaphor should not be processed as a special (and especially troublesome) use of language that demands its own bolt-on module with its own specialist and rather ad-hoc processes. Rather, metaphor, metonymy, synecdoche, and related figurative phenomena should be handled as organic applications of the same selective-inference procedures that deal with other, more mundane aspects of language comprehension—such as "*forcing congruence between predicates and their arguments, and anaphora and ambiguity resolution*"—and that set out to construct the most coherent understanding of a text and its discourse structure using a small number of very general principles such as viewing *interpretation as abduction* (Hobbs et al. [1993]). As shown by the work of Martin [1990], even practical, domain-specific NLP systems—such as the *Unix Consultant* of Wilensky et al. [1988]—demand a robust fluency in metaphor. Although metaphor is the stuff of fanciful poetry and high-flying oratory, it is also the stuff of everyday communication. The ultimate NLP application of metaphor *is* NLP.

If a computational model of metaphor is to make our NLP systems more robust, it must itself exhibit robustness if it is not to become yet another source of brittleness in an already complex processing pipeline. Yet robustness is not a function of the specific theory to which one subscribes, as every theoretical approach has its own strengths and its own weaknesses. Each views metaphor as a different kind of process—as a means of divergent categorization, or as a correctable deviation from the norm, or as a relational projection from one domain into another, or as the final product of a conceptual blueprint that can be used to build many variations on the same theme. But, if metaphor acts like a knife in one context and a corkscrew in another, we should not aim to build the computational equivalent of a *Swiss-army knife*, a single baroque system that incorporates a fold-out module for every possible perspective on the phenomenon. Rather than hide the multiplicity of metaphor, our solutions should allow an NLP system to select the particular approaches to figurative language that are best suited to a given text. NLP systems should thus have the latitude to decide on the most appropriate level at which to apply different approaches and the most effective order in which to invoke them. For example, an NLP system may prefer a particular approach to interpret copula metaphors, or to disentangle obviously metaphorical uses of the copula form, such as "*marriage is slavery*," from divergent but not obviously figurative uses of categorization such as "*marriage is a legal contract*" or "*marriage is a partnership*." It may choose to employ a different approach to disentangle potential metonymies from possible metaphors, as in the statement "*You speak treason, sir*" (response: "*fluently!*"). One NLP system may be satisfied by a metonymic interpretation, in which "*treason*" simply stands for "*the expression of treasonous sentiments*," while another may wish to look deeper, to see "*treason*" as a reference to an entire language of meaningful—if politically subversive—possibilities. One NLP system may be satisfied with a superficial, conventional reading of the metaphor "*Chris Christie, Republican heavyweight*" (as used on the cover of the *Economist* newspaper), in which Christie is simply seen as a *powerful* member of the Republican party. Another, however, may seek a reading that also takes account of the far-from-subtle pun in this metaphor; Christie is not just a powerful politician but a famously *heavy* and rotund politician, too, to the extent that the man's diet is also a source of political fodder. Or indeed, one NLP system may be satisfied to take the *Economist* at its word and treat it as a *newspaper*; another may use the flexible categorization offered by metaphor to reconcile the *Economist*'s description of itself with the fact that it is packaged and sold as a weekly *magazine*. Figurative processing needs vary from application to application and context to context, thus it makes sense to package the diverse algorithms and resources for handling various types of figurative phenomena as *web services*, online systems that hide the complexity of metaphor processing yet which can be called upon to generate and understand linguistic metaphors on demand.

There are compelling reasons to see metaphor as a solution rather than as a problem, as a service (or ecology of services) that can be called upon to inject variety and novelty into our own language, or to appreciate variety and novelty in the language of others (see Veale [2013c]). Many creative language tasks—such as poetry, joke, and story generation—require the conceptual and linguistic divergence offered by metaphor, to say nothing of the semantic challenges posed by the ubiquity of metaphor in everyday language. When figurative competence is offered via reusable and composable web services, NLP systems need not implement their own metaphor solutions, and are instead freed to focus on providing their own unique competences. Whether we view it as a problem or as a solution, metaphor is not yet a *standardized* phenomenon in NLP, and so different researchers focus on diverse aspects of metaphor using a wide range of bespoke models and linguistic resources. But when these models are provided as public services, researchers are free to draw from a rich ecology of complementary solutions without inheriting either their complexity or their resource-dependence. New approaches to metaphor, and to broader problems of linguistic creativity, may then emerge as researchers and developers mix and match services to meet their own specific application needs.

Large business organizations frequently outsource their creative needs to external agencies that specialize in *thinking differently*. These agencies provide services that broaden the range of options that are accessible to an organization, and have the benefit of learning from their many different commissions in diverse genres, areas of business, and modes of creative expression. While organizations aim to attract and retain creative people of their own, external agencies provide a constant, reliable, and informative service that greatly reduces the overheads associated with creative decision-making. Large software systems, like large business organizations, can also benefit from the services of an external creative agency, in the form of a suite of web services rather than a company of creative professionals. This outsourcing to the Web makes particular sense when dealing with creative services like metaphor, analogy, conceptual blending, knowledge discovery, etc., because these services offer much more than simple algorithms. Rather, such services need to integrate a complex array of algorithms, world knowledge, and large sources of evidential data (such as text corpora). Moreover, theories and models of these creative phenomena are still very much in flux, while the knowledge they hungrily consume needs to be continuously acquired, maintained, and updated. It is thus far more convenient for a third-party software application to tap into dynamically updated web services that hide their complexity behind a simple interface than to re-implement these services and resources for themselves. Creative web services, for metaphor and related figurative phenomena, offer a more compelling value proposition—to businesses, application developers, and researchers—than the traditional combination of published algorithms and laboratory prototypes. In turning metaphor into a reliable service, we also transform it from a vexing problem into a versatile solution. This is the kind of transformation that our metaphor-processing systems might one day appreciate for themselves, or indeed *suggest* for themselves.

Bibliography

Jan Aarts and Joseph Calbert. *Metaphor and Non-Metaphor: The Semantics of Adjective Noun Combinations.* Niemeyer, Tübingen, 1979. 35, 36, 38

James Allen, Mary Swift, and Will de Beaumont. Deep semantic analysis of text. In *Proceedings of the 2008 Conference on Semantics in Text Processing*, STEP '08, pages 343–354, Venice, Italy, 2008. DOI: 10.3115/1626481.1626508. 76

Antonietta Alonge and Margherita Castelli. Encoding information on metaphoric expressions in WordNet-like resources. In *Proceedings of the ACL 2003 Workshop on Lexicon and Figurative Language*, pages 10–17, 2003. DOI: 10.3115/1118975.1118977. 75

Joanne Arciuli and James Thompson. Improving the assignment of lexical stress in text-to-speech systems. In *Proceedings of the 11th Australasian International Conference on Speech Science and Technology*, pages 296–300, Auckland, New Zealand, 2006. 62

Ron Artstein and Massimo Poesio. Inter-coder agreement for computational linguistics. *Computational Linguistics*, 34(4):555–596, 2008. DOI: 10.1162/coli.07-034-r2. 58

Olga Babko-Malaya, Ann Bies, Ann Taylor, Szuting Yi, Martha Palmer, Mitch Marcus, Seth Kulick, and Libin Shen. Issues in synchronizing the English treebank and prop-bank. In *Proceedings of the Workshop on Frontiers in Linguistically Annotated Corpora 2006*, pages 70–77, Sydney, Australia, July 2006. Association for Computational Linguistics. DOI: 10.3115/1641991.1642000. 62

Yulia Badryzlova, Yekaterina Isaeva, Ruslan Kerimov, and Natalia Shekhtman. Using the linguistic metaphor identification procedure (MIPVU) on a Russian corpus: rules revised and extended. *Humanitarian Vector*. Series: Philology, vostoko-management, 36 (4), 2013a. 63

Yulia Badryzlova, Natalia Shekhtman, Yekaterina Isaeva, and Ruslan Kerimov. Annotating a russian corpus of conceptual metaphor: a bottom-up approach. In *Proceedings of the First Workshop on Metaphor in NLP*, pages 77–86, Atlanta, GA, 2013b. 63

Timothy Baldwin and Su Nam Kim. Multiword expressions. In N. Indurkhya and F. J. Damerau, editors, *Handbook of Natural Language Processing, Second Edition*, pages 267–292. CRC Press, Taylor and Francis Group, Boca Raton, FL, 2010. 89

Timothy Baldwin and Aline Villavicencio. Extracting the unextractable: A case study on verb-particles. In *Proceedings of the Sixth Conference on Computational Natural Language Learning*, pages 98–104, Taipei, Taiwan, August-September 2002. DOI: 10.3115/1118853.1118854. 62

Valentina Bambini, Donatella Resta, and Mirko Grimaldi. A Dataset of metaphors from the Italian literature: Exploring psycholinguistic variables and the role of context. *PLoS ONE*, 9 (9), 2014. DOI: 10.1371/journal.pone.0105634. 66

John Barnden. Consciousness and common-sense metaphors of mind. In S. O'Nuallain, P. McKevitt, and E. Mac Aogain, editors, *Two Sciences of Mind: Readings in Cognitive Science And Consciousness*, pages 311–340. John Benjamins Publishing Company, 1997. 65

John Barnden. Artificial intelligence, figurative language and cognitive linguistics. In G. Kristiansen, M. Achard, R. Dirven, and F. J. Ruiz de Mendoza Ibanez, editors, *Cognitive Linguistics: Current Application and Future Perspectives*, pages 431–459. Mouton de Gruyter, Berlin, 2006. DOI: 10.1515/9783110197761. 15, 48, 50, 86

John Barnden. Metaphor and metonymy: Making their connections more slippery. *Cognitive Linguistics*, 21(1):1–34, 2010. DOI: 10.1515/cogl.2010.001. 26

John Barnden. Metaphor and simile: Fallacies concerning comparison, ellipsis and inter-paraphrase. *Metaphor and Symbol*, 27(4):265–282, 2012. DOI: 10.1080/10926488.2012.716272. 12

John Barnden and Mark Lee. An artificial intelligence approach to metaphor understanding. *Theoria et Historia Scientiarum*, 6(1):399–412, 2002. 15, 48, 50, 86

Eric Baumer, Bill Tomlinson, and Lindsey Richland. Computational metaphor identification: A method for identifying conceptual metaphors in written text. In *Proceedings of Analogy '09*, Sofia, Bulgaria, 2009. 90

Beata Beigman Klebanov and Eyal Beigman. A game-theoretic model of metaphorical bargaining. In *Proceedings of the 48th Annual Meeting of the Association for Computational Linguistics*, pages 698–709, Uppsala, Sweden, Association for Computational Linguistics, July 2010. 111

Beata Beigman Klebanov and Michael Flor. Argumentation-relevant metaphors in test-taker essays. In *Proceedings of the First Workshop on Metaphor in NLP*, pages 11–20, Atlanta, GA. Association for Computational Linguistics, June 2013. 58, 59, 69, 98, 111

Beata Beigman Klebanov, Daniel Diermeier, and Eyal Beigman. Lexical cohesion analysis of political speech. *Political Analysis*, 16:447–463, 2008. DOI: 10.1093/pan/mpn007. 111

Beata Beigman Klebanov, David Kaufer, and Hillary Franklin. A figure in a field: Semantic fields based analysis of antithesis in political speech. *Cognitive Semiotics*, 6:121–154, 2010. DOI: 10.1515/cogsem.2010.6.spring2010.121. 111

Beata Beigman Klebanov, Chee Wee Leong, Michael Heilman, and Michael Flor. Different texts, same metaphors: Unigrams and beyond. In *Proceedings of the Second Workshop on Metaphor in NLP*, pages 11–17, Baltimore, MD, 2014. DOI: 10.3115/v1/w14-2302. 98, 106

Melanie Bell and Ingo Plag. Informativeness is a determinant of compound stress in english. *Journal of Linguistics*, 48:485–520, 11 2012. ISSN 1469-7742. DOI: 10.1017/s0022226712000199. 62

Benjamin K. Bergen and Nancy C. Chang. Embodied construction grammar in simulation-based language understanding (technical report 02- 004). Technical report, International Computer Science Institute, 2002. DOI: 10.1075/cal.3.08ber. 52

Adam L. Berger, Stephen A. Della Pietra, and Vincent J. Della Pietra. A maximum entropy approach to natural language processing. *Computational Linguistics*, 22:39–71, 1996. 94

Janice Bibik. *Metaphors for Teaching: How Health and Physical Education Teachers Describe their Roles.* Georgetown, DE: McGraw Hill, 1997. 110

Kim Binsted and Graeme Ritchie. Computational rules for generating punning riddles. *Humor, International Journal of Humor Res.*, 10(1):25–76, 1997. DOI: 10.1515/humr.1997.10.1.25. 114

Julia Birke and Anoop Sarkar. A clustering approach for the nearly unsupervised recognition of nonliteral language. In *Proceedings of EACL-06*, pages 329–336, 2006. 66, 95, 101, 102, 105

Max Black. *Models and Metaphors: Studies in Language and Philosophy.* Cornell University Press, NY, 1962. 5, 10, 24

Max Black. How metaphors work: A reply to Donald Davidson. *Critical Inquiry*, 6(1):131–143, 1979. DOI: 10.1086/448033. 11

David Blei, Andrew Ng, and Michael Jordan. Latent dirichlet allocation. *Journal of Machine Learning Research*, 3:993–1022, 2003. 89, 103

Frank Boers and Murielle Demecheleer. Measuring the impact of cross-cultural differences in learners' comprehension of imageable idioms. *ELT Journal*, 55(3):255–262, 2001. DOI: 10.1093/elt/55.3.255. 112

Danushka Bollegala and Ekaterina Shutova. Metaphor interpretation using paraphrases extracted from the web. *PLoS ONE*, 8(9):e74304, 2013. DOI: 10.1371/journal.pone.0074304. 15, 79, 85, 92

Jan Bosman. Persuasive effects of political metaphors. *Metaphor and Symbolic Activity*, 2:97–113, 1987. DOI: 10.1207/s15327868ms0202_2. 111

Ram Boukobza and Ari Rappoport. Multi-word expression identification using sentence surface features. In *Proceedings of the 2009 Conference on Empirical Methods in Natural Language Processing: Volume 2 - Volume 2*, EMNLP '09, pages 468–477, Stroudsburg, PA, 2009. Association for Computational Linguistics. ISBN 978-1-932432-62-6. DOI: 10.3115/1699571.1699573. 63

Brian Bowdle and Dedre Gentner. The career of metaphor. *Psychological Review*, 112(1):193–216, 2005. DOI: 10.1037/0033-295x.112.1.193. 19, 39

David Bracewell, Marc Tomlinson, Michael Mohler, and Bryan Rink. A tiered approach to the recognition of metaphor. *Computational Linguistics and Intelligent Text Processing*, 8403:403–414, 2014. DOI: 10.1007/978-3-642-54906-9_33. 105

Thorsten Brants and Alex Franz. *Web 1T 5-gram Version 1*. Linguistic Data Consortium, 2006. 81, 85, 105

Susan Brennan and Herbert Clark. Conceptual pacts and lexical choice in conversation. *Journal of Experimental Psychology: Learning, Memory and Cognition*, 22(6):1482–1493, 1996. DOI: 10.1037/0278-7393.22.6.1482. 7

Geert Brône and Kurt Feyaerts. Headlines and cartoons in the economic press: Double grounding as a discourse supportive strategy. In G. Jacobs and G. Erreygers, editors, *Discourse and Economics*, Amsterdam, 2005. John Benjamins. 24

Marc Brysbaert, Amy Warriner, and Victor Kuperman. Concreteness ratings for 40 thousand generally known English word lemmas. *Behavior Research Methods*, 46(3):904–911, 2013. DOI: 10.3758/s13428-013-0403-5. 98

Jill Burstein, John Sabatini, Jane Shore, Brad Moulder, and Jennifer Lentini. A user study: Technology to increase teachers' linguistic awareness to improve instructional language support for English language learners. In *Proceedings of the Workshop on Natural Language Processing for Improving Textual Accessibility*, pages 1–10, Atlanta, GA, June 2013. Association for Computational Linguistics. 112

Lynne Cameron. *Metaphor in Educational Discourse*. Continuum, London, 2003. 55, 110, 111

Lynne Cameron. Patterns of metaphor use in reconciliation talk. *Discourse and Society*, 18(2): 197–222, 2007. DOI: 10.1177/0957926507073376. 20, 31

Mark Cannice and Arthur Bell. Metaphors used by venture capitalists: Darwinism, architecture and myth. *Venture Capital*, 12(1):1–20, 2010. DOI: 10.1080/13691060903184787. 110

Jaime Carbonell. Metaphor: An inescapable phenomenon in natural language comprehension. In Wendy Lehnert and Martin Ringle, editors, *Strategies for Natural Language Processing*, pages 415–434. Lawrence Erlbaum, 1982. 39, 40, 42, 46, 48, 64

Eileen Cardillo, Gwenda Schmidt, Alexander Kranjec, and Anjan Chatterjee. Stimulus design is an obstacle course: 560 matched literal and metaphorical sentences for testing neural hypotheses about metaphor. *Behavior Research Methods*, 42(3):651–664, 2010. DOI: 10.3758/brm.42.3.651. 65

Helena Caseli, Aline Villavicencio, André Machado, and Maria José Finatto. Statistically-driven alignment-based multiword expression identification for technical domains. In *Proceedings of the Workshop on Multiword Expressions: Identification, Interpretation, Disambiguation and Applications*, pages 1–8, Singapore, August 2009. Association for Computational Linguistics. DOI: 10.3115/1698239.1698241. 63

Marco Casonato. *Immaginazione e Metafora*. Roma, Italy: Laterza, 2003. 110

Arthur Cater. Conceptual primitives and their metaphorical relationships. In *Proceedings of the 1985 International Symposium on Discourse Processing*, St. Patrick's College, Dublin, Ireland, 1985. 37, 38, 52

Jonathan Charteris-Black. Speaking with forked tongue: A comparative study of metaphor and metonymy in English and Malay phraseology. *Metaphor and Symbol*, 18(4):289–310, 2003. DOI: 10.1207/s15327868ms1804_5. 110

Jonathan Charteris-Black. *Politicians and Rhetoric: The Persuasive Power of Metaphor*. Palgrave, 2005. 55, 111

Jonathan Charteris-Black and Timothy Ennis. A comparative study of metaphor in Spanish and English financial reporting. *English for Specific Purposes*, 20(3):249–266, 2001. DOI: 10.1016/s0889-4906(00)00009-0. 95, 110

Rudi Cilibrasi and Paul Vitanyi. The Google similarity distance. *IEEE Transactional on Knowledge and Data Engineering*, 19(3):370–383, 2007. DOI: 10.1109/tkde.2007.48. 97

Rodney Clarken. Five metaphors for educators. In *Proceedings of the Annual Meeting of the American Education Research Association*, Chicago, March 1997. 110

Allan Collins and Elizabeth Loftus. A spreading-activation theory of semantic processing. *Psychological Review*, 82(6):407–428, 1975. DOI: 10.1037/0033-295x.82.6.407. 42

Corinna Cortes and Vladimir Vapnik. Support-vector networks. *Machine Learning*, 20(3):273–297, 1995. 96

Garrison W. Cottrell. Toward connectionist semantics. In *Proceedings of TINLAP '87, the 1987 workshop on Theoretical issues in natural language processing*, TINLAP '87, pages 65–70, 1987. DOI: 10.3115/980304.980318. 37, 38, 51

DR Cox. The regression analysis of binary sequences (with discussion). *Journal of the Royal Statistical Society B*, 20:215–242, 1958. 94

William Croft. The role of domains in the interpretation of metaphors and metonymies. In René Dirven and Ralf Porings, editors, *Metaphor and Metonymy in Comparison and Contrast*, pages 161–206, Mouton de Gruyter, Berlin, 1993. 2003. 51, 52

Silviu Cucerzan. Large-scale named entity disambiguation based on Wikipedia data. In *Proceedings of the 2007 Joint Conference on Empirical Methods in Natural Language Processing and Computational Natural Language Learning (EMNLP-CoNLL)*, pages 708–716, Prague, Czech Republic, June 2007. Association for Computational Linguistics. 62

Marcel Danesi. Metaphorical competence in second language acquisition and second language teaching: The neglected dimension. *Language, communication and social meaning*, pages 489–500, 1993. 111

Donald Davidson. What metaphors mean. *Critical Inquiry (Special Issue on Metaphor)*, 5(5): 31–47, 1978. DOI: 10.1086/447971. 10, 11, 24

Luciana de Castro Salgado, Clarisse de Souza, and Carla Leitão. Using metaphors to explore cultural perspectives in cross-cultural design. In *Internationalization, Design and Global Development*, pages 94–103. Springer, 2011. DOI: 10.1007/978-3-642-21660-2_11. 110

Paul Deane. A nonparametric method for extraction of candidate phrasal terms. In *Proceedings of the 43rd Annual Meeting of the Association for Computational Linguistics (ACL'05)*, pages 605–613, Ann Arbor, MI, June 2005. Association for Computational Linguistics. DOI: 10.3115/1219840.1219915. 63

Alice Deignan. Metaphorical expressions and culture: An indirect link. *Metaphor and Symbol*, 18 (4):255–271, 2003. DOI: 10.1207/s15327868ms1804_3. 110

Alice Deignan and Liz Potter. A corpus study of metaphors and metonyms in English and Italian. *Journal of Pragmatics*, 36:1231–1252, 2004. DOI: 10.1016/j.pragma.2003.10.010. 110

Alice Deignan, Danuta Gabrys, and Agnieszka Solska. Teaching English metaphors using cross-linguistic awareness-raising activities. *ELT Journal*, 51(4):352–360, 1997. DOI: 10.1093/elt/51.4.352. 112

Ton den Boon and Dirk Geeraerts, editors. *Van Dale Groot Woordenboek van de Nedelandse taal, 14th edition*. Utrecht & Antwerp: Van Dale Lexicografie, 2005. 63

Javier Diaz-Vera and Rosario Caballero. Exploring the feeling-emotions continuum across cultures: Jealousy in English and Spanish. *Intercultural Pragmatics*, 10(2):265–294, 2013. DOI: 10.1515/ip-2013-0012. 95, 110

Zhendong Dong and Qiang Dong. *HowNet and the Computation of Meaning*. World Scientific, Singapore, 2006. DOI: 10.1142/9789812774675. 74, 78, 82

Qing Dou, Shane Bergsma, Sittichai Jiampojamarn, and Grzegorz Kondrak. A ranking approach to stress prediction for letter-to-phoneme conversion. In *Proceedings of the Joint Conference of the 47th Annual Meeting of the ACL and the 4th International Joint Conference on Natural Language Processing of the AFNLP*, pages 118–126, Suntec, Singapore, August 2009. Association for Computational Linguistics. DOI: 10.3115/1687878.1687897. 62

Jonathan Dunn. Evaluating the premises and results of four metaphor identification systems. In *Proceedings of CICLing'13*, pages 471–486, Samos, Greece, 2013a. DOI: 10.1007/978-3-642-37247-6_38. 78, 94

Jonathan Dunn. What metaphor identification systems can tell us about metaphor-in-language. In *Proceedings of the First Workshop on Metaphor in NLP*, pages 1–10, Atlanta, GA, 2013b. 78, 94, 95

Michele Emanatian. Metaphor and the expression of emotion: The value of cross-cultural perspectives. *Metaphor and Symbolic Activity*, 10(3):163–182, 1995. DOI: 10.1207/s15327868ms1003_2. 110

Robert Entman. Language: The loaded weapon. *Political Communication*, (20):415–432, 2003. 110

Katrin Erk and Sebastian Padó. A structured vector space model for word meaning in context. In *Proceedings of the Conference on Empirical Methods in Natural Language Processing*, pages 897–906, Waikiki, HI, USA, 2008. DOI: 10.3115/1613715.1613831. 104

Katrin Erk and Sebastian Padó. Paraphrase assessment in structured vector space: Exploring parameters and datasets. In *Proceedings of the Workshop on Geometrical Models of Natural Language Semantics*, pages 57–65, Athens, Greece, 2009. DOI: 10.3115/1705415.1705423. 104

Katrin Erk and Sebastian Padó. Exemplar-based models for word meaning in context. In *Proceedings of the ACL 2010 Conference Short Papers*, pages 92–97, Uppsala, Sweden, 2010. 104

Thomas Evans. A heuristic program to solve geometric-analogy problems. In *Proceedings of AFIPS (American Federation of Information Processing Societies) joint computer conference*, pages 327–338, NY, 1964. DOI: 10.1145/1464122.1464156. 39

Theresa Eynon. Cognitive linguistics. *Advances in Psychiatric Treatment*, 8:399–407, 2002. DOI: 10.1192/apt.8.6.399. 110

Norman Fairclough. *Language and Power*. NY: Pearson Education Ltd., 2nd ed., 2003. 111

Brian Falkenhainer, Kenneth D. Forbus, and Dedre Gentner.   Structure-mapping engine: Algorithm and examples. *Artificial Intelligence*, 41:1–63, 1989. DOI: 10.1016/0004-3702(89)90077-5. 42

Dan Fass. Collative semantics: A semantics for natural language processing. Technical report, New Mexico State University, NM, 1988. 34

Dan Fass. met*: A method for discriminating metonymy and metaphor by computer. *Computational Linguistics*, 17(1):49–90, 1991. 75, 90

Gilles Fauconnier. *Mental spaces: aspects of meaning construction in natural language*. Cambridge University Press, 1994. DOI: 10.1017/cbo9780511624582. 25

Gilles Fauconnier. *Mappings in Thought and Language*. Cambridge University Press, 1997. DOI: 10.1017/cbo9781139174220. 25

Gilles Fauconnier and Mark Turner. Conceptual projection and middle spaces (technical report 9401). Technical report, University of California at San Diego, Department of Computer Science, 1994. 53

Gilles Fauconnier and Mark Turner. *The Way We Think: Conceptual Blending and the Mind's Hidden Complexities*. Basic Books, NY, 2002. 10, 25, 26, 28

Jerome Feldman. *From Molecule to Metaphor: A Neural Theory of Language*. The MIT Press, 2006. 23, 51

Jerome Feldman and Srini Narayanan. Embodied meaning in a neural theory of language. *Brain and Language*, 89(2):385–392, 2004. DOI: 10.1016/s0093-934x(03)00355-9. 51, 52, 53

Christiane Fellbaum, editor. *WordNet: An Electronic Lexical Database (ISBN: 0-262-06197-X)*. MIT Press, 1st ed., 1998. 63, 73, 82

Charles Fillmore, Christopher Johnson, and Miriam Petruck. Background to FrameNet. *International Journal of Lexicography*, 16(3):235–250, 2003. DOI: 10.1093/ijl/16.3.235. 77, 94

Jenny Finkel, Trond Grenager, and Christopher Manning. Incorporating non-local information into information extraction systems by Gibbs sampling. In *Proceedings of the 43rd Annual Meeting of the Association for Computational Linguistics (ACL'05)*, pages 363–370, Ann Arbor, MI, June 2005. Association for Computational Linguistics. DOI: 10.3115/1219840.1219885. 62

David Fishelov. Poetic and non-poetic simile: Structure, semantics, rhetoric. *Poetics Today*, 14 (1):1–23, 1992. DOI: 10.2307/1773138. 80

W. Nelson Francis and Henry Kučera. A Standard Corpus of Present-Day Edited American English. Technical report, Brown University. Providence, RI, 1979. 96

Lisa Gandy, Nadji Allan, Mark Atallah, Ophir Frieder, Newton Howard, Sergey Kanareykin, Moshe Koppel, Mark Last, Yair Neuman, and Shlomo Argamon. Automatic identification of conceptual metaphors with limited knowledge. In *Proceedings of AAAI 2013*, 2013. 77, 99, 106, 107

Matt Gedigian, John Bryant, Srini Narayanan, and Branimir Ciric. Catching metaphors. In *Proceedings of the 3rd Workshop on Scalable Natural Language Understanding*, pages 41–48, NY, 2006. DOI: 10.3115/1621459.1621467. 77, 94

Dedre Gentner. Structure-mapping: A theoretical framework. *Cognitive Science*, 7(2):155–170, 1983. 6, 18, 40, 42, 48

Dedre Gentner, Brian Falkenhainer, and Janice Skorstad. Metaphor: The good, the bad and the ugly. In Yorick Wilks, editor, *Theoretical Issues in NLP*. Lawrence Erlbaum Associates, Hillsdale, NJ., 1989. 39, 41

Rachel Giora, Ofer Fein, Ann Kronrod, Idit Elnatan, Noa Shuval, and Adi Zur. Weapons of mass distraction: Optimal innovation and pleasure ratings. *Metaphor and Symbol*, 19(2):115–141, 2004. DOI: 10.1207/s15327868ms1902_2. 114

Rachel Giora, Ofer Fein, Nili Metuki, and Pnina Stern. Negation as a metaphor-inducing operator. In L. R. Horn, editor, *The Expression of Negation*. Mouton de Gruyter, Berlin, 2010. DOI: 10.1515/9783110219302. 16

Sam Glucksberg. Understanding metaphors. *Current Directions in Psychological Science*, 7:39–43, 1998. DOI: 10.1111/1467-8721.ep13175582. 17

Sam Glucksberg. How metaphor creates categories – quickly! In Jr. Raymond W. Gibbs, editor, *The Cambridge Handbook of Metaphor and Thought*. Cambridge University Press, Cambridge, 2008. DOI: 10.1017/cbo9780511816802.001. 17

Sam Glucksberg and Catherine Haught. On the relation between metaphor and simile: When comparison fails. *Mind and Language*, 21(3):360–378, 2006. DOI: 10.1111/j.1468-0017.2006.00282.x. 12, 80

Joseph A. Goguen and Fox D. Harrell. Style: A computational and conceptual blending-based approach. In *The Structure of Style: Algorithmic Approaches to Understanding Manner and Meaning*, page 147–170. Berlin, 2010. DOI: 10.1007/978-3-642-12337-5_12. 53

Adele E. Goldberg. *Constructions: A Construction Grammar Approach to Argument Structure*. University of Chicago Press, Chicago and London, 1995. 51

Joe Grady. Foundations of meaning: primary metaphors and primary scenes. Technical report, Ph.D. thesis, University of California at Berkeley, 1997. 21, 51, 96, 104

Joseph Grady. Primary metaphors as inputs to conceptual integration. *J. Pragmatics*, 37:1595–1614, 2005. DOI: 10.1016/j.pragma.2004.03.012. 26, 96

Paul Grice. Logic and conversation. In P. Cole and J. Morgan, editors, *Syntax and Semantics 3: Speech Acts*, pages 41–58. Academic Press, NY, 1978. 10

Yanfen Hao and Tony Veale. An ironic fist in a velvet glove: Creative mis-representation in the construction of ironic similes. *Minds and Machines*, 20(4):483–488, 2010. DOI: 10.1007/s11023-010-9211-1. 85

Marti Hearst. Automatic acquisition of hyponyms from large text corpora. In *Proceedings of the 14th Conference on Computational Linguistics - Volume 2*, COLING '92, pages 539–545, Stroudsburg, PA, 1992. Association for Computational Linguistics. DOI: 10.3115/992133.992154. 80, 85, 87

Ilana Heintz, Ryan Gabbard, Mahesh Srivastava, Dave Barner, Donald Black, Majorie Friedman, and Ralph Weischedel. Automatic extraction of linguistic metaphors with LDA topic modeling. In *Proceedings of the First Workshop on Metaphor in NLP*, pages 58–66, Atlanta, GA, 2013. 102, 103

Christian Hempelmann. Computational humor: Beyond the pun. In Victor Raskin, editor, *The Primer of Humor Research*. Mouton de Gruyter, Berlin, 2008. DOI: 10.1515/9783110198492. 114

John Heywood, Elena Semino, and Mich Short. Linguistic metaphor identification in two extracts from novels. *Language and Literature*, 1:35–54, 2002. DOI: 10.1177/096394700201100104. 55

Hung Huu Hoang, Su Nam Kim, and Min-Yen Kan. A re-examination of lexical association measures. In *Proceedings of the Workshop on Multiword Expressions*, pages 31–39. Association for Computational Linguistics, 2009. DOI: 10.3115/1698239.1698246. 89

Jerry Hobbs. Metaphor, metaphor schemata and selective inferencing (technical note 204). Technical report, SRI International, Artificial Intelligence Center, 1979. 44, 45

Jerry Hobbs. Metaphor interpretation as selective inferencing. In *Proceedings of the 7th International Joint Conference on Artificial Intelligence - Volume 1*, IJCAI'81, pages 85–91, Vancouver, BC, Canada, 1981. DOI: 10.2190/5kje-327r-felr-gawl. 16, 44, 119

Jerry Hobbs. Metaphor and abduction (technical note 508). Technical report, SRI International, Artificial Intelligence Center, 1991. 44, 45, 49, 77

Jerry Hobbs, Mark Stickel, Douglas Appelt, and Paul Martin. Interpretation as abduction. *Artificial Intelligence*, 63(1-2):69–142, 1993. DOI: 10.1016/0004-3702(93)90015-4. 44, 119

Keith Holyoak and Paul Thagard. Analogical mapping by constraint satisfaction. *Cognitive Science*, 13:295–355, 1989. DOI: 10.1207/s15516709cog1303_1. 39, 42

Dirk Hovy, Taylor Berg-Kirkpatrick, Ashish Vaswani, and Eduard Hovy. Learning whom to trust with mace. In *Proceedings of the 2013 Conference of the North American Chapter of the Association for Computational Linguistics: Human Language Technologies*, pages 1120–1130, Atlanta, GA, June 2013a. Association for Computational Linguistics. 67, 96

Dirk Hovy, Shashank Shrivastava, Sujay Kumar Jauhar, Mrinmaya Sachan, Kartik Goyal, Huying Li, Whitney Sanders, and Eduard Hovy. Identifying metaphorical word use with tree kernels. In *Proceedings of the First Workshop on Metaphor in NLP*, pages 52–57, Atlanta, GA, 2013b. 59, 67, 77, 90, 96

Shelby Hunt and Anil Menon. Metaphors and competitive advantage: Evaluating the use of metaphors in theories of competitive strategy. *Journal of Business Research*, 33:81–90, 1995. DOI: 10.1016/0148-2963(94)00057-l. 110

James Hutton. *Aristotle's Poetics (English translation)*. Norton, NY, 1982. 6

Bipin Indurkhya. *Metaphor and Cognition: an interactionist approach*. Studies in Cognitive Systems. Kluwer Academic, Amsterdam, 1992. 10, 39

Eric Iverson and Stephen Helmreich. Metallel: An integrated approach to non-literal phrase intrepretation. *Computational Intelligence*, 8:477–493, 1992. DOI: 10.1111/j.1467-8640.1992.tb00376.x. 35

Sattar Izwaini. Corpus-based study of metaphor in information technology. In *Proceedings of the Workshop on Corpus-based Approaches to Figurative Language, Corpus Linguistics 2003*, Lancaster, 2003. 110

Hyeju Jang, Mario Piergallini, Miaomiao Wen, and Carolyn Rose. Conversational metaphors in use: Exploring the contrast between technical and everyday notions of metaphor. In *Proceedings of the Second Workshop on Metaphor in NLP*, pages 1–10, Baltimore, MD, June 2014. Association for Computational Linguistics. DOI: 10.3115/v1/w14-2301. 59, 70, 110

Christopher Johnson. Metaphor versus conflation in the acquisition of polysemy: the case of see. In M.K Hiraga, C. Sinha, and S. Wilcox, editors, *Cultural, Typological and Psychological Perspectives in Cognitive Linguistics*, pages 155–169. John Benjamins, Amsterdam, 1999. DOI: 10.1075/cilt.152. 21, 51

Mark Johnson, editor. *The Body in the Mind: The Bodily Basis of Meaning, Imagination, and Reason*. University of Chicago Press, Chicago, IL, 1987. DOI: 10.2307/431155. 20, 22, 46

Yael Karov and Shimon Edelman. Similarity-based word sense disambiguation. *Computational Linguistics*, 24(1):41–59, 1998. 101

Sujata Kathpalia and Heah Lee Hah Carmel. Metaphorical competence in ESL student writing. *Journal of Language Teaching and Research (RELC)*, 42(3):273–290, 2011. DOI: 10.1177/0033688211419379. 111

Jerrold Katz and Jerry Fodor. The Structure of Semantic Theory. In J. Katz and J. Fodor, editors, *The Structure of Language*, pages 479–518, Prentice Hall, Englewood Cliffs, NJ, 1964. 35

Hossein Kaviani and Robabeh Hamedi. A quantitative/qualitative study on metaphors used by Persian depressed patients. *Archives of Psychiatry and Psychotherapy*, 4:5–13, 2011. 110

Kevin Keller. *Strategic Brand Management: Building, Measuring and Managing Brand Equity*. Prentice Hall, NY, 2003. 114

Walter Kintsch. Metaphor comprehension: A computational theory. *Psychonomic Bulletin and Review*, 7:257–266, 2000. DOI: 10.3758/bf03212981. 38

Walter Kintsch. Predication. *Cognitive Science*, 25:173–202, 2001. DOI: 10.1016/s0364-0213(01)00034-9. 38, 53

Karin Kipper-Schuler. *VerbNet: A broad-coverage, comprehensive verb lexicon*. Dissertation. University of PA. 2005. 76

Rob Koeling, Diana McCarthy, and John Carroll. Domain-specific sense distributions and predominant sense acquisition. In *Proceedings of Human Language Technology Conference and Conference on Empirical Methods in Natural Language Processing*, pages 419–426, Vancouver, British Columbia, Canada, October 2005. Association for Computational Linguistics. DOI: 10.3115/1220575.1220628. 98

Veronika Koller. *Metaphor and Gender in Business Media Discourse: A Critical Cognitive Study*. Palgrave Macmillan, Basingstoke: NY, 2004. DOI: 10.1057/9780230511286. 55, 110

Zoltán Kövecses. Language, figurative thought, and cross-cultural comparison. *Metaphor and symbol*, 18(4):311–320, 2003. 110

Zoltán Kövecses. *Metaphor in Culture: Universality and Variation*. Cambridge University Press, Cambridge, 2005. DOI: 10.1017/cbo9780511614408. 95

Zoltán Kövecses. Universality and variation in the use of metaphor. In *Selected Papers from the 2006 and 2007 Stockholm Metaphor Festivals*, pages 51–74. 2008. 110

Saisuresh Krishnakumaran and Xiaojin Zhu. Hunting elusive metaphors using lexical resources. In *Proceedings of the Workshop on Computational Approaches to Figurative Language*, pages 13–20, Rochester, NY, 2007. DOI: 10.3115/1611528.1611531. 77, 90, 106

Solomon Kullback and Richard Leibler. On information and sufficiency. *Annals of Mathematical Statistics*, 22(1):79–86, 1951. DOI: 10.1214/aoms/1177729694. 91

Oliver Kutz, John Bateman, Fabian Neuhaus, Till Mossakowski, and Mehul Bhatt. E pluribus unum: Formalisation, use-cases, and computational support for conceptual blending. In A. Smaill T.R. Besold, M. Schorlemmer, editor, *Computational Creativity Research: Towards Creative Machines, Thinking Machines*. Atlantis/Springer, Berlin, 2014. 53

George Lakoff. Metaphor and war: The metaphor system used to justify war in the Gulf. *Peace Research*, 23:25–32, 1991. DOI: 10.1515/cogsem.2009.4.2.5. 111

George Lakoff. What is metaphor? In J. A. Barnden and K. J. Holoyak, editors, *Advances in Connectionist and Neural Computation Theory: Analogy, Metaphor and Reminding*, Norwood, NJ, 1994. Ablex. 22

George Lakoff. *Moral Politics: How Liberals and Conservatives Think*. University of Chicago Press, 2002. DOI: 10.7208/chicago/9780226471006.001.0001. 111

George Lakoff and Mark Johnson. *Metaphors We Live By*. University of Chicago Press, Chicago, 1980. DOI: 10.7208/chicago/9780226470993.001.0001. 20, 22, 37, 46, 48

George Lakoff and Mark Johnson. *Philosophy in the Flesh: The Embodied Mind and Its Challenge to Western Thought*. Basic Books, New York, 1999. 26

George Lakoff, Jane Espenson, and Alan Schwartz. The Master Metaphor List. Technical report, University of California at Berkeley, 1991. 60, 64, 69, 90

Mark Landau, Daniel Sullivan, and Jeff Greenberg. Evidence that self-relevant motives and metaphoric framing interact to influence political and social attitudes. *Psychological Science*, 20 (11):1421–1427, 2009. DOI: 10.1111/j.1467-9280.2009.02462.x. 111

Thomas Landauer and Susan Dumais. A solution to Plato's problem: The latent semantic analysis theory of acquisition, induction, and representation of knowledge. *Psychological review*, 104: 211–240, 1997. DOI: 10.1037/0033-295x.104.2.211. 38, 105

J. Richard Landis and Gary Koch. The measurement of observer agreement for categorical data. *Biometrics*, 33(1):159–174, 1977. DOI: 10.2307/2529310. 58

Mark Lee. Methodological issues in building a corpus of doctor-patient dialogues annotated for metaphor. In *Proceedings of the German Cognitive Linguistics Association*, Munich, Germany, 2006. 110

Anna-Liisa Leino and Margareth Drakenberg. Metaphor: An educational perspective. *Research Bulletin*, 84, 1993. 110

Beth Levin. *English Verb Classes and Alternations*. University of Chicago Press, Chicago, 1993. 76

Lori Levin, Teruko Mitamura, Davida Fromm, Brian MacWhinney, Jaime Carbonell, Weston Feely, Robert Frederking, Anatole Gershman, and Carlos Ramirez. Resources for the detection of conventionalized metaphors in four languages. In *Proceedings of the Language Resources and Evaluation Conference*, pages 498–501, 2014. 110

David Lewis, Yiming Yang, Tony Rose, and Fan Li. Rcv1: A new benchmark collection for text categorization research. *Journal of Machine Learning Research*, 5:361–397, 2004. 106

Hongsong Li, Kenny Q. Zhu, and Haixun Wang. Data-driven metaphor recognition and explanation. *Transactions of the Association for Computational Linguistics*, 1:379–390, 2013. 86, 93

Linlin Li and Caroline Sporleder. Classifier combination for contextual idiom detection without labelled data. In *Proceedings of the 2009 Conference on Empirical Methods in Natural Language Processing*, EMNLP '09, pages 315–323, 2009. DOI: 10.3115/1699510.1699552. 90, 96

Linlin Li and Caroline Sporleder. Using gaussian mixture models to detect figurative language in context. In *Human Language Technologies: The 2010 Annual Conference of the North American Chapter of the Association for Computational Linguistics*, pages 297–300, 2010. 90, 96

William Little, Henry Fowler, Jessie Coulson, and Charles Onions, editors. *The Shorter Oxford Dictionary on Historical Principles*, (3rd ed.). Oxford, UK: Clarendon, 1973. 58

Jeannette Littlemore. The effect of cultural background on metaphor interpretation. *Metaphor and Symbol*, 18(4):273–288, 2003. DOI: 10.1207/s15327868ms1804_4. 110, 112

Jeannette Littlemore and Graham Low. Metaphoric competence and communicative language ability. *Applied Linguistics*, 27:268–294, 2006. 111

Jeannette Littlemore, Tina Krennmayr, James Turner, and Sarah Turner. An investigation into metaphor use at different levels of second language writing. *Applied Linguistics*, 35(2):117–144, 2014. DOI: 10.1093/applin/amt004. 111

Birte Lönneker. Lexical databases as resources for linguistic creativity: Focus on metaphor. In *Proceedings of the LREC 2004 Workshop on Language Resources for Linguistic Creativity*, pages 9–16, Lisbon, Portugal, 2004. 75

Birte Lönneker and Carina Eilts. A current resource and future perspectives for enriching WordNets with metaphor information. In *Proceedings of the Second International WordNet Conference—GWC 2004*, pages 157–162, Brno, Czech Republic, 2004. 75

Louis Lu and Kathleen Ahrens. Ideological influences on building metaphors in Taiwanese presidential speeches. *Discourse and Society*, 19(3):383–408, 2008. DOI: 10.1177/0957926508088966. 111

Milla Luodonpää-Manni and Johanna Viimaranta. Metaphoric expressions on vertical axis revisited: An empirical study of Russian and French material. *Metaphor and Symbol*, 25(2):74–92, 2010. DOI: 10.1080/10926481003715994. 110

Zouhair Maalej. Figurative language in anger expressions in Tunisian Arabic: An extended view of embodiment. *Metaphor and Symbol*, 19:51–75, 2004. DOI: 10.1207/s15327868ms1901_3. 110

Fiona MacArthur. Metaphorical competence in EFL: Where are we and where should we be going? a view from the language classroom. *Applied Cognitive Linguistics in Second Language Learning and Teaching: AILA Review*, 23(1):155–173, 2010. DOI: 10.1075/aila.23.09mac. 111

Mitchell Marcus, Beatrice Santorini, and Mary Marcinkiewicz. Building a large annotated corpus of English: The Penn treebank. *Computational Linguistics*, 2:313–330, 1993. 62

James Martin. *A Computational Model of Metaphor Interpretation*. Academic Press Professional, Inc., San Diego, CA, 1990. 15, 23, 37, 47, 50, 52, 86, 90, 119

Zachary Mason. Cormet: a computational, corpus-based conventional metaphor extraction system. *Computational Linguistics*, 30(1):23–44, 2004. DOI: 10.1162/089120104773633376. 77, 90, 99

Keiko Matsuki. Metaphors of anger in Japanese. In *Language and the cognitive construal of the world*. Berlin: Gruyter, 1995. DOI: 10.1515/9783110809305.137. 110

Marina Meila and Jianbo Shi. A random walks view of spectral segmentation. In *AISTATS*, 2001. 100

Dan Melamed. Automatic discovery of non-compositional compounds in parallel data. *CoRR*, cmp-lg/9706027, 1997. 63

Tomas Mikolov, Kai Chen, Greg Corrado, and Jeffrey Dean. Efficient estimation of word representations in vector space. *arXiv preprint arXiv:1301.3781*, 2013. 105

Taniya Mishra and Srinivas Bangalore. Predicting relative prominence in noun-noun compounds. In *Proceedings of the 49th Annual Meeting of the Association for Computational Linguistics: Human Language Technologies*, pages 609–613, Portland, Oregon, June 2011. Association for Computational Linguistics. 62

Jeff Mitchell and Mirella Lapata. Vector-based models of semantic composition. *Proceedings of ACL-08: HLT*, pages 236–244, 2008. 104

Michael Mohler, David Bracewell, Marc Tomlinson, and David Hinote. Semantic signatures for example-based linguistic metaphor detection. In *Proceedings of the First Workshop on Metaphor in NLP*, pages 27–35, Atlanta, Georgia, 2013. 77, 97, 99, 105

Michael Mohler, Bryan Rink, David Bracewell, and Marc Tomlinson. A novel distributional approach to multilingual conceptual metaphor recognition. In *Proceedings of COLING 2014, the 25th International Conference on Computational Linguistics: Technical Papers*, pages 1752–1763, Dublin, Ireland, 2014. 104, 105

Marco Moreno. *Metaphors in Hugo Chávez's Political Discourse: Conceptualizing Nation, Revolution, and Opposition*. ProQuest, 2008. 111

Gareth Morgan. *Images of Organizations*. Beverly Hills, CA: Sage, 1997. 110

Alessandro Moschitti, Daniele Pighin, and Roberto Basili. Tree kernel engineering for proposition re-ranking. In *Proceedings of Mining and Learning with Graphs (MLG)*, 2006. 96

Maria Teresa Musacchio. Metaphors and metaphor-like processes across languages: Notes on English and Italian language of economics. In Khurshid Ahmad, editor, *Affective Computing and Sentiment Analysis*, volume 45 of *Text, Speech and Language Technology*, pages 79–88. Springer Netherlands, 2011. ISBN 978-94-007-1756-5. DOI: 10.1007/978-94-007-1757-2. 110

Andreas Musolff. *Mirror images of Europe: Metaphors in the public debate about Europe in Britain and Germany*. Iudicium, Muenchen, 2000. 55, 110

Preslav Nakov and Marti Hearst. Using verbs to characterize noun-noun relations. In *Artificial Intelligence: Methodology, Systems, and Applications (AIMSA)*, page 233–244, Berlin, 2006. Springer. DOI: 10.1007/11861461_25. 85

Srini Narayanan. Knowledge-based Action Representations for Metaphor and Aspect (KARMA). Technical report, Ph.D. thesis, University of California at Berkeley, 1997. 46

Yair Neuman, Dan Assaf, Yohai Cohen, Mark Last, Shlomo Argamon, Newton Howard, and Ophir Frieder. Metaphor identification in large texts corpora. *PLoS ONE*, 8(4):e62343, 2013. DOI: 10.1371/journal.pone.0062343. 106

Larisa Nikitina and Fumitaka Furuoka. Measuring metaphors: A factor analysis of students' conceptions of language teachers. *Metaphor.de*, 15:161–180, 2008. 110

Ian Niles and Adam Pease. Towards a standard upper ontology. In *Proceedings of the International Conference on Formal Ontology in Information Systems - Volume 2001*, FOIS '01, pages 2–9, New York, NY, 2001. ACM. DOI: 10.1145/505168.505170. 77, 94

Ian Niles and Adam Pease. Linking lexicons and ontologies: Mapping WordNet to the suggested upper merged ontology. In *Proceedings of the 2003 international conference on Information and Knowledge Engineering (IKE'03), Las Vegas*, pages 412–416, 2003. 77, 94

Peter Norvig. Inference in text understanding. In *Proceedings of the American National Conference on Artificial Intelligence (AAAI-87)*, Seattle, WA, page 561–565, 1987. 35, 42

Geoffrey Nunberg. Transfers of meaning. *Journal of Semantics*, 12(1):109–132, 1995. DOI: 10.1093/jos/12.2.109. 35

Gozde Özbal and Carlo Strapparava. A computational approach to automatize creative naming. In *Proceedings of ACL'12, the 50th annual meeting of the Association of Computational Linguistics*, 2012. 86, 114

Martha Palmer, Paul Kingsbury, and Daniel Gildea. The proposition bank: An annotated corpus of semantic roles. *Computational Linguistics*, 1:71–106, 2005. DOI: 10.1162/0891201053630264. 62, 76

Alan Partington. A corpus-based investigation into the use of metaphor in British business journalism. *ASp*, 7-10:25–39, 1995. DOI: 10.4000/asp.3718. 55, 110

Brad Pasanek. Eighteenth Century Metaphors of the Mind, a Dictionary. Doctoral Dissertation, Stanford University, 2006. 65

Brad Pasanek. *Metaphors of Mind: An Eighteenth-Century Dictionary*. Johns Hopkins University Press, 2015. 65

Brad Pasanek and D. Sculley. Mining millions of metaphors. *Literary and Linguistic Computing*, 23(3):345–360, 2008. DOI: 10.1093/llc/fqn010. 65

Trijntje Pasma. Metaphor identification in Dutch discourse. In Fiona MacArthur, José Luis Oncins-Martinez, Manuel Sánchez-Garcia, and Ana María Piquer-Piriz, editors, *Metaphor in Use: Context, Culture, and Communication*, pages 69–83. John Benjamins Publishing Company, Amsterdam, 2012. DOI: 10.1075/hcp.38. 63

Francisco C. Pereira. *Creativity and Artificial Intelligence: A Conceptual Blending Approach*. Walter de Gruyter, Berlin, 2007. 53

Wim Peters and Ivonne Peters. Lexicalised systematic polysemy in WordNet. In *Proceedings of LREC 2000*, Athens, 2000. 75

Karl Pichotta and John DeNero. Identifying phrasal verbs using many bilingual corpora. In *Proceedings of the 2013 Conference on Empirical Methods in Natural Language Processing*, pages 636–646, Seattle, Washington, October 2013. Association for Computational Linguistics. 62

Pragglejaz Group. MIP: A method for identifying metaphorically used words in discourse. *Metaphor and Symbol*, 22:1–39, 2007. DOI: 10.1207/s15327868ms2201_1. 55, 56, 57, 58, 59, 60, 61, 63, 68

James Pustejovsky. The generative lexicon. *Computational Linguistics*, 17(4), 1991. 36

James Pustejovsky. *The Generative Lexicon.* MIT Press, Cambridge, MA, 1995. 36

Felicity Rash. *The Language of Violence: Adolf Hitler's Mein Kampf.* Peter Lang, NY, 2006. 65, 111

Lev Ratinov and Dan Roth. Design challenges and misconceptions in named entity recognition. In *Proceedings of the Thirteenth Conference on Computational Natural Language Learning (CoNLL-2009)*, pages 147–155. Association for Computational Linguistics. Boulder, Colorado, June 2009. DOI: 10.3115/1596374.1596399. 62

Michael Reddy. The conduit metaphor: A case of frame conflict in our language about language. In Andrew Ortony, editor, *Metaphor and Thought*. Cambridge University Press, Cambridge, MA., 1979. 52

Astrid Reining and Birte Lönneker-Rodman. Corpus-driven metaphor harvesting. In *Proceedings of the HLT/NAACL-07 Workshop on Computational Approaches to Figurative Language*, pages 5–12, Rochester, NY, 2007. DOI: 10.3115/1611528.1611530. 75

Philip Resnik. Selection and Information: A Class-based Approach to Lexical Relationships. Technical report, University of PA, 1993. 90, 91

John Roberts, editor. *Metaphor and Simile in The Oxford Dictionary of the Classical World*. Oxford University Press, Oxford, UK, 2007. 16

Shani Robins and Rochard Mayer. The metaphor framing effect: metaphorical reasoning about text-based dilemmas. *Discourse Processes*, 30:57–86, 2000. DOI: 10.1207/s15326950dp3001_03. 111

Michael Rundell and Gwyneth Fox, editors. *Macmillan English Dictionary for Advanced Learners*. Oxford, UK: Macmillan Education, 2002. 58

Sylvia Weber Russell. Metaphoric coherence: Distinguishing verbal metaphor from "anomaly." *Computational Intelligence*, 8(3):553–574,, 1992. DOI: 10.1111/j.1467-8640.1992.tb00379.x. 36, 38, 52

Evan Sandhaus. The New York Times annotated corpus. *Linguistic Data Consortium*, 2008. 98, 106

Roger Schank and Robert Abelson. *Scripts, Plans, Goals and Understanding*. Psychology Press, NY, 1977. DOI: 10.1016/b978-1-4832-1446-7.50019-4. 36

Elena Semino, John Heywood, and Mick Short. Methodological problems in the analysis of a corpus of conversations about cancer. *Journal of Pragmatics*, 36(7):1271–1294, 2004. DOI: 10.1016/j.pragma.2003.10.013. 110

Samira Shaikh, Tomek Strzalkowski, Ting Liu, George Aaron Broadwell, Boris Yamrom, Sarah Taylor, Laurie Feldman, Kit Cho, Umit Boz, Ignacio Cases, Yuliya Peshkova, and Ching-Sheng Lin. A multi-cultural repository of automatically discovered linguistic and conceptual metaphors. In Nicoletta Calzolari (Conference Chair), Khalid Choukri, Thierry Declerck, Hrafn Loftsson, Bente Maegaard, Joseph Mariani, Asuncion Moreno, Jan Odijk, and Stelios Piperidis, editors, *Proceedings of the Ninth International Conference on Language Resources and Evaluation (LREC'14)*, Reykjavik, Iceland, May 2014. European Language Resources Association (ELRA). 72, 110

Ekaterina Shutova. Automatic metaphor interpretation as a paraphrasing task. In *Proceedings of NAACL 2010*, pages 1029–1037, Los Angeles, 2010. 69, 77, 79, 91, 92, 93, 104

Ekaterina Shutova. Metaphor identification as interpretation. In *Proceedings of *SEM 2013*, Atlanta, GA, 2013. 77, 90, 92, 93

Ekaterina Shutova and Lin Sun. Unsupervised metaphor identification using hierarchical graph factorization clustering. In *Proceedings of NAACL 2013*, Atlanta, GA, 2013. 99, 100, 101, 102

Ekaterina Shutova and Simone Teufel. Metaphor corpus annotated for source - target domain mappings. In *Proceedings of LREC 2010*, pages 3255–3261, Malta, 2010. 59, 68, 93

Ekaterina Shutova, Lin Sun, and Anna Korhonen. Metaphor identification using verb and noun clustering. In *Proceedings of Coling 2010*, pages 1002–1010, Beijing, China, 2010. 93, 99, 100, 101

Ekaterina Shutova, Tim Van de Cruys, and Anna Korhonen. Unsupervised metaphor paraphrasing using a vector space model. In *Proceedings of COLING 2012*, Mumbai, India, 2012. 15, 92, 104

Ekaterina Shutova, Barry Devereux, and Anna Korhonen. Conceptual metaphor theory meets the data: a corpus-based human annotation study. *Language Resources and Evaluation*, 47(4): 1261–1284, 2013. DOI: 10.1007/s10579-013-9238-z. 68

Sidney Siegel and John Castellan. *Nonparametric statistics for the behavioral sciences*. McGraw-Hill Book Company, NY, 1988. DOI: 10.1097/00005053-195707000-00032. 69

Hanna Skorczynska and Alice Deignan. Readership and purpose in the choice of economics metaphors. *Metaphor and Symbol*, 21(2):87–104, 2006. DOI: 10.1207/s15327868ms2102_2. 110

Richard Sproat. English noun-phrase accent prediction for text-to-speech. *Computer Speech & Language*, 8(2):79 – 94, 1994. ISSN 0885-2308. DOI: 10.1006/csla.1994.1004. 62

Gerard Steen. When is metaphor deliberate? In N.L. Johannesson, C. Alm-Arvius, and D. Minugh, editors, *Selected Papers from the Stockholm 2008 Metaphor Festival*, pages 43–63. Stockholm: Acta Universitatis Stockholmiensis, 2008. 58, 62

Gerard Steen, Aletta Dorst, Berenike Herrmann, Anna Kaal, Tina Krennmayr, and Trijntje Pasma. *A Method for Linguistic Metaphor Identification: From MIP to MIPVU*. John Benjamins, Amsterdam/Philadelphia, 2010. DOI: 10.1075/celcr.14. 58, 59, 60, 61, 62, 67, 68, 95, 98

Anatol Stefanowitsch. HAPPINESS in English and German: A metaphorical-pattern analysis. In M. Altenberg and S. Kemmer, editors, *Language, Culture, and Mind*, Stanford, 2004. CSLI Publications. 110

Biz Stone. *Things A Little Bird Told Me*. Grand Central Publishing, NY, 2014. 2, 30

Tomek Strzalkowski, George Broadwell, Sarah Taylor, Laurie Feldman, Samira Shaikh, Ting Liu, Boris Yamrom, Kit Cho, Umit Boz, Ignacio Cases, and Kyle Elliot. Robust extraction of metaphor from novel data. In *Proceedings of the First Workshop on Metaphor in NLP*, pages 67–76, Atlanta, GA, 2013. 77, 99, 102, 103, 107

Karen Sullivan. *Grammar in Metaphor: A Construction Grammar Account of Metaphoric Language*. Ph.D. thesis, University of California, Berkeley, 2007. 51, 52

Karen Sullivan. *Frames and Constructions in Metaphoric Language*. John Benjamins, Amsterdam, 2013. DOI: 10.1075/cal.14. 51

Lin Sun and Anna Korhonen. Improving verb clustering with automatically acquired selectional preferences. In *Proceedings of EMNLP 2009*, pages 638–647, Singapore, August 2009. DOI: 10.3115/1699571.1699596. 91

Archer Taylor. *Proverbial Comparisons and Similes from California. Folklore Studies 3*. University of California Press, CA, 1954. 8, 113

Stefan Thater, Georgiana Dinu, and Manfred Pinkal. Ranking paraphrases in context. In *Proceedings of the 2009 Workshop on Applied Textual Inference*, pages 44–47, Suntec, Singapore, 2009. DOI: 10.3115/1708141.1708149. 104

Stefan Thater, Hagen Fürstenau, and Manfred Pinkal. Contextualizing semantic representations using syntactically enriched vector models. In *Proceedings of the 48th Annual Meeting of the Association for Computational Linguistics*, pages 948–957, Uppsala, Sweden, 2010. 104

Paul H. Thibodeau and Lera Boroditsky. Metaphors we think with: The role of metaphor in reasoning. *PLoS ONE*, 6(2):e16782, 02 2011. DOI: 10.1371/journal.pone.0016782. 111

Roger Tourangeau and Robert Sternberg. Aptness in metaphor. *Cognitive Psychology*, 13, 1981. DOI: 10.1016/0010-0285(81)90003-7. 68

Kristina Toutanova, Dan Klein, Christopher Manning, and Yoram Singer. Feature-rich part-of-speech tagging with a cyclic dependency network. In *Proceedings of the HLT-NAACL*, pages 252–259. Association for Computational Linguistics. Edmond, Canada, May–June 2003. DOI: 10.3115/1073445.1073478. 62

Yulia Tsvetkov and Shuly Wintner. Identification of multiword expressions by combining multiple linguistic information sources. *Computational Linguistics*, 40:449–468, 2014. DOI: 10.1162/coli_a_00177. 63

Yulia Tsvetkov, Elena Mukomel, and Anatole Gershman. Cross-lingual metaphor detection using common semantic features. In *Proceedings of the First Workshop on Metaphor in NLP*, pages 45–51, Atlanta, GA, 2013. 77, 95, 106

Yulia Tsvetkov, Leonid Boytsov, Anatole Gershman, Eric Nyberg, and Chris Dyer. Metaphor detection with cross-lingual model transfer. In *Proceedings of the 52nd Annual Meeting of the Association for Computational Linguistics (Volume 1: Long Papers)*, pages 248–258, Baltimore, MD, June 2014. Association for Computational Linguistics. DOI: 10.3115/v1/p14-1024. 59, 66

Yuancheng Tu and Dan Roth. Sorting out the most confusing English phrasal verbs. In **SEM 2012: The First Joint Conference on Lexical and Computational Semantics – Volume 1: Proceedings of the main conference and the shared task, and Volume 2: Proceedings of the Sixth International Workshop on Semantic Evaluation (SemEval 2012)*, pages 65–69. Association for Computational Linguistics. Montréal, Canada, 7-8 June 2012. 62

Peter Turney, Yair Neuman, Dan Assaf, and Yohai Cohen. Literal and metaphorical sense identification through concrete and abstract context. In *Proceedings of the Conference on Empirical Methods in Natural Language Processing*, EMNLP '11, pages 680–690. Association for Computational Linguistics. Stroudsburg, PA, 2011. 105, 106, 107

Akira Utsumi. Interpretive diversity explains metaphor-simile distinction. *Metaphor and Symbol*, 22:291–312, 2007. DOI: 10.1080/10926480701528071. 12

Akira Utsumi. Computational exploration of metaphor comprehension processes using a semantic space model. *Cognitive Science*, 35(2):251–296, 2011. DOI: 10.1111/j.1551-6709.2010.01144.x. 12, 38, 39, 53

Tim Van de Cruys, Thierry Poibeau, and Anna Korhonen. Latent vector weighting for word meaning in context. In *Proceedings of EMNLP*, Edinburgh, UK, 2011. 104

Tony Veale. Analogy generation with hownet. In *Proceedings of IJCAI'2005, the International Joint Conference on Artificial Intelligence*. Morgan Kaufmann, 2005. 78

Tony Veale. Re-representation and creative analogy: A lexico-semantic perspective. *New Generation Computing*, 24:223–240, 2006a. DOI: 10.1007/bf03037333. 78, 79

Tony Veale. Tracking the lexical Zeitgeist with Wikipedia and WordNet. In *Proceedings of ECAI'2006, the 17th European Conference on Artificial Intelligence*, Trento, Italy, 2006b. John Wiley. 114

Tony Veale. Creative language retrieval: A robust hybrid of information retrieval and linguistic creativity. In *Proceedings of ACL'2011, the 49th Annual Meeting of the Association for Computational Linguistics: Human Language Technologie*, 2011. 115

Tony Veale. A context-sensitive, multi-faceted model of lexico-conceptual affect. In *Proceedings of ACL'2012, the 50th Annual Conference of the Association for Computational Linguistics*, 2012a. 28, 29, 115

Tony Veale. From conceptual mash-ups to bad-ass blends: A robust computational model of conceptual blending. In *Proceedings of ICCC-2012, the 3rd International Conference on Computational Creativity*, 2012b. 53

Tony Veale. The agile cliché: Using flexible stereotypes as building blocks in the construction of an affective lexicon. In A. Oltramari, P. Vossen, L. Qin, and E. Hovy, editors, *New Trends of Research in Ontologies and Lexical Resources*, Theory and Applications of Natural Language Processing. Springer, Berlin, 2013a. DOI: 10.1007/978-3-642-31782-8. 81, 82, 83

Tony Veale. Linguistic readymades and creative reuse. *Transactions of the SDPS: Journal of Integrated Design and Process Science*, 17(4):37–51, 2013b. 115

Tony Veale. A service-oriented architecture for computational creativity. *Journal of Computing Science and Engineering*, 7(3):159–167, 2013c. DOI: 10.5626/jcse.2013.7.3.159. 120

Tony Veale. Coming good and breaking bad: Generating transformative character arcs for use in compelling stories. In *Proceedings of ICCC-2014, the 5th International Conference on Computational Creativity*, Ljubljana, Slovenia, 2014. 116

Tony Veale and Yanfen Hao. Comprehending and generating apt metaphors: A web-driven, case-based approach to figurative language. In *Proceedings of AAAI'2007, the 22nd Conference of the Association for the Advancement of Artificial Intelligence*, 2007. 81, 82, 84

Tony Veale and Mark Keane. Conceptual scaffolding: A spatially founded meaning representation for metaphor comprehension. *Computational Intelligence*, 8(3):494–519, 1992. DOI: 10.1111/j.1467-8640.1992.tb00377.x. 23, 37, 39, 49

Tony Veale and Mark Keane. Belief modeling, intentionality and perlocution in metaphor comprehension. In *Proceedings of the 16th Annual Meeting of the Cognitive Science Society, Atlanta, Georgia*, Hillsdale, NJ, 1994. Lawrence Erlbaum Associates. 39, 73

Tony Veale and Mark Keane. The competence of sub-optimal structure mapping on 'hard' analogies. In *Proceedings of IJCAI'97, the 15th International Joint Conference on Artificial Intelligence*, San Mateo, CA, 1997. Morgan Kaufmann. 40, 42, 43

Tony Veale and Guofu Li. Creative introspection and knowledge acquisition: Learning about the world thru introspective questions and exploratory metaphors. In *Proceedings of AAAI'2011, the 25th Conference of the Association for the Advancement of Artificial Intelligence*. AAAI press, 2011. 85, 86

Tony Veale and Guofu Li. Creating similarity: Lateral thinking for vertical similarity judgments. In *Proceedings of ACL 2013, the 51st Annual Meeting of the Association for Computational Linguistics*, 2013. 83

Tony Veale and Guofu Li. Analogy as an organizational principle in the construction of large knowledge-bases. In H. Prade and G. Richard, editors, *Computational Approaches to Analogical Reasoning: Current Trends*, volume 548 of *Studies in Computational Intelligence*. Springer, Berlin, 2014. DOI: 10.1007/978-3-642-54516-0. 85

Tony Veale and Guofu Li. Distributed divergent creativity: Computational creative agents at web scale. *Cognitive Computation*, May 2015. ISSN 1866-9956. DOI: 10.1007/s12559-015-9337-9. 74

Tony Veale and Diarmuid O'Donoghue. Computation and blending. *Cognitive Linguistics*, 11 (3-4):253–281, 2000. DOI: 10.1515/cogl.2001.016. 42, 53

Tony Veale, Guofu Li, and Yanfen Hao. Growing finely-discriminating taxonomies from seeds of varying quality and size. In *Proceedings of EACL 2009, The 12th Conference of the European Chapter of the Association for Computational Linguistics*, 2009. DOI: 10.3115/1609067.1609160. 83

Tony Veale, Alessandro Valitutti, and Guofu Li. Twitter: The best of bot worlds for automated wit. In *Proceedings of DAPI/HCII-2015, the 3rd International Conference on Distributed, Ambient and Pervasive Interactions at the 17th International Conference on Human-Computer Interaction*, Los Angeles, CA, 2015. DOI: 10.1007/978-3-319-20804-6_63. 86, 116

Eileen Cornell Way. *Knowledge Representation and Metaphor. Studies in Cognitive systems*. Kluwer Academic, Amsterdam, 1991. 39, 82

Robert Wilensky, David Chin, Marc Luria, James Martin, James Mayfield, and Dekai Wu. The Berkeley Unix consultant project. *Computational Linguistics*, 14(4):35–84, 1988. DOI: 10.1007/978-3-642-88719-2_25. 48, 119

Yorick Wilks. A preferential pattern-seeking semantics for natural language inference. *Artificial Intelligence*, 6:53–74, 1975. DOI: 10.1016/0004-3702(75)90016-8. 34, 36, 49

Yorick Wilks. Making preferences more active. *Artificial Intelligence*, 11(3):197–223, 1978. DOI: 10.1016/0004-3702(78)90001-2. 34, 36, 38, 75, 76, 89

Yorick Wilks, Adam Dalton, James Allen, and Lucian Galescu. Automatic metaphor detection using large-scale lexical resources and conventional metaphor extraction. In *Proceedings of the First Workshop on Metaphor in NLP*, pages 36–44, Atlanta, GA, 2013. 75, 76, 90

Patrick Winston. Learning and reasoning by analogy. *Communications of the ACM*, 23(12):689–703, 1980. DOI: 10.1145/359038.359042. 39, 40, 42

Ian Witten and Eibe Frank. *Data Mining: Practical Machine Learning Tools and Techniques*. Morgan Kaufmann Series in Data Management Sys. Morgan Kaufmann, second edition, June 2005. DOI: 10.1145/507338.507355. 95

Ning Yu. Metaphorical expressions of anger and happiness in English and Chinese. *Metaphor and Symbolic Activity*, 10:59–92, 1995. DOI: 10.1207/s15327868ms1002_1. 110

Shipeng Yu, Kai Yu, and Volker Tresp. Soft clustering on graphs. *Advances in Neural Information Processing Systems*, 18:1553, 2006. 100

Gerald Zaltman and Lindsay Zaltman. *Marketing metaphoria: What deep metaphors reveal about the minds of consumers*. Harvard Business Press, 2008. 110

Yi Zhang, Valia Kordoni, Aline Villavicencio, and Marco Idiart. Automated multiword expression prediction for grammar engineering. In *Proceedings of the Workshop on Multiword Expressions: Identifying and Exploiting Underlying Properties*, pages 36–44. Association for Computational Linguistics. Sydney, Australia, July 2006. DOI: 10.3115/1613692.1613700. 63

Authors' Biographies

TONY VEALE

Dr. Tony Veale is a computer scientist at University College Dublin, Ireland, where his research focuses on the computational modeling of creative linguistic phenomena, including metaphor, blending, simile, analogy, and verbal irony. He leads the European Commission's PROSECCO network (PROSECCO-network.eu and @PROSECCOnetwork), an international coordination action that aims to promote the scientific exploration of computational creativity. Veale is particularly interested in the generative creativity of metaphor, and builds generative models of metaphor, simile, and blending, which are made publicly available as reusable Web services to promote the integration of figurative language-processing capabilities in third-party applications. He is the author of the 2012 monograph on computational linguistic creativity titled *Exploding the Creativity Myth: The Computational Foundations of Linguistic Creativity* from Bloomsbury Press, and creator of the metaphor-generating Twitterbot @MetaphorMagnet. Veale is also the founder of the educational website RobotComix.com, which promotes the philosophy and practice of computational creativity to the general public via online tutorials and free textbooks such as *Hand-Made By Machines? An Illustrated Guide to Creativity in Humans and Machines.*

EKATERINA SHUTOVA

Ekaterina Shutova is a Leverhulme Early Career Fellow at the University of Cambridge Computer Laboratory. Her research is in the area of natural language processing with a specific focus on computational semantics and figurative language processing using statistical learning. Previously, she worked at the International Computer Science Institute and the Institute for Cognitive and Brain Sciences at the University of California, Berkeley and the Department of Theoretical and Applied Linguistics at the University of Cambridge. Ekaterina received her Ph.D. in computer science from the University of Cambridge in 2011 and her doctoral dissertation concerned computational modeling of figurative language.

BEATA BEIGMAN KLEBANOV

Beata Beigman Klebanov is a Senior Research Scientist in the research and development division at Educational Testing Service in Princeton, NJ. She received her Ph.D. in computer science in 2008 and her B.S. degree in computer science in 2000—both from The Hebrew University of Jerusalem. She received her M.S. degree (with distinction) in cognitive science from the University of Edinburgh in 2001. Before joining ETS, she was a post-doctoral fellow at the Northwestern Institute for Complex Systems and Kellogg School of Management, where she researched computational approaches to political rhetoric. Her interests include discourse modeling, analyzing argumentative and figurative language, and automated semantic and pragmatic analysis of text. At ETS, her focus is on automatically scoring content in student writing. She researches methods to analyze cohesion in student essays, as well as metaphor, topicality, personalization, use of sourced content, and sentiment, among others.

Printed in the United States
by Baker & Taylor Publisher Services